The concept of possible worlds, has recently gained interdiscipli tool when borrowed by literary theory to explain the notion of fictional worlds. In this book Ruth Ronen develops a comparative reading of the use of possible worlds in philosophy and in literary theory, and offers an analysis of the way the concept contributes to our understanding of fictionality and the structure and ontology of fictional worlds. Dr. Ronen suggests a new set of criteria for the definition of fictionality, making rigorous distinctions between fictional and possible worlds; and through specific studies of domains within fictional worlds – events, objects, time and point of view – she proposes a radical rethinking of the problem of fictionality in general and fictional narrativity in particular.

Possible worlds in literary theory

Literature, Culture, Theory

❖❖

General editors

RICHARD MACKSEY, *The Johns Hopkins University*
and MICHAEL SPRINKER, *State University of New York at Stony Brook*

The Cambridge *Literature, Culture, Theory* series is dedicated to theoretical studies in the human sciences that have literature and culture as their object of enquiry. Acknowledging the contemporary expansion of cultural studies and the redefinitions of literature that this has entailed, the series includes not only original works of literary theory but also monographs and essay collections on topics and seminal figures from the long history of theoretical speculation on the arts and human communication generally. The concept of theory embraced in the series is broad, including not only the classical disciplines of poetics and rhetoric, but also those of aesthetics, psychoanalysis, semiotics, and other cognate sciences that have inflected the systematic study of literature during the past half century.

Titles published

Return to Freud: Jacques Lacan's dislocation of psychoanalysis
SAMUEL WEBER
(*translated from the German by Michael Levine*)

Wordsworth, dialogics, and the practice of criticism
DON H. BIALOSTOSKY

The subject of modernity
ANTHONY J. CASCARDI

Onomatopoetics: theory of language and literature
JOSEPH GRAHAM

Parody: ancient, modern, and post-modern
MARGARET ROSE

The poetics of personification
JAMES PAXSON

Possible worlds in literary theory
RUTH RONEN

Possible worlds in literary theory

RUTH RONEN

Senior Lecturer in Poetics and Comparative Literature
Tel Aviv University

CAMBRIDGE
UNIVERSITY PRESS

Published by the Press Syndicate of the University of Cambridge
The Pitt Building, Trumpington Street, Cambridge, CB2 1RP
40 West 20th Street, New York, NY 10011-4211, USA
10 Stamford Road, Oakleigh, Melbourne 3166, Australia

First published 1994

Printed in Great Britain at the University Press, Cambridge

A catalogue record for this book is available from the British Library

Library of Congress cataloguing in publication data

Ronen, Ruth.
Possible worlds in literary theory / Ruth Ronen.
p. cm. – (Literature, culture, theory: 7)
Includes bibliographical references and index.
ISBN 0 521 45017 9. – ISBN 0 521 45648 7 (paperback)
1. Fiction – Technique. 2. Possibility in literature. 3. Reality in literature. 4. Possibility.
5. Logic. I. Title. II. Series.
PN3355.R66 1994
809.3–dc20 93-8033 CIP

ISBN 0 521 45017 9 hardback
ISBN 0 521 45648 7 paperback

In memory of my beloved mother
who departed too soon.

Contents

ix

Contents

Acknowledgments

Earlier versions of parts of chapters in this book have appeared in various journals in recent years. Although these have been radically revised in the preparation of this book, I would like to express my gratitude to the following journals for permission to make further use of the relevant material. Parts of chapter 1 were published in the journal *Semiotica* in a paper titled "Possible Worlds in Literary Theory: A Game in Interdisciplinarity." Part of chapter 2 was published as "Possible Worlds between the Disciplines" in *The British Journal of Aesthetics*. Part of chapter 4 is based on a paper published in *Poetics Today* under the title "Completing the Incompleteness of Fictional Entities." A version of chapter 5 was published in *Poetics Today*, under the title "Paradigm Shift in Plot Models: An Outline of the History of Narratology." An early version of chapter 6 appeared (in French) in *Poétique* as "La focalisation dans les mondes fictionnels" and a version of chapter 7 appeared in *Style* as "The Semiotics of Fictional Time: Three Metaphors in the Study of Temporality in Fiction."

A number of people have either directly or indirectly influenced my work, and I would like to express my indebtedness and gratitude to them. I am grateful to Benjamin Harshav, who was the first to stimulate my interest in the problem of fictionality. Thanks are also due to Lubomir Doležel who introduced me to problems of logic and semantics in the study of literature; his influence on my work is indeed immeasurable. I am also grateful to Amos Funkenstein who has helped me to feel at ease when addressing philosophical problems. Yeshayahu Shen, Gerald Prince, Yael Levo and Brian McHale have been devoted readers and stringent critics of both earlier versions of this material and of chapters of the book itself; they have helped me to improve and revise my thoughts on the matters involved. I would like to thank people at the Porter Institute and in the Department of Poetics and Comparative Literature at Tel Aviv University for creating the intellectual atmosphere appropriate for research, and especially Itamar

Acknowledgments

Even-Zohar for making available certain financial support during the preparation of this book. In particular I would like to thank Sonja Laden for her style-editing and Sharon Himmelfarb for her less specific, yet no less valuable help. Last but not least, I would like to thank my family, and especially my daughter Dana, who has proven, beyond doubt, that anything is possible.

Introduction

Fictionality as an interdisciplinary problem

The concept of *fictionality* participates in the discourses of more than one discipline and understanding fictionality therefore requires an interdisciplinary approach. Fictionality is a distinctive property of literary texts and as such it forms a natural topic for literary research. Fictional texts also posit a reality of their own that casts doubt on basic notions in logic and semantics and as such fictional worlds can be expected to interest philosophers. Yet the histories of the two disciplines show that fictionality has attracted only sporadic and limited attention from both literary and philosophical quarters. It is only in recent years that the two disciplines have come to share an interest in fictionality; furthermore, it is only in recent years that the two disciplines, when addressing the question of fiction, have started to refer to the same object of research. Until the mid seventies fictionality was an object of separate disciplinary pursuits: it was interpreted as a property of texts by literary theorists and either excluded as logical abnormality or entirely ignored by philosophers. That is, although traditional literary theory did not ignore the problem of fiction, it has regarded the fictionality of texts as an inner type of organization, largely disregarding the fact that being fictional, by definition, refers to the relations between a world and what lies beyond its boundaries. Recent years have witnessed a serious attempt on the part of literary theorists to go beyond the boundaries of the literary text and to address the concept of *fictionality* in a larger cultural context. Parallel to these developments, philosophy (and in particular philosophical logic) has developed analytical tools for dealing with problems raised by fictional worlds. It is at this stage that the philosophical and the literary discourses on fictionality started to interact (and sometimes overlap), and it is at this point that interdisciplinary dialogue on issues related to fictionality began to be marked in both disciplines.[1]

As noted above, fictionality, as a literary property, is obviously not a new topic in literary studies in either the Anglo-American (Wellek and Warren, 1963: 142 ff. and 212 ff.; Frye, 1957: esp. 248 ff., 303 ff.)[2] or in the German tradition (Auerbach, 1968). Yet, although literary theory has always regarded fictionality as the distinctive feature of literary texts (and hence equated fictionality with literarity), the canonized orientation toward fiction, largely influenced by the formalist–structuralist tradition and by the tenets of the New Criticism, attempted to locate the fictional property of texts in some textual component, making various proposals in this direction (Hamburger, 1973: the epic preterite; Banfield, 1982: free indirect discourse; Jakobson, 1960: equivalence patterns). From a theoretical point of view this direction of approach to fictionality reflects an attempt to isolate the literary object from all other objects of culture and to show that all properties and categories relevant to the understanding of literature, including its fictionality, can be clarified and defined by way of the literary text itself. Imposing a "centripetal" perspective, which confines research to the limits of the literary, to inner-systemic considerations, has left the fictionality of worlds and texts practically unexplicated within literary studies. Traditional branches of literary studies departing from such a centripetal position, would not and could not address the question of the relationship between fiction and reality, or the question of how the fictional mode is related to other non-actual states and events (such as myths, dreams, wishes and so on). Recent years are however marked by a growing interest shown

1 See Brinker, 1987, for an analytical survey of the recently noticeable interchange between philosophy and literary theory around questions of interpretation and meanings. Here, as elsewhere, Brinker is one philosopher who rejects the situation where philosophical meta-positions (realism, pragmatism) serve as literary "themes"; he rather advocates an interchange between the two disciplines so that a systematic paradigm is constructed for the literary discipline (a stand shared by the author of the present study).

2 Note however that whereas Wellek and Warren dedicate a chapter to the problem of the relations between fiction and reality, Frye subsumes the problem of fiction under a generic study of forms where he identifies fiction with specific novelistic forms. Other Anglo-American critics like Scholes and Kellogg, Forster and Booth do not refer to fictionality directly at all, but only indirectly through the issue of realism. In any case, for traditional theory of literature fictionality is not a theoretical issue in itself unless it involves specific forms and devices of literary composition.

within the literary discipline in questions of ontology, in the distinction between fictional and nonfictional literary texts, in problems of representation, mimesis and the like. Fictionality is no longer defined as a property of texts: it is either viewed as a type of speech situation, as a position within a culture, or as a particular type of logic or semantics. In any of these definitions, the approach to fictionality legitimates a new set of problems not addressed before by literary theory.

The need to understand fictionality and to legitimize this new set of referential considerations has taken theorists beyond literary models in a search for explanatory tools and methods in other fields. From speech-acts theory to possible worlds semantics, interdisciplinary models that were not originally meant to explicate literary phenomena have emerged in the literary research domain to serve the acute need to explain a notion of fictionality, which has changed both in status and meaning. The primary sources of models suggesting a broader view on the literary phenomenon, and a more general conception of fictionality, naturally lie in the philosophical domain: in philosophical logic, in the philosophy of language and in aesthetics. Concepts that originated from these various philosophical branches have indeed been adopted by literary theorists, and this borrowing did not stop on the level of terminology. The currency of concepts such as *world projection, make-believe, mimesis, representation* and others drawn from aesthetics, alongside modal notions – like *possible states of affairs, cross-world identity, accessibility* – developed in philosophical logic, attests not only to the search on the part of literary theorists for explanatory models for fictionality beyond the confines of traditional literary theory; it reveals that this search has created an area of cross-disciplinary research. By now both clusters of concepts have been fully incorporated into the literary lexicon and are widely used in literary discourse.

In order to analyze the influence of philosophical logic and aesthetics on the literary discourse on fictionality, it is yet not enough to focus on the literary discourse itself. It is necessary to explore more deeply this area of interdisciplinary conceptualization. For this purpose the specific source of the philosophical influence on literary theory of fictionality and the particular area of interchange between the two disciplines have to be precisely located to account for the change in the literary and philosophical disciplines and for the concept of *fictionality* produced by these changes. Since the new interest in the problem of fictionality in literary studies is marked by the influence of specific areas in philosophy, it is the first aim of this study to trace the sources, route and functions of this influence. That is, in order to understand the place of fictionality in current literary theory and explore this concept further, the interchange between the two disciplines has to be fully traced and grasped. The fact that the nature of fiction touches on some basic questions in philosophical logic and the philosophy of language does not imply that fictionality is a purely philosophical concept that necessarily exceeds the explanatory tools of literary models. Nor does it imply that the relations between the philosophical and literary discourses about fictionality are straight-forward; there is a whole complex of issues related to the interdisciplinary exchange around the problem of fiction.

Note that in tracing the various philosophical traditions that tackle the problem of fiction I will not deal with their separate influences on the literary discipline. Although, at least in the Anglo-American tradition of thought, logic and aesthetics are distinct modes of philosophical discourse (crudely speaking, the former representing the "left-overs" of analytical–formal philosophy, and the latter manifesting a more speculative, humanistic philosophical tendency), independent developments in the philosophical domain are not in themselves a direct object of the present study. Fictionality and related notions can be described indiscriminately as objects of logic and of aesthetics, particularly because it is the philosophical, even the metaphysical insights behind formal logic and semantics (and not the formalizations themselves) that pertain to the present study. The work of aestheticians (like Goodman, Walton, Wolterstorff, Brinker and others) will therefore be referred to alongside works of logicians (from Hintikka and Kripke to Lewis and Adams), but only insofar as their work pertains to the links between philosophical notions and the problem of fiction. I will also refrain from surveying the philosophical discourse on the logic of fiction for its own sake. To some extent the state-of-the-art in this regard, is well summarized in specific collections of essays to which formal semanticians and logicians contributed their work.[3] Although the solutions for fiction proposed by philosophers have been varied and even contradictory, these solutions will not be surveyed for their own sake. Specific aspects of the philosophical discussion on fiction and related topics will be brought up at various

3 The primary source in this respect is the issue of the journal *Poetics* (vol. 8, 1979).

stages of the present study to illuminate the sources and the implications of the influence of philosophical logic on literary theory. These will also show what can ultimately be learnt from the process in which literary theory has become receptive to the discourse on non-actual states of affairs in general and on fictionality in particular developed in another discipline.

Possible worlds and fictionality

This study concentrates on one central metaphor, that of *possible worlds*, whose origins lie with Leibnitz. Within philosophy possible worlds serve diverse purposes: they are used as a metaphysical term, as a concept of modal logic, as a way for describing epistemic accessibility and even as a metaphor in the philosophy of science denoting relationships between mutually exclusive paradigms. Possible worlds are also widely employed in aesthetic discussions of representation, mimesis and artistic reference. Possible worlds have not only been used across philosophical domains but also across disciplines and have, above all, permeated the field of literary theory (but also linguistics, art theory and the natural sciences). Possible worlds stand in this study first as a general label for a set of modal and referential concepts developed in logic and borrowed by other disciplines to describe diverse issues: from universes of discourse in linguistics, through fictional worlds and narrative multi-perspectives in literary theory, to physical reality in natural sciences. This set includes the concepts of necessity and possibility, that of world, world-set and transworld relations, concepts referring to world constituents, and to modes of existence (nonexistence, incomplete being, and so on). These concepts have permeated the literary theoretical discourse as evidenced in the re-introduction of referential issues into the literary domain and in the terminology prevailing in areas of literary theorizing that address the problem of fictionality. Possible worlds hence provide a general framework and context for describing the most notable influence of philosophical discourse on the literary theory of fictionality and they supply the grounds for reorienting literary theory toward questions of reference, ontology and representation. "Possible worlds" is also a specific term that has re-emerged in modal logic in the seventies to provide the abstract notions of modal logic with concrete content: possibility and necessity are described in this context as *worlds* or as *states of affairs*. *Possible worlds*, in itself, has gained a marked currency in the literary area of discourse. In this specific sense the idea of possible worlds is symptomatic of modifications and revisions in the philosophical discipline itself in the last two decades. Both in its specific and its more general sense the concept of *possible worlds* represents a larger context behind it and it does not appear as an isolated concept in philosophy. Discussions about possible worlds and related issues in philosophy, represent more general changes in this domain. These changes proceed in the direction of relaxing philosophical notions of *truth*, *existence* and *world-language relations*, notions that traditionally received rigid delimitations. Understanding the influence of the philosophical discourse on literary theory hence cannot proceed without due attention being paid to these changes. In applying possible worlds to the literary discipline there is no reason to assume that the concept can be detached from its broader philosophical context. The impact of philosophical conceptualization and theorizing on literary theory of fictionality indeed transcends the notion of possible worlds in its restricted sense, and to explain this impact one must hence draw from wider philosophical resources. In this regard possible worlds can again serve as a handy metaphor, as a lens through which changes in the philosophical domain can be surveyed and the extent of their influence gauged. The way possible worlds and related concepts (like accessibility, necessity, contingency) are interpreted in literary theory reflects a specific phase in the history of cross-disciplinary fertilization around the problem of fiction, as this study aims to demonstrate. The nature of this phase is particularly conspicuous not only because it is encapsulated in the very notion of possible worlds and in the ontological connotations this concept carries, but also because it marks the first stage of interdisciplinary exchange in a history that has for the most part been a history of separate disciplinary undertakings. It is for this reason that possible worlds can reflect deeper-rooted changes of direction and orientation in both disciplines.

The essentials of the interdisciplinary exchange around possible worlds can be summarized in the following way (and they will be fully elaborated in chapter 1 of this study):

(1)   Possible worlds (and related concepts) borrowed from philosophical logic, indicate the legitimization of referential problems and of issues that have to do with the relations fiction–reality in literary theory.

(2)   Possible worlds provide for the first time a philosophical

explanatory framework that pertains to the problem of fiction. This is an exception in view of the long philosophical tradition, from Plato to Russell, that has excluded fiction from the philosophical discussion (fiction has been viewed, for instance, as a sequence of propositions devoid of a truth value).

(3) Possible worlds indicate that fiction is logically and semantically not an exceptional phenomenon. Although fiction is constituted by propositions that seem like regular assertions yet do not refer to actual states of affairs or to anything at all, there are other cultural products with similar features, products that present non-actual states of affairs through the power of language (conditionals, propositions relating the wishes, anticipations or memories of a speaker, myth-constructing propositions, etc.). Fiction is hence not seen as an isolated exceptional phenomenon but is part of a larger context of discourses that do not refer to the way things actually are in the world.

(4) Possible worlds breach the hermetics of literariness and the inner-systemic orientation that had been a prevalent characteristic of literary theory for some decades. This is achieved however without hindering the possibility of formalism in literary theory. In this respect the logico-semantic source of possible worlds matches the needs of literary researchers anxious to retain formal methods of description in literary studies.

These four points that supply the grounds and the motivation for the literary use of possible worlds portray only one side of the picture of interdisciplinary exchange. The other side of this exchange reveals symptomatic difficulties that cross-disciplinary conceptual borrowing involves. In this context a twofold problem with the literary use of possible worlds requires explanation. First, literary theory gives insufficient account of the philosophical sources of thinking about possible worlds, and, second, in the process of transferring possible worlds to the literary domain, the concept loses its original meaning and becomes a diffuse metaphor. In short, possible worlds is a concept that seems to have been fully incorporated into the literary discipline without a sufficient clarification of its original meaning. The result is a naive adaptation or an inadvertent metaphorization of a concept whose original (philosophical and literary) nonfigurative significance is far from self-evident. A similar situation occurs in relation to other concepts such as accessibility, actuality and nonexistents. Often then, the literary use of these concepts deviates from their original philosophical meaning: it ignores the purposes these concepts were destined to serve and the problems they aimed to solve in the philosophical domain. In addition to this partial account of the original significance of possible worlds, it sometimes seems that in the literary arena possible worlds function as "modern" substitutes for more traditional concepts and thereby the explanatory potential possible worlds carry with them for literary phenomena is not fully exhausted. Thus, although the interdisciplinary interaction around the concept of *possible worlds* did give rise to some insights concerning literary fiction and enabled new directions of thought, this interaction has still not been fully explored in some respects, while in other respects it has been misleading. The problems involved in using possible worlds across disciplines will be described in the second chapter of this study where it will be shown that fictional worlds can be seen as possible worlds only when part of the logico-semantic features of the latter concept are ignored. Although possible worlds talk marks the birth of a new type of discourse on fictionality within the literary discipline, fictional worlds, unlike possible worlds, manifest a world-model based on the notion of *parallelism* rather than *ramification*. Possible worlds are based on a logic of ramification determining the range of possibilities that emerge from an actual state of affairs; fictional worlds are based on a logic of parallelism that guarantees their autonomy in relation to the actual world.

A world of any ontological status contains a set of entities (objects, persons) organized and interrelated in specific ways (through situations, events and space-time). A world as a system of entities and relations, is an autonomous domain in the sense that it can be distinguished from other domains identified with other sets of entities and relations. A fictional world is likewise composed of sets of *entities* (characters, objects, places) and of networks of relations that can be described as *organizing principles*: spatio-temporal relations, event and action sequences. Worlds, whether fictional, possible or actual, are hence distinguishable from one another. Yet the fictional world is constructed as a world having its own distinct ontological position, and as a world presenting a self-sufficient system of structures and relations. Possible worlds however, despite being distinguishable worlds, do not share this ontological autonomy. One central symptom of the kind of autonomy attributed to fictional worlds is manifested in the way fiction constitutes an independent *modal structure*. Constructed as a parallel world, every fictional world includes a core of facts around which orbit sets of states of affairs of diminishing fictional actuality. The fictional modal structure manifests the parallelism of fictional ontologies indicating that fictional facts do not relate *what could have or could not have occurred in actuality, but rather, what did occur and what could have occurred in fiction.*

Fictionality and the pragmatics of fiction

The importance of delimiting the area of interchange between the two disciplines, of grasping the source of the philosophical influence on literary theory of fictionality and of distinguishing fictional from possible worlds, lies in the new approach to fictionality that this analysis generates. To some extent the mere use of concepts borrowed from philosophical logic, and particularly the use of concepts that belong to the framework of *possible worlds* goes hand in hand with a new conception of fictionality. It is the aim of chapter 3 of this study to elucidate the nature and significance of the notion of fictionality that emerges from the interdisciplinary domain of theorizing about referential issues. The work of a group of literary researchers working within a formalist tradition (Doležel, Pavel, Eco, Ryan, Vaina, Margolin) anticipates, implies and sometimes explicitly implements a reconsideration of fictionality. The terminology these theorists have borrowed from the logical framework is applied in order to tackle a variety of issues: to clarify the concept of *fictionality* (Pavel, 1986; Doležel, 1988), to clarify generic distinctions (Ryan, 1991; Doležel, 1985), to analyze the speech act distinctive of fiction-making (Martinez-Bonati, 1981; Ryan, 1984; Petrey, 1990) and even to solve the poetical problems raised by particular literary trends (McHale, 1987) or to describe the reading process and semiotic deciphering of the literary text (Eco, 1979). This range of issues to which logical concepts are applied ratifies the recent interest of literary theorists in general questions related to the logic and semantics that derive from the "fictional" position of a text in a culture. Yet beyond this variety of issues, and upon a closer look at these models, a common trait emerges: what characterizes this whole direction, directly influenced by the philosophical discussion of necessity, possibility and possible worlds, is that there is no longer an attempt to locate the fictionality of texts in a textual property. Although not often explicitly stated, the position presented in these studies implies that a logic of fiction does not base itself on textually immanent features. The state of being fictional is identified with a complex of literary, cultural and institutional considerations. This direction of research shows that the fictional property of texts can be defined relative to a given cultural context, as a pragmatically decided feature of texts. Every culture adduces its own relative criteria for classification of texts: some texts are viewed as fictional but only relative to texts that are considered within this same context to be nonfictional – history, or scientific versions of the actual world. Fictionality is hence no longer viewed as immanent: only as a pragmatically determined property can fictionality distinguish *Anna Karenina* as a fiction from Michelet's nonfictional *History of France* despite the considerable number of fictional components that the latter contains. Fictionality can also contextually distinguish fiction from myth (texts that can be considered fictional or factual according to the historical moment chosen) and from scientific texts (texts that present authoritative versions of how the world is).

Chapter 3 would therefore aim to propose a systematic model of what a pragmatic definition of fictionality involves by integrating the results of the critique on the interdisciplinary use of possible worlds with a description of the logico-semantic properties of fiction. If a fictional world is not a possible world, the question remains as to what characterizes fictional ontologies and what is their position in relation to their producers and understanders. To explore the unique nature of fiction we should first ask how far the analogy between possible and fictional worlds has brought us in this respect. Possible worlds have evidently had a long-lasting and profound impact on the literary discipline in its dealings with fictionality. The situation looks like this: the impact of possible worlds and other logical concepts on literary theory is demonstrated in what can be described as the rendering of fictionality into a pragmatic concept; the pragmatics of fiction, in its turn, is the basis for defining the kind of context-dependent dividing line between fictional and nonfictional ontologies, and also the basis for describing the logic and semantic properties related to the fictional modality.

A pragmatically determined dividing line between fiction and nonfiction means that the way fictionality is approached in the present study contrasts with both "segregationist" and "integrationist" approaches to fiction.[4] Contrary to the type of dividing line between fiction and nonfiction proposed in this study, segregationists tend to

4 The distinction between segregationist and integrationist approaches to fiction was proposed in Pavel, 1986.

impose a categorical dividing line between fiction and nonfiction and explain the nature of fiction as a *deviation* from the actual state of affairs, from standard logic or from normal rules of semantics. The pragmatics of fiction described in the present study also opposes the view of integrationists who tend from the start to *blur the differences* between conflicting ontologies. Integrationist approaches repress the ontological differentiation between worlds and posit an unproblematic accessibility between world-systems. Furthermore, both integrationist and segregationist approaches tend to view the nature of fictional entities as dictated by a metaphysical and epistemic view on the nature of reality. Theories of fiction, I claim, should be neither segregationist nor integrationist in their approach; a certain autonomy should be granted to the logic and semantics of fiction, an autonomy that would prevent unwarranted attempts, on the part of literary theorists, to forward or imply claims about what is the "actual state of affairs."

Despite the relativity with which the property of being fictional is imbued, the fictionality of a text does entail specific logico-semantic rules according to which the fictional world is read. Under certain pragmatic circumstances or in a specific cultural context, a decision is made to categorize texts under the rubric "fiction." Once the label "fiction" has been attributed, conventions dictating the status and proper interpretation of fictional propositions are activated. When a text is considered to be fictional, its set of propositions are read according to *fictional world-constructing conventions* and it is made to signify by observing the set of *fictional world-reconstructing conventions* (described in chapter 3). From the former set of conventions follows the ontological separation of fiction from actuality, and from the second set it follows that, granted this separation, the domains constituting the fictional world (characters and objects, events, time and space) obey modes of organization that are unique to fiction.[5] That is, when the propositions of a text are indexed by the property "fictional" in a given cultural context, the characters, for instance, constructed by these propositions, are viewed as participants in a parallel fictional world-system, and in view of this parallelism (that is, logico-semantic autonomy relative to other world systems) these characters are regarded as demonstrating a unique mode of

---

5 It should be noted that possible worlds hover on this notion of fictionality. The pragmatic definition of fictionality specified on the basis of logico-semantic properties directly derives from the type of logico-semantics that possible worlds introduced into the study of modalities and nonactual worlds.

organization (for example, according to the appropriate world-reconstructing convention, we assume that characters in fictional worlds are organized in central and secondary sets, that characters are of a flat or round nature, etc.). Each fictional domain hence functions both as an *ontological* domain and as a *structural* domain: it identifies the unique ontological status of fiction relative to other worlds of non-actual existence and it identifies the structural modus of fiction that emerges from world-bound principles of organization.[6]

This view on the autonomy of fictional worlds implies that fictional worlds are ontologically and structurally distinct: facts of the actual world have no a priori ontological privilege over facts of the fictional world. The fictional world system is an independent system whatever the type of fiction constructed and the extent of its drawing on our knowledge of the actual world. Since fictional worlds are autonomous, they are not more or less fictional according to degrees of affinity between fiction and reality: facts of the actual world are not constant reference points for the facts of fiction. Drawing a pragmatic distinction between fiction and reality, that both underlines the relativity of the fictional category and at the same time the autonomy of worlds of fiction, hence does not impose a specific notion of what reality is, or how it is related to fiction. The activation of conventions for fiction-reading means that the fictional world is grasped as logically autonomous relative to any notion of reality (although it might heavily rely on such reality notions).

Fictionality and narrativity

Whereas the first part of this study is dedicated to the interaction between possible worlds and fictionality, the second part will concentrate on the relations between fictional worlds and narrativity. It would be claimed that the fictionality of literary worlds is a composite phenomenon assuming both inter-world relations (fiction cannot be defined outside a cultural system that defines also nonfictional modes of being) and intra-world organization. In the case of narrative worlds intra-world organization is determined by narrativity.

6 "... very many of the worlds of universal semantics [possible worlds of most modern semantics] are not fictional worlds, for two reasons: they have no author or set of authors; and they lack structural requirements of coherence, continuity, organisation, and so forth that distinguish fictional worlds, even those of bad works of fiction, from other worlds" (Routley, 1979: 7).

This study focuses on the meeting place of fictionality and narrativity although dramatic texts as well as lyrical poetry and narrative prose all construct worlds or fragments of worlds. One could therefore equally study the meeting place of fictionality with the lyrical or dramatic qualities of worlds. The emphasis on narrativity is yet motivated by the generally held belief that among literary genres, narrative fiction most clearly constructs those systematic sets and states of affairs to which the concept of *world* pertains. Such an intuitive belief may explain why among fields of literary theory, narrative theory is still more occupied with the problem of world construction than the theory of drama or of the lyric, although it can be shown that worlds are not confined to narrative construction. Since narrative fiction most clearly constructs worlds one could expect, from a point of view that examines the overall state of the literary discipline, that any theoretical attempt to describe fictional worlds would rely on a combination of these two concepts: *fictionality* and *narrativity*.

The recent interest of literary theorists in problems of reference, representation and fictionality is indeed particularly marked in the discourse of narratologists (theorists of narrative).[7] This institutional intersection (and personal identity) of professionals known as narratologists and those who work on problems of fictionality and of fictional ontology should not however create a misleading impression. Until very recently it has been exceptionally rare in narrative studies that referential issues and new theories of fictionality were made to bear on the core of narrative research. As remarked above, the emphasis on the susceptibility of the category of the fictional to cultural-historical fluctuations represents a radical change of conception about the nature of literary worlds. Yet, until the late eighties, this change of conception has by and large remained detached from the mainstream of narrative theory. In other words, the impact of philosophical concepts on the literary discipline has been restricted to very limited areas of research, or at least, the implications of this impact have not been fully appropriated. That is, although a newly developed pragmatics of fiction welcomes a new conception of plot-structures, points of view and perspectives, characters and objects, and

---

7 Both an interdisciplinary orientation and a preoccupation with referential issues are manifested in recent issues of the journals *Poétique* (1989) and *Poetics Today* (1990, 1991) dedicated to narratology. Such publications reflect the fact that referential considerations have started to permeate the mainstream of literary theory.

temporal structure, these mostly continue to be addressed with traditional terms, or at least so it seems on face value. The mainstream of narrative theory, in other words, pays little heed to the way fictionality affects the inner organization of narrative texts. Thus, although in the sense explained above, fictionality and narrativity are inseparable facets of literary worlds of the narrative kind, the question is why combination of the two figures so little in literary theory. The history of literary dealings with the problem of fictionality indirectly answers this problem: a theory that incorporates both terms faces some obvious difficulties of method and methodology. Whereas narrativity developed almost solely within literary studies and reflects the "centripetal" tendencies prevalent in the history of this discipline, the point of departure for dealing with the concept of fictionality necessarily lies outside the study of literature and requires a "centrifugal" approach. It is for this reason that until recent changes in the literary discipline, attempts on the part of narrative theorists to deal with the problem of fictionality stopped at the intra-systemic level.

Chapters 4 to 7 of this study aim to counterbalance the demands of a theory of fictionality with a matching view on narrative concepts. The "centripetal" tendencies detectable in narrative theory demand an appropriate theory that will grant fictional narrative with an autonomy, that will delineate the literary boundaries of narrative worlds, distinguishing the narrative system from what lies beyond it. I would claim that the autonomy and self-sufficiency presupposed for narrative worlds are compatible with some principal aspects of the pragmatic definition of fictionality. The pragmatics of fiction hence presents these two facets of narrative worlds as inseparable: fictionality imposes inter-world determination and the narrativity of worlds imposes intra-world principles of organization on the fictional system. A central aim of the present study is therefore to examine the implications of the interdisciplinary interchange on fictionality for the inner structure of fictional worlds. The interdisciplinary game, centered on the concept of *possible worlds*, which affects the way fictionality is defined by literary theorists, can also prove significant for our understanding of some of the basic concepts and modes of descriptions of the world constructed by narrative texts. First, a systematic description of fictional worlds must tackle the concept of fictionality: to explicate the particular property of fictional worlds that detaches them from the actual states of affairs composing what is viewed as reality or a version thereof. Yet addressing the fictionality of worlds constitutes only a first step in describing the particular entities, relations, and modes of organization unique to worlds of fiction. The narrativity of worlds seems to be an indispensable complement to their fictionality that would account for the specific mode of being of narrative worlds.

Events, setting, characters and space-time are modes of narrative organization that reflect the nature and concerns of fictional world-construction. In this study four fictional domains are examined: the domain of *fictional entities*, the domain of *fictional events*, the domain of *fictional perspectives* and the domain of *fictional time*; in the construction of each domain both ontological and structural aspects of inner-world modes of organization will be investigated. This view of the way a fictional world is provides a possible access to narrative organization through the prism of its fictional mode of being. A fictional world can be described as a unique system separate from, although dependent on cultural-historical reality in which it is created and with which it holds more or less obvious affinities. The qualities characteristic of fictional worlds are not only reflected in the relation between the fictional position of a world and alternative positions of other worlds; being fictional is also reflected in the narrative and compositional structures of literary worlds. Although narrative worlds are not restricted to the domain of fiction, when narrativity is combined with fictionality the world produced has its own distinctive traits. An ontological dividing line between narrative fiction and nonfiction is hence not immanent; it is implied in our assigning, within a given cultural context, the property "fiction" to a narrative text and its world, and by our reconstructing the narrative structures of this world in view of its fictionality. This assignment can take place even if what lies outside fiction are more texts of fiction or other narratives that constitute no more than versions of reality.

Fictional texts and worlds have been claimed to possess no a priori properties distinguishing them from nonfictional texts and worlds. Yet I do claim that these texts are susceptible or they enable an autonomization and that what makes them susceptible to cultural autonomization are the specific modes of organization manifested by fictional worlds. I will show however that the structural aspect of narrative fiction is a derivative of the ontological aspect: once a world is assigned the category of fiction, understanding fiction requires identifying modes of organization unique to this world-type.

Examining the interaction between fictionality and narrativity demonstrates why fictionality, defined as a contextual position of a text, as a relativized property, is an object of research that naturally belongs to the literary discipline. When questions of fictionality are integrated rather than detached from "literary" and "narrative" concerns, when referential considerations are made to bear on problems concerning inner-world modes of organization, fictionality becomes an integral part of a theory of literary worlds.

I

Possible worlds, fictional worlds

This chapter will reconstruct and examine the motivation and logic behind the conceptual link between possible worlds and fictional worlds. I will attempt to motivate this link both in terms of the more or less apparent properties of possible worlds that appeal to literary theorists, and in terms of more general disciplinary considerations (concerning the philosophical discipline in particular) that may further justify the attempt at interdisciplinary exchange around the concept of *possible worlds*.

My intention in this chapter is mainly to explain why the interdisciplinary link between the possible worlds framework and the problem of fictionality is fundamental to the nature of both although the productivity of this link has certain limitations. My first concern would be to reveal the basic and most obvious similarities between possible and fictional worlds thus formulating and explaining the initial attraction possible worlds hold for literary theory, and to reveal the advantages gained by literary theory from marrying possible with fictional worlds. I would secondly discuss the motivations for tying fictionality with possible worlds in view of more global disciplinary concerns, thus providing at least a partial explanation as to how and why fiction has become a relatively important object of philosophical discussions. Hence, although the connection between fictionality and the philosophical concept of *possible worlds* is far from self-evident, I intend to deal here with what philosophy has to offer on the subject of fiction which would account for the penetration of possible worlds' talk into the literary discourse about fictionality. It is in the next chapter that the literary side of the picture will be further explored, yet this time in order to reveal both the limitations involved in tying possible to fictional worlds and the misapprehensions that the literary interpretation of possible worlds manifests.

Stage I   The philosophical notion of possible worlds and its basic relevance to fictional worlds

It is assumed in literary studies that most literary works, especially narrative types, construct fictional worlds. Yet, despite the longevity and acceptance of this assumption by literary theory and criticism, the concept of fictionality has almost been entirely neglected until recent years. This neglect is mainly due to a long tradition of massively focusing on the mimetic function of literary worlds: literary criticism has been traditionally preoccupied with the representational and mimetic relations between the worlds of literature and an actual reality, paying no heed to the logical and semantic implications of the fact that literary worlds are fictional, imaginative constructions. The neglect of the problem of fictionality should be surprising neither in relation to traditional, mimetic literary criticism, nor in relation to formalist–structuralist theories. Regarding views of the latter bent; here as a result of an ideologically motivated orientation toward the "literary" and the "intra-poetic" since the New Criticism, literary studies were not "equipped" to deal with the relations between the world constructed by a literary text and nonliterary or nonfictional states of affairs.

In the last decade however, the discipline of literature has undergone radical change which caused, among other things, the legitimation of a set of problems related to reference and existence in fiction, and with this a new interest in the problem of fictionality. These changes explain the general growing interest within the literary discipline in concepts developed by philosophy of language, philosophical logic, aesthetic theory, and the popularity of a concept like *possible worlds*.[1]

The current influence of philosophical logic on literary theory is intertwined with the evolution of each of the disciplines in isolation. The present chapter attempts to explain how the separate courses of each of these disciplines produced a convenient domain of exchange around the concept of *possible worlds*. Literature's borrowing from philosophy reflects, as claimed above, developments in literary studies and the re-orientation of literary research toward questions related to

1 Speech act theory manifests another marked influence of philosophical discourse on the literary one. As in the case of possible worlds, speech acts were borrowed from another discipline in order to explicate and account for aspects of literary communication which immanent literary concepts could not handle (see Petrey, 1990; Campbell, 1975; Pratt, 1977; Felman, 1983).

the referential functions of literature. Furthermore, from the perspective of literary theory, philosophy would seem of late to have become more apt for supplying solutions to pressing literary problems of fictionality because recent trends in philosophy offer more flexible approaches to questions surrounding reference, truth values, modalities, and possible and inactual situations; these developments in philosophy (which will be fully discussed later in this chapter) intuitively suit a literary discipline engaged in an attempt to grasp an elusive cultural phenomenon such as fiction. Literary theory of fictionality hence coincides with and benefits from the non-dogmatic and generally non-metaphysical framework of modern philosophy as reflected in the treatment of problems such as possibility, truth and reference. This non-dogmatism necessary for clarifying the concept of fictionality is reflected with particular intensity in the framework of possible worlds. Literary theorists who attempt, in various ways, to link literary fictionality with modal concepts in philosophy (Eco, Vaina, Margolin, Doležel, Pavel, Ryan and others) hence do not make this link in a disciplinary vacuum: within the world of philosophy itself there is a growing arsenal of philosophical models dealing with possibility, existence, nonexistence, and even with fiction and with other phenomena that undermine standard two-valued logic. The growing dominance of concepts such as possible worlds, accessibility among worlds, necessity and possibility, nonexistence, counterfactuality, cross-world identity and epistemic worlds, thus reflects epistemologically less restrained ways of thinking about philosophical problems.

The group of literary theorists mentioned above who, crudely speaking, continue the formalist tradition in literary studies, were among the first to use concepts derived from philosophical logic in general and the framework of possible worlds in particular. These have been used in order to clarify literary issues: to explain the notion of *fictionality* (Pavel, 1986; Doležel, 1988); to clarify generic distinctions (Doležel, 1985; Ryan, 1991); to analyze the speech act distinctive of fiction-making (Doležel, 1980; Martinez-Bonati, 1981; Ryan, 1984; Petrey, 1990); or to describe the reading process and semiotic deciphering of the literary text (Eco, 1979); and even solve some of the poetic problems raised by specific literary trends, such as postmodernism (McHale, 1987). What characterizes this direction, directly influenced by the philosophical discussion of necessity, possibility and possible worlds, that there is no longer an attempt to locate the fictionality of texts in a textual property. In all its manifestations, literary research influenced by philosophical logic, implies a different view on fictionality: fictionality is identified with a *pragmatic* position of certain texts relative to a given cultural context (relative to texts with a different cultural position, such as history, or relative to texts considered to be versions of reality, such as scientific theories). A key to understanding this interdisciplinary link lies in the fact that fictionality is no longer regarded as immanent, and is not identified with components of the literary text itself. As will be shown below, a pragmatic definition of fictionality derives from merely adapting possible worlds and related terms to the literary discipline. Some of the literary theorists even use the notion of possible worlds to show that the fictionality of texts is a property deriving from cultural and historical decisions (according to which *War and Peace* is a fictional text although it documents historical and social facts, myths are considered fictional texts or historical texts according to the specific historical moment at which they are received, and the *Histoire de la France* by Michelet is a historical text despite the invented elements that recur in it). When such a pragmatic (or non-immanent) understanding of fictionality is accepted, the questions about literary fiction arise concerning the logical and semantic principles that derive from a *pragmatic–contextual* definition of fictionality. That is, the fictional position of texts entails a specific logic and semantics for literature although this logico-semantics does not ground itself on textual facts and is not activated but by a cultural decision.

Put in general terms then, a growing philosophical interest in nonexistence and possibilism, combined with a shift in the way fictionality is comprehended and theorized by literary theorists, have created a convenient context for disciplinary interchange.

More specifically, in the context of explaining the logico-semantic implications of the fictionality of literary worlds (and as this chapter will explore) possible worlds serve literary theory in a variety of ways:

(1) Possible worlds legitimize an interest in referential problems and in everything that concerns the relations between literature and the actual world.

(2) Possible worlds supply, for the first time, a philosophical framework for explaining fiction, thereby turning fiction into a legitimate topic of philosophical discussion. This is a radical shift in a long tradition, from Plato to Russell, that viewed fiction as a sequence of propositions devoid of truth value or simply false.

(3)   The framework of possible worlds attests to the fact that fiction is not an extraordinary phenomenon. It is one among other categories of cultural products that present non-actual states of affairs through language (the same is true of conditionals, descriptions of worlds of desire, belief, and anticipation, and mythical versions of the world).

(4)   Possible worlds offer a way of escaping hermeticist claims about the literary text and the intra-systemic tendency of literary studies without sabotaging the possibility of formalization in dealing with the structure of a fictional world. In this respect the logical source of possible worlds is appropriate to the aims of literary theorists who decline any essentialist approaches to literature while aspiring to maintain formal methods of description in literary theory as much as possible.

The development of a conceptual framework of possible worlds hence at first glance seems to offer a new outlook on the problem of fictionality, on the ontology of fictional worlds and fictional objects, and on generic problems such as realism. Yet, is there indeed such a straightforward relevance between the two domains of theorizing? Are the premises underlying the philosophical framework of possible worlds clear enough to allow the adaptation of possible worlds for the questions surrounding fiction?

The basic intuition behind possible worlds states that there are other ways things could have been, that there exist other possible states of affairs (see Bradley and Swartz, 1979: 1–8). Yet, in fact, the nature of these other ways the world could have been is a polemical issue. Possible worlds create a heterogenous paradigm that allows various conceptions for possible modes of existence. Philosophical debates about the validity of possible worlds center on the sense and extent to which by engaging ourselves in a counterfactual or modal discourse we commit ourselves to an alternative ontology. The core of this debate can be clarified if we look more closely at specific versions of possible worlds models. The various positions on possible worlds are in fact various views on the degree of *realism* to be ascribed to possible worlds.[2] There we can discover three basic views on the validity of talking about possible states of affairs and about the actuality of these alternative worlds.

(1)   According to the radical view known as *modal realism*, all

---

2 See Putnam, 1990: 71; Kripke, 1972: 44.

modal possibilities we might stipulate, as well as the actual world, are equally realized in some logical space where they possess a physical existence. Thus according to Lewis (1973), who is the major proponent of such a view in modern times, "actual" does not refer to the world we inhabit or to a specific notion of what reality is. "Actual" is rather an indexical term; the inhabitants of each world see their universe as the actual one. The way Lewis interprets possible worlds may assist us in grasping the ontological extravagance implied in his position: for Lewis possible worlds are parallel worlds, autonomous "foreign countries" with their own laws and with an actuality of their own. Such worlds do not exist in a way that differs from the mode of existence of the actual world.[3]

(2)   To the second view, commonly termed *moderate realism*, a more heterogeneous variety of positions can be attributed. Some versions of moderate realism are known as "actualism" according to whose supporters (Plantinga, van Inwagen, Adams, Rescher and Stalnaker) possible worlds necessarily exist within the confines of the actual world and are viewed as components of the actual world. The actual world is a complex structure that includes both its actual elements and non-actual possibilities, that is, the ways things might have been (whether these non-actual possibilities exist as *mental constructs*, as postulated by Rescher, as *non-obtaining states*, as proposed by Plantinga, or as a *set of propositions* about things in our world, as suggested by Adams). Possible worlds in any case are the result of rational behavior which only admits one world. That is, the ways things might have been are components of reality since a rationalist cannot believe that possibilities are literally there in a space causally disconnected from our world. The moderate realist, rejecting speculation about what happens in worlds unattached to our own, hence attributes possibilities to our world. Possible worlds yet produce explanations in modal contexts because they can be employed, for instance, to account for the meaning of modal propositions as propositions true in possible worlds: modal propositions do not impose quantifying over nonexistents; they only require that we quantify over things similar to actualities.

Another version of moderate realism acknowledges the explanatory force of possible worlds yet accentuates the difference between possible worlds and the actual state of things. Kripke (1972) as well as

3 Such a version also exists in the New Physics postulating a proliferation of parallel worlds. For a popularized account, see Davies's *Other Worlds* (1980).

other philosophers approach the question of the mode of existence of possible worlds by claiming that possible worlds are *abstract entities*, hypothetical situations, not real "parallel worlds." They differentiate between the modality of the actual world, and the modality of hypothetical possible constructs which form the non-actualized part of the world. Thus whereas Kripke emphasizes the abstractness of alternative possibilities, a moderate realist in the actualist vein, like Plantinga, claims that had things been different, an alternative state of affairs would not only be possible, but there would have been such a state of affairs, although not an obtaining (or exemplified) state. The actual world has the distinction of actually obtaining while all other possible worlds exist in the actual world, yet they do not actually obtain (Plantinga, 1974: 47–48).

The various advocates of moderate realism hence distinguish in a variety of modes the actual state of affairs from possible states of affairs without however subsuming to the ontological "extravagant" assumption that these possibilities are literally "out there."

(3) A third approach adopts an *anti-realist* view on possible worlds. Here possible worlds are denied any kind of heuristic or explanatory power, any pertinence to questions of being and existence, and are definitely refused any kind of actuality. The most common argument for rejecting these notions maintains that a belief in possible worlds assumes the existence, or at least the accessibility, of an actual world, a belief that is basically misguided. Possible worlds are rejected because there is no way to qualify the reality of *the actual* or *the real* in relation to which other worlds present a variety of alternate possibilities. An anti-realism toward possible worlds is therefore part and parcel of a general anti-realist philosophical position. The notion of an actual world as a constant background to non-actual possibilities serves both a metaphysical stand that accepts the actual world as the best, inevitable or at least the only world that could have been actualized, but it is also part of a moderate stand that chooses to see the actual world only as a contingency. Yet, if the actual is a contingency, a myth that manifests no essential difference from non-actual states of the world, possible worlds claims the anti-realist, will also prove to constitute a relative notion, of no avail when the distinction between the actual and the non-actual is at stake. Note that although on the level of logic this may seem as another version of a Lewis approach, these views radically diverge in terms of the metaphysical suppositions motivating them. While Lewis' radical

realism attributes concrete existence to all worlds, for an anti-realist like Goodman existence and actuality are attributed to none. Lewis sees all worlds as equally real and concrete (although he distinguishes between genres of worlds); Goodman sees all worlds as versions subject to radical relativism.

These three views on the degree of realism to be ascribed to possibilities, on the heuristic significance of possible worlds, and their position in relation to the actual world, first explain why possible worlds cannot be approached as a *monolithic notion* by any discipline that would choose to adopt the concept. Second, the variety of ways of interpreting the notion of possible worlds shows that philosophers themselves do not take possible worlds as a conceptual given. Philosophical debates about possible worlds relate to the very presuppositions behind using this concept and they examine and sometimes question the very relevance of this basic metaphysical tool, carrying clear ontological implications, for problems of logic and semantics.[4] These debates thus reveal the core and rationale behind the entire philosophical notion of possible worlds.

The different views on possible worlds also indicate the main problem in adopting this concept in the description of fictional worlds. Whereas a view of possible worlds of the sort that Lewis proposes suits the intuitions of readers of literature about the concrete existence of fictional worlds (for readers a fictional Anna Karenina is at least as concrete and familiar as one's actual friend), it leads to an ontological extravagance that few philosophers would endorse. A more common conception of possible worlds as abstract entities or hypothetical states describing the ways the world might have been, although more acceptable from a philosophical point of view, seems intuitively less suitable for fiction where one would be reluctant to consider fictional worlds as abstract states of affairs. At the same time, an (almost) absolute relativism of the kind that Goodman promotes contradicts a sense of division throughout the culture between fiction and reality; treating all worlds as versions of an equal status defies the very idea that a culture differentiates among its various ontological domains.

---

4 Kripke, who first introduced possible worlds into modal logic (1963), dedicates considerable parts of his later *Naming and Necessity* to examining the "philosophy" behind this notion. It is indeed this distance between the usefulness of possible worlds as a formal semantic tool in the context of logic and its implications for a philosophy of logic, which instigates debates among philosophers over the validity of using possible worlds.

Although in certain contexts the dividing line between fictional and nonfictional domains can prove to be rather fuzzy or transitory (as extensively shown in Pavel 1986, 1989), acknowledging and identifying these divides seem to be part of our basic cultural competence.

Since *possible worlds* is a vague concept in itself, reflecting diverse philosophical methods and approaches, applying it to any other context requires prior interpretation and qualification. The philosophical divergence of interpretations given to possible worlds is hence bound to counteract any attempt to apply possible worlds directly to literary phenomena, as if the concept were not open to interpretation and its potential explanatory power subject to a polemic within the source-discipline itself. A literary use of possible worlds necessarily imposes a deviation from the original plurality of meanings that characterized the use of possible worlds in philosophy. For instance, philosophers use possible worlds' concepts in order to describe the world as a complex modal structure, consisting of subsystems of worlds of various degrees of possibility (accessibility) relative to the world actually obtaining. Literary theorists and aestheticians make use however of possible worlds because notions of possibility and alternativity enable them to examine the accessibility relations between fictional worlds and *reality*. That is, literary theorists translate the general notion of accessibility into one particular type of possibility relations between fiction and *reality*. The philosophical notion of accessibility relations is thus interpreted so that possible worlds would be able to explain the distance between fiction and the real world (Pavel, 1986; Walton, 1978/9; Paskins, 1977: 344–47). As will be shown in detail in the next chapter, possible worlds are often used in the literary discipline with no prior clarification of their original meaning and with no account of the particular interpretation attributed to them in the literary field.

Despite the diversity of philosophical opinions about possible worlds, the idea common to all of them is that non-actual possibilities make perfectly coherent systems which can be described and qualified, imagined and intended and to which one can refer. Whatever the logical status of such possibilities, in all interpretations of possible worlds the non-obtaining or non-actuality of a state of affairs does not preclude or stipulate one's ability to make propositions about this state of affairs. By attributing concrete content to our modal talk, that is, by showing that talk about things that are not actual is talk about possible worlds, philosophical discourse provides a convenient way to describe other non-actualized, yet coherent, describable systems. Possible worlds also enable us to describe the relation holding between worlds; possible worlds can account for the links between the actual world and other worlds of a non-actual nature because each world (or set of states of affairs) is presented as a system under closure (as relatively autonomous), and a system ramifying in describable ways from the one world actually obtaining. Approaching the problem of fiction with the framework of possible worlds not only assumes an ability to refer to non-actualized alternatives, it also explores fiction as one among the various modal possibilities that orbit the actual world. Possible worlds "must be conceived not so much as alternatives to the real world but as worlds connected with it" (Castañeda, 1979: 59). Possible worlds, in any of their philosophical versions, thus can work as a descriptive tool both for the notion of alternativeness and for analyzing accessibility relations among worlds (for further analysis of *accessibility* defining the relative possibility of worlds, see chapter 2).

One of the more interesting points about possible worlds, a point missed by literary theorists, is that not only consensual domains among philosophers who refer to the framework of possible worlds can be employed in the context of fiction. That is, areas of debate in philosophy, like the one about the nature of actuality, or about the ontological value connoted by the notion of *world*, can also illuminate polemical points in discussions about fictionality. Let us look at one concrete polemical area which can prove prolific for literary theorizing. One of the more fundamental problems the logic of possible worlds poses for philosophers relates to the type of metaphysics implied by this framework and its conceptual components. Some philosophers would claim that by assuming possible states of affairs we are bound also to assume, although hypothetically, that we can adopt an *extra-systemic viewpoint*. To put it differently, since possibility is a relation between worlds as well as an attribute of worlds, to say about a world that it is possible involves considering it in relation to "other worlds" and hence requires a position outside any possible world under consideration. We would only then be able to describe the logical status of each given state of affairs and its accessibility relative to the actualized center of the system of worlds. The question of whether possible worlds involve an attempt to define the links between possible states of affairs and the actual world, and to determine whether the actual world is privileged over other alternatives is one area of disaccord in the philosophical context. Assuming an extra-systemic viewpoint on a system of worlds is a Platonist concretization of the notion of relative possibility, a type of concretization assumed by some proponents of possible worlds and one of the difficulties philosophers raise against this framework.[5] More modest proposals will just see possibility as an operator over a variety of world-models and disregard the metaphysical implications that can be drawn from such an operator. This problem has its counterpart in a pressing question in the context of a theory of fiction where the question of how is a fictional world positioned relative to other worlds, of primary importance: can we assume that a given fictional world holds stable describable relations with some notion of "the real"? Does fictionality manifest a stable position of one category of worlds relative to the actual world or relative to other categories of non-actual possibilities (that is, are all types of fiction subsumed under one category), or does fiction allow different degrees of fictionality and a variety of possibility relations established differently in each fictional world? Are the worlds of *Germinal, Slaughterhouse 5, Everyman* and "The Sandman" fictional in the same way, or does each assume a different relation of possibility with the actual world and hence posit a different mode of fictionality? Does each of these fictional worlds considered possible or impossible in relation to one and the same world-picture? Although a fictional world does not necessarily manifest one type of relative possibility (for example, E. T. A. Hoffmann's "The Sandman" contains more than one ontological structure), some philosophers would consider the fictional world to entertain a stable type of accessibility relation with the actual world for its construction (these philosophers would consider fictionality as a modal category manifested, for instance, in a fictionality operator subjecting all propositions of fiction to one unified modality). Yet others see fictional worlds as a non-actualized set which depends to varying degrees on a "horizon of actuality"; the degree of reliance on reality's resources affects the way one perceives fiction and the way one might define the nature of fiction. To sum up this point, the entire spectrum of philosophical debate about the nature of possibility is reflected in the variety of conceptions about the logic of fiction held by philosophers and literary theorists.

5 Against the metaphysical overtones attached to possible worlds by some of its proponents, linguists, for instance, claims Partee, would be perfectly happy to keep the structure of possible worlds semantics while ignoring the possible worlds themselves for the most part (1989: 120).

For most philosophers possible worlds are characterized by their being *intensional worlds,* a feature that distinguishes them from the actual world and brings out their similarity to fictional worlds. Intensions are treated in possible worlds semantics as functions from possible worlds to extensions; a possible world is a world where the meaning of words determines the collection of things referred to by these words or to which these words are applied. That is, a possible world is a world where "Shakespeare" and "the author of *King Lear*" diverge in meaning, and this divergence carries referential implications; the denotative values of expressions might change from one possible world to another (in another possible world, "Shakespeare" and "the author of *King Lear*" might denote two separate beings). Possible worlds semantics hence does not deal with the denotative value of expressions in the actual world, but with the ways in which denotations are determined in a possible world (Heintz, 1979; Woods, 1974; Ihwe, 1979). Possible worlds' notions thus allow us to see the fictional world as a universe of discourse constructing its own world of referents.

Finally, possible worlds aid our understanding of fiction since within its framework the autonomy of world systems is secured. In possible worlds semantics each world is considered to be closed under implication; that is, subjecting a proposition to a modal operator (of necessity or possibility), changes the structure of the proposition. Since a modal operator binds the propositions contained in its range (in other words, it dominates the proposition to which it is connected), the overall logical structure of a proposition is also dominated by the operator. This is reflected in the way logical inference works when a range of propositions is subjected to one modal operator (of necessity, for instance), or to another operator (of possibility). In each case rules of inference may produce different results and sometimes rules of inference might not be applicable at all. In this way, through logical operation, one can demonstrate the way in which modal operators dominate logical procedures and determine the structure of propositions in their range.[6] The idea is then that logical inferences derived from a set of possible states of affairs are confined by that set's

---

6 For instance, compare:
"It is necessary that if it rains, the ground wets," to "it is possible that if it rains, the ground wets." From the first one can infer that if it rains the ground is wet; from the second one cannot make such an inference (in another possible world the ground might be covered with insulating fabric).

boundaries. This notion of closedness is clearly relevant to the case of fiction where it can be used (somewhat metaphorically) to account for the intuitive sense of autonomy one tends to attach to fictional worlds. Philosophers' notions regarding fiction have led them to identify fictionality with a specific operator that works as an analogue to modal operators as explained above. Applying such a fiction-operator hence produces a closed set of propositions bound by a common operator. This procedure undertaken on a logical level can explain the autonomy of fiction understood and accepted intuitively by readers and interpreters of literature. This operator, signaling the fictionality of states of affairs, can be interpreted as indicating the unique ontological perspective characteristic of a fictional world. Logic and literary theory thus "join forces" to represent the unique autonomy of fiction in terms of the appropriate modal or intensional (binding) operator: "it is fictional in the world of *Madame Bovary* that ...," "it is fictional" being viewed as a modality that secures the ontological autonomy of the states of affairs included in the world of *Madame Bovary*. Although philosophers might disagree as to the specific logical implications drawn from a fiction-operator (the type of logic such an operator imposes on a closed set of propositions),[7] the notion of an intensional operator marking out fictional discourse is a widely shared and recurrent solution representing the independent rules of logical reference and inference in a fictional system.

The specificity of boundaries enclosing the propositions that make up a fictional world can also explain why a world of fiction constitutes a discrete system with a modal structure of its own. Although possible worlds are viewed by most philosophers as causally linked to the actual world, it is the whole system of relations among the actual world and possible worlds that can help to define the autonomy of fiction. A "world" connotes a whole complex of states of affairs, whether the world is actual or fictional. A fictional world, like any possible world, is analogous to the actual world in that it has its own set of facts and its own subworlds and counter-worlds. As a *world* it contains "an actual world" and a set of possibilities, alternatives, predictions and forecasts non-actualized in the fictional world (Ryan,

---

7 A fictionality operator can be interpreted as imposing a modality *de dicto* (i.e., modality that subsumes the whole proposition under its range) or as a modality *de re* (i.e., modality that only has the predicative part of the proposition in its scope). See, for instance, Castañeda, 1979: 46.

1984; Doležel, 1981; Martinez-Bonati, 1981). In sum, introducing the semantics and logic of possible worlds into literary discourse on fictionality opens up a variety of intriguing solutions to this problem.

Stage II   Philosophers' approach to fiction

The previous section explicated how some aspects of "being fictional" can be illuminated through a similarity allegedly held with "being possible." Yet acknowledging that things might have been different does not necessarily lead to a belief in possible worlds. Possible worlds presuppose a difference between actual existence and possible existence in states of affairs (between the actual and the possible, between a necessary mode of being and a contingent mode), and not all philosophers would acknowledge this difference, and even if they do, would not necessarily see possible worlds as a satisfactory account of this difference.[8] For those philosophers who talk about possible worlds, the philosophical motivation for developing the concept beyond Leibnitz emanates from the desire to explicate our intuitive sense of alternativeness to the actual course of events and the need to explain propositions whose truth value is contingent or indefinite despite having a logico-semantic structure similar to propositions with necessary or definite truth values ("Nixon is a human" as opposed to "Nixon was the president of the U.S." or "a unicorn just galloped by"). Philosophical investigations strive to distinguish between modes of being and explain the difference between the way things could have been and the way things actually are. Following these questions, fictional propositions representing fictional states of affairs have become an object of interest for philosophers and part of their considerations.

Philosophers working on possible worlds, however, do not focus on the ontological status of fictional states of affairs *per se*. On the contrary, many philosophical analyses of possible worlds attempt to exclude fictional propositions from the realm of the possible since these do not refer to possible states of affairs but rather to nonexistents and sometimes to impossible states. Generally speaking, the analysis

8 Note however that even Goodman who rejects the notion of possible worlds differentiates between a *constructed* version of the world, the merely *possible* version, and the *right* version. Thus, even within a highly relativistic framework like Goodman's, world versions are not all on an equal footing.

of fiction from a philosophical perspective often aims to qualify and check "the explanatory power of certain logical hypotheses and models" (Woods & Pavel, 1979: 1), and not to solve the particular literary problems raised by fiction. Fiction introduces non-actual states of affairs that have no claim for truth or actuality. Yet, fiction poses a problem for philosophers because unlike other possible but non-actual occurrences, fictional states of affairs dissimulate their fictionality and may be presented *as facts*.[9] Moreover, fiction constructs alternative courses of events and states of affairs, and these are attributed to *nonexistent beings* (Raskolnikov's crime or Natasha's wedding). For this reason, even philosophers who acknowledge modes of being beyond the actual world might resist possible worlds that introduce non-existents and diverge from (expand, restrict, invent or totally revise) the inventory of entities composing the actual world. Actualists, but also philosophers adopting a more lenient approach to possible worlds, would find it difficult to accept the idea of nonexistents and fictional obtaining.[10] Can worlds that introduce nonexistent and sometimes impossible entities as if these were actually existing be considered possible worlds without affecting the basic tenets of the logic of possibility? In face of the difficulties fiction raises before modal logicians, the interest many philosophers have paid to the logic of fiction, and their preoccupation with the truth of fiction, has often emerged from a "segregationist" ideology,[11] from the wish to separate fiction from other non-actuals. Philosophy would much rather tie language to existent things than loosen the hinges of reality with fictional propositions.[12] Even in post-Russellian times, some philosophers would claim that "the very idea of a nonexistent object is a confusion, or at best a notion, like that of a square circle, whose exemplification is impossible" (Plantinga, 1976: 143). Possible worlds, even within the actualist orientation that Plantinga represents (attributing existence to all possible beings), do not necessarily admit the notion of nonexistent objects.

9 Most literary worlds contain a core of fictional facts but also nonfactual elements like the beliefs, desires or predictions of a character or narrator, elements that do not *obtain* in the fictional world.

10 In an extreme actualist formulation, although there could have been some things that don't *in fact* exist, there are no things that don't exist but could have. Thus, according to Plantinga (1979) and the actualist conception of possible worlds that he represents, all things exist but not all of them obtain.

11 The terms "segregationist" vs. "integrationist" semantics were coined by Pavel (1986: 11ff.).　　　　12 As pointed out by Rorty, 1982.

Philosophers use a variety of modes for distinguishing nonexistents from existents and for underlining the fact that the former breach standard mechanisms of logic. The deviational nature of nonexistents is stressed by claiming, for instance, that in naming of nonexistents one cannot reconstruct a moment when a name was assigned to an entity (the history of naming a nonexistent object ends in a "block," Donnellan, 1974); by assuming that propositions about nonexistent entities require a different logic (Woods, Routley); a different semantic characterization (Parsons) or a different pragmatics (Searle). By employing these modes philosophers attempt to separate fictional propositions from "serious" ones and from propositions about existents. The author "writes a sentence which has the form of an assertion beginning with a reference, but is in fact neither asserting nor referring ... " (Urmson, 1976: 155). Philosophers who are concerned with fiction are bothered especially by the fact that fiction attributes its assertions to nonexistents, or by the fact that one can make truthful propositions about nonexistents. In their dealing with fiction philosophers seem to be looking for a conceptual niche where the distinctive features of fiction will both secure a place for it among non-actual beings and ensure that fiction stays within its unique logical domain. Fiction should be defined in terms that would prevent it from permeating the domain of standard logic.

Oftentimes philosophers refer to the logic of fiction in terms of *nonlogic*:

the logic of fictional worlds is ... much more anarchical than that of relevant worlds: the logic of a world associated with a work of fiction may be any logic that the author chooses to impose ... Given that the logic of a fictional world may be any logic, it follows that *there is no general uniform logic of fiction*. For the intersections of all logics is a null logic, no logic, as each purported logical principle is cancelled out by a logic where it does not hold good (Routley, 1979: 10).

This idea of nonlogic lurks behind any philosophical discussion we might pick from among the available philosophical models for the logic of fiction: whether it is Castañeda (1979) who describes the unique status of fictional entities as that of quasi-indexical beings exhibiting a specific mode of predication; or Parsons (1980) for whom nonexistent beings resemble actual beings in their nuclear, but not in their extranuclear, properties. Zemach (forthcoming) who promotes what is, from the standpoint of a theory of fiction, a flexible view of existence, treats existence as a property like any other property that an entity can either have or lack; however he also resumes a typically philosophical position and concludes his paper by claiming that fictional nonexistent beings exceed their worlds because, unlike existents, they cannot be exhausted in referential terms. In this manner, a dividing line reappears in his model between fiction and nonfiction, between referring to nonexistents and referring to existents.

Introducing a story- or fiction-operator is one of the most widely proposed segregationist solutions for fiction. A fiction-operator segregates the world of a story from the actual world by delineating the logical domain for a set of fictional propositions. A fiction-operator hence explains how the same proposition can be true when stated in a journal, false when stated by a literary text, but true again when considered under implication of the fictional operator. In other words, a fiction operator closes a domain under implication and subjects it to laws of inference obtaining in this domain, and regardless of what lies beyond the domain's boundaries (the proposition "it is raining in London today" can be true in the context of a novel by Dickens regardless of the truth value of this proposition in the actual world). Although this ambiguity of truth value cannot be explained by syntactic ambiguity, it can be accounted for when truth in fiction is treated in terms of a closedness under implication of sets of propositions in the scope of a fiction-operator. The idea of fictional objects as non-actual entities existing in possible worlds can also solve other logical features of our claims about fiction; it can handle, for instance, the incompleteness of fictional objects (as will be discussed in chapter 4).[13] In short, philosophical logic offers solutions to some of the problems that fiction poses for a logic of possibility. Yet, philosophers posit for fiction a unique type of logic that will not threaten the logical foundations of formal semantics in general and of possible worlds thinking in particular.

Crossing from possible to fictional worlds would seem to violate a "segregationist" function of possible worlds as of other philosophical models for fiction. The very idea of using possible worlds semantics for explicating the idea of fiction counteracts philosophers' approach to fiction (within or without the possible world framework), an approach that aims to create a separate logical domain for fiction. Clearly, no cross-disciplinary borrowing can operate automatically

13 See Howell, 1979: 137–140.

and would always require some adjustments, yet, in the case of the interdisciplinary link between possible and fictional worlds, the motivation for establishing a link between modal logic and the problem of fiction emerged in the first place for different, and even opposing reasons, in the philosophical and literary disciplines. This incompatibility is reflected in the fact that *literary theorists use possible worlds to reveal the common denominator between fictional and other modes of non-actual world construction.* Many philosophical attempts to deal with fiction are however produced with an opposite purpose in mind. In this context of the incompatible viewpoints of the two disciplines, the need to explain the motivation for initially coupling the two concepts turns out to touch upon some intricate problems of interdisciplinary cross-fertilization. To reveal the profound motivations behind coupling possible worlds with fictional worlds requires that the place of possible worlds within a broader philosophical context is reconstructed. The next stage would hence provide an explanation for the attempt to solve fictionality with possible worlds. Only on this level of global disciplinary concerns can we understand the deep-level motivations for this inter-disciplinary link.

Stage III Possible worlds in a wider context: the key to a semiotization of worlds

The possible worlds framework reflects a broader philosophical attempt to relax the meaning of certain philosophical concepts by questioning the relations holding between language and the world. Possible worlds represent current trends in philosophy that aim to show that linguistic and logical mechanisms operate independently of the states of affairs to which they refer. Backed by this conception, possible worlds would be shown here to offer a convenient support for a view of fictionality in terms of semiotic world models. I am referring here mostly to the trend, represented by philosophers such as Putnam and Kripke, which opens the way for a semiotic approach to the concept of *world* in general and of *possible worlds* in particular.

Recent developments in the philosophy of language and in modal logic offer possible solutions to various aspects of fictionality. These developments, of which the growing interest in possible worlds forms an important part, allow us to define worlds as semiotic models: worlds whose construction is language-dependent and unimpeded by the absence of a corresponding state of affairs "out there." In order to trace the steps by which this conclusion can be reached, I will examine two areas of philosophical discussion that pertain to the problem of fictionality:

(1) The logico-semantic problem of the truth value of fictional discourse.

(2) The problem of referring to fictional entities: the ontological status of fictional entities and of their properties.

These two areas of discussion recently reveal new interpretations of concepts that have traditionally prevented the incorporation of fiction into a broader theory of logic or semantics. New interpretations of truth and of reference manifest most clearly a relaxation of logical standards, and hence introduce a renewed relevance of philosophical issues to solving aspects of fictionality. To avoid wider philosophical considerations in the present context and the blurring of the discussion by specific debates between rival views, I will tackle these current philosophical topics from the standpoint of the interests of a theory of fictionality and show how this theory can benefit from current philosophical positions towards truth and reference.

The truth value of fictional discourse

The problem of the truth value of fictional discourse forms part of a more general question: does fictional discourse obey the same rules of logic and semantics as nonfictional discourse? Since fictional discourse does not refer to actual states of the world, it is doubtful whether it can be regarded as a truth-valued type of discourse. The logical problem of truth emerges with particular strength in the context of fiction because fiction questions the applicability of standard logic to a discourse about nonexistent individuals or objects, granted that the propositions about those individuals carry no unique semantic markers to indicate their nonexistence. According to views held by philosophers until recent years, a fictional proposition like, "Emma Bovary committed suicide" does not fulfill the basic requirement of a factual statement: there is no true existential presupposition attributing existence to Emma (Emma simply does not exist). The proposition is thus regarded as either false (Russell) or as neither true nor false (Strawson). This view forms part of what is called *a correspondence theory of truth*, according to which the truth value of propositions is determined by a corresponding state of affairs obtaining in the world. The view of truth as correspondence between concepts and facts had dominated twentieth-century philosophy from Russell to Searle. Within such a tradition the truth value of propositions in general and of fictional propositions in particular is solved along a definite line of argument. If a statement refers to a nonexistent individual, that statement can not correspond to reality and is therefore false (or lacks a truth value). When truth is regarded as a relation between an extralinguistic state of affairs and a linguistic expression, it cannot be applied to fiction since fiction does not commit itself to extralinguistic states. Fictional discourse is obviously deviant from the point of view of such a truth standard based on correspondence.

Alternatively, truth can be defined not in terms of a correspondence but in pragmatic terms. *A pragmatic theory of truth* replaces a metaphysical vision of truth as an essential correspondence between world and language (à la Russell) with a more flexible view of truth. A statement or proposition can be true in some sense even if what the proposition refers to (corresponds to) does not exist (or we cannot definitely know if it exists or not). According to a pragmatic theory of truth, the truth of a proposition can rely on weaker standards. Donnellan, Putnam and Kripke (although still relying in their theories of reference on a correspondence between language and world), have at least paved the way to a pragmatic theory of truth by severing the bond between the relation language-world and a speaker's knowledge and familiarity with the object of his utterance. That is, epistemological considerations were disconnected by these philosophers from the ability to refer. According to Donnellan, for instance, what ties words to the world is not the speaker's knowledge but some causal (non-epistemic) association between them. For pragmatists like Dewey or Rorty (who dissociate themselves from Putnam and Kripke),[14] language-world correspondence is no longer at issue for a theory of reference. Language can be used on the basis of relative and pragmatic standards alone; these determine the warranted assertibility of a proposition according to criteria of belief, convention etc. Truth is not a fixed over-all standard but is rather changing and tentative; it is the

---

14 Although Donnellan or Kripke disjoin the condition of existence entirely from the condition of identification (that is, epistemic access to the referred-to existent), their philosophy of language still develops an account of "how words relate to the world," and relies on existence as what ensures successful reference. The fact that Donnellan and Kripke have kept some notion of reference shows that "semantics has not become completely disjoined from epistemology, despite advertisements to that effect" (Rorty, 1982: 128).

practical uses to which we put a statement which determine its truth value. A statement is true if it "works," if its assertion is warranted by a state of affairs it produces regardless of referential questions.

The move from the correspondence theory of truth to the pragmatic view on truth (for present purposes, Kripke, Putnam and Rorty can be grouped together) marks a clear relaxation of the philosophical standard of truth. Current philosophy allows us to refer to objects even though we might know these objects only vaguely or partially. In our use of language, we can decide whether a proposition is true or assertible even when the proposition does not refer to an object existing in a definite time and space. We can even distinguish between true and false assertions when the existence or mode of being of the objects within a given discourse is doubtful or indeterminate. Note that this relaxation of truth standards came about because of developments of logical models for possible worlds and for counter-factual situations, because of the attempt to examine the standard of truth in modal contexts. By viewing assertions relative to their distinctive contexts, we can transfer the world where truth is assessed from the real world to an alternative or fictional world (Woods, 1974: 12; Routley, 1979: 18).

Truth in fiction is evidently treated very differently within a correspondence theory of truth on the one hand and a pragmatic (contextual) theory of truth on the other. The correspondence theory cannot solve the problem of fiction since it denies any attempt to talk about the truth of propositions relating to nonexistents. Some features of this theory of truth are, however, reflected in specific attempts, on the part of philosophers, to solve the question of truth in fiction. Following the rationale of a correspondence theory of truth, the problem of fictional discourse is solved by interposing a borderline between fictional and nonfictional discourse, by segregating the two types of discourse. According to one typical way of dealing with fiction from a segregationist perspective, fictional speech-acts are described by Searle (1979) as *pretended* referring acts. Pretense provides a way of separating fictional discourse from nonfictional discourse; it prefixes every fictional statement with an indicator of its being not more than a pretended referring, questioning, or asserting. When a speech act is pretended its standard truth values are suspended. As mentioned earlier in this chapter, the suspension of logical laws by means of attaching an operator indicating fictionality has been another widely proposed solution. Lewis (1978), for instance, describes a fictionality operator as an "intensional operator that may be analyzed as a restricted universal quantifier over possible worlds." In other words, when an assertion is prefixed by "in fiction f(p)," the truth of the given fictional proposition (p) is closed under implication of a fictional operator (f), which restricts the inferences drawn from such assertions. Similarly, Castañeda (1979) describes the difference between a sentence in a newspaper and a sentence in a literary text as a difference of operator in the range of which the sentence appears. All the sentences of a literary text are subsumed under a story-operator that indicates the title of the text "In the story x ..." or the subworld in which the proposition represented by that sentence obtains (in the belief world of character a ...). Despite the problems raised by the modal-operator solution for fiction (within this proposition the existence of extrafictional objects within fiction, of objects that exist outside, as well as inside fiction, cannot be solved),[15] philosophers seem to believe that the appropriate modal operator solves, to some extent, the problem of truth in fiction.

Modal operators that define and delimit fictional discourse do indeed serve to separate fictional from nonfictional discourse both in philosophical and in literary discussions of fictionality. Yet, whereas philosophers conceive of such operators as controlling propositions about nonexistents (propositions about existents, even within fiction, would require a different modal operator), literary theorists regard the modality of fiction as operating in a very different manner. Literary theorists view the fiction operator as a liberating rather than a restrictive logical principle. For them a fiction operator is an overall defining principle that reveals one aspect of the nature of fiction. Within literary theory, such operators serve to explain the partial insulation of fictional discourse from nonfictional contexts and not to solve the truth-value-problem of fiction; Emma Bovary's world is insulated from the world of Raskolnikov and also from our world: we are therefore unable to meet her in any but her own world. Whereas for a philosopher, a fiction-operator confines propositions about nonexistents to a well-delineated logical domain, according to a literary theorist like Pavel (1975), fictionality is a global strategy of texts and as such it secures the autonomy of a fictional universe. Instead of describing fictional worlds as worlds diverging at certain points from the actual world, fictionality is defined as a kind of *cordon*

15 See, for instance, Castañeda, 1979: 46.

sanitaire which binds together the constituents of the fictional world. The fictionality operator also enables fictional inferences to deviate from legitimate inferences in factual contexts. Such a view also carries implications for the status of the actual world: it enables us to see the actual world not as a given but as a set of propositions indexed by a different operator ("it is actual that p"). Following this type of logic the actual world can be viewed as any version of reality which, like fictional versions, is convention-dependent. Literary theorists are hence preoccupied with securing a legitimate logical space for fiction and not with establishing "norms" of truthful and valid assertions.

Yet when the norm of truth and validity is relaxed and relativized, it becomes possible to consider *internal standards of truth*. At the same time the need to distinguish between fiction and truth, between existence and nonexistence becomes less acute. Fictional discourse creates its own *universe of discourse* in relation to which statements are either true or false. Thus philosophical problems associated with fiction disappear once a metaphysical conception of truth is discarded. Moreover, as Rorty (1982) suggests, the strong semantic relation between words and reality should be replaced by the weaker semantic relation of "talking about" because the physical relations between language and reality can lead to absurdities such as those to which Searle is driven: Russell's axiom of existence is attributed to objects with no physical existence. Rorty proposes to see the relation of "talking about" as "one which may be *constituted* by discourse – since no more is required for talking about Sherlock Holmes ... than that the words Sherlock Holmes ... be systematically bandied about" (132). According to this view of truth in fiction, referring does not tie an expression to a physical object; the truth of a reference is determined by the very laws of discourse. Discourse creates an object that exists in some logical space, allowing us to refer to it and to make true assertions about it. This truth standard derives from the laws in operation in that universe of discourse.

Current philosophical discussions acknowledge the fact that truth cannot be regarded as a standard, relating states of the world to corresponding descriptions of these states. An extreme pragmatist like Rorty rejects the correspondence theory of truth, the concept of necessary truth, and any kind of metaphysical realism which regards statements as absolutely true or false. His stand, but also Kripke's position, reflects a philosophical relaxation of truth regardless of epistemic limitations on validation. Truth cannot be regarded as an absolute standard, or as a relevant notion at all in considering the meaning of a proposition. From Goodman's radical perspective the concept of truth as a whole is rejected:

> many world versions – some conflicting with each other, some so disparate that conflict or compatibility among them is indeterminable – are equally right ... Rightness, however, is neither constituted nor tested by correspondence with a world independent of all versions. (1984: 39)

Goodman rejects any epistemological or ontological considerations in the weighing of world-versions. Pragmatists of similar conviction, simply do not believe that philosophy has anything interesting to say about truth. In any of its current formulations the concept of truth is thus in a way an altered logical standard in modern philosophy: from a metaphysical absolute principle responsible for establishing the relation between language and world, the standard of truth has changed into what one might interpret as a semiotic-oriented principle in terms of which one can describe the way a universe of discourse is constructed and is operated.

I mentioned above, somewhat sporadically, some of the philosophical attempts to approach the truth of fiction in the context of the truth of a discourse uncommitted to actual states of affairs. Fiction, like possible worlds and counterfactuals, requires a different truth standard. A truth standard applied to fiction should account for one's ability to refer to possible and impossible objects and states with equal success; it should at the same time, take into consideration the distance between fictional states of affairs and other actual or non-actual worlds (a fictional proposition requires a different validation standard from a proposition relating a dream). A more relaxed notion of truth should also be able to account for both truthful *and* false propositions within a possible (or impossible) fictional world.

The attempt to solve the problem of truth in fiction requires that a fictional text be studied in terms of some specific principle of validation. Philosophy allows us to talk about reference and truth in non-actual contexts. Yet, if we isolate the case of fiction from other discourses on non-actual beings,[16] relaxing the standard of truth would still leave us with the pressing problem regarding the specific features of fictional discourse that determine which assertions are regarded as

---

16 The proposition "John was a king" can hardly be attributed a truth value when appearing in an oneiric context, yet it does require a validation principle in a fictional state of affairs.

true in the fictional universe. In other words, in the context of fiction we cannot give up on some notion of truth, a notion that would yield criteria for distinguishing true from false *fictional assertions*. The textual assertion that "Charles [Bovary] finished by rising in his own esteem for possessing such a wife" is subjected to the limited point of view of Charles, a point of view that puts the fictional validity of the assertion under reservation; it is only within the character's universe of beliefs that the statement is validated. As a fictional fact the situation Charles depicts in his mind seems doubtful. Thus, we can see that a fictional world-model requires a whole set of semiotic conventions to account for its modal stratifications. To account for degrees of validation of fictional propositions, various suggestions were made in order to define more specifically the notion of truth in fiction.[17]

Within the fictional universe of discourse, truth is not determined relative to an extratextual universe, but relative to a fictional world in which only some of the textual assertions can establish facts. Doležel (1980), for instance, talks about degrees of *authentication* where an authentication function attributes factuality or nonfactuality to propositions. A fictional universe has its own complex modal structure, in which some states are factual and others are hypothetical, or impossible. An analogous modal structure accounts for the relationship between the actualized world of fiction (the factual center of that world) and other possible worlds of belief, memory, prediction and so on.[18]

The rejection of metaphysical realism and any type of correspondence as a criterion for truth, the replacement of the concept of truth with that of warranted assertibility (or with other context-bound flexible criteria of validation), and the recognition that the notion of truth should be relative to other versions and languages – all these ideas demonstrate progress for a theory of fiction. Truth no longer involves a fixed and absolute standard by which true and false world-versions are judged, and by which fictional worlds are rejected from the realm of the true. This radical change in the concept of truth supports attempts to describe alternative standards of validation within fictional worlds because as Putnam claims, "any superiority of

---

17 A similar and related problem is the one of the truth of propositions *about* fiction. If fictional discourse is closed under implication, rules of inference should undergo a considerable change to determine legitimate inferences from fictional discourse. Here we enter the problem of valid laws of inference in fiction, which I approach in chapter 3. 18 See also Ryan, 1984.

our versions over other versions must be judged and claimed from *within* our collection of versions; there is no neutral place to stand" (168). In this sense, possible worlds mark a re-conception of truth and a move from understanding truth as an absolute metaphysical principle to interpreting it as a semiotic standard relative to a universe of discourse.

Truth is one of the logical principles questioned by fiction. Possible worlds, which enter philosophical discussions on non-actual states and objects, mark a change of attitude toward the concept of truth. The less metaphysical and rigid the concept of truth becomes, the more appropriate it proves to be for a definition of truth in fiction, and this change of philosophical perspective can prove to be productive for the understanding of fiction.

The problem of referring to fictional entities

Traditional theories of meaning claimed that the meaning of a term is formed by a conjunction (or disjunction) of properties associated with that term. The concept corresponding to a term is hence fixed by an intensional set. In other words, the meaning properties of a term determine its extension, and the intension of a term can be often taken to reflect the essence of the kind of thing named (the meaning of the name Socrates is fixed by the property "a Greek philosopher"). In recent years, though, a group of philosophers, notably Putnam, Kripke and Donnellan, have established a new theory of reference.[19] In opposition to traditional theories of reference, Kripke and Donnellan argue that proper names refer independently of identifying descriptions: a name will refer to a given individual whether or not that individual satisfies the set of descriptions associated with it. We can refer to Nixon, for instance, even if we assume that none or almost none of his properties obtain ("imagine Nixon was not elected president"). In other possible worlds or counterfactual situations, an individual needs only those properties, if any, that are essential to it. A name is tied to its referent not by identifying properties necessarily, but by the discursive practice in which such a tie is assumed.

The significance of this new theory of reference is threefold. First it implies that meanings are not fixed paradigms of concepts: the term "water" includes the concept of H_2O as part of its meaning only after the appropriate chemical formula was discovered. The basis for using

19 For a survey of these theories of meaning see Schwartz, 1977.

a term referentially is hence variable and, one might even claim, conventional. Second, a term can fix a reference regardless of whether the essence of the thing, or any of its essential properties, are known. Third, names act as *rigid designators* and can be used in modalized contexts when the entity denoted by the name retains very little with its other possible actualizations. The affinity between possible worlds semantics and the new theory of reference is hence obvious; as Loux (1979: 35) claims, meaning is a referential concept and it must be analyzed in terms of extension, but it is also a modal notion to be explicated in possible worlds terms. The new theory of reference, enables us to talk about objects not completely known, to refer just through the power of language, and to think about possible worlds in which objects retain none of their identifying or essential descriptions.

By allowing all this, it seems, the new theory of naming can explain fictional referring and the way fictional discourse creates worlds. Yet the relaxation of the rules of reference is not destined by philosophers to incorporate fictional naming into a general theory of naming. Let us see in what way the new theory of reference insists on excluding fictional names from the domain of legitimate naming. The philosophical debate over the meaning of names, as surveyed above, focuses on one main issue: does the meaning of a name and its referring-capacity depend on identifying the name with a set of descriptions and is naming dependent on knowledge of some property essential to the referent? In Kripke's and Donnellan's theories of reference names can rigidly designate a referent independently of the speaker's ability to identify the referent and its essential or contingent properties. A name rigidly refers in contexts that radically diverge from what we know or do not know of the referent in the actual world. The use of the name "Paris" can result in a successful referring even if we know nothing of this city. Each discursive context can prompt another set of properties to be associated with the referent concerned. Designation is fixed and rigid, so promises the theory, even when we cross the lines from the domain of the actual to possible worlds. Kripke for instance, ensures the identity of the referent across worlds by relying on the genetic code of a Socrates, who will remain himself even if denied the property of being a philosopher in another possible world. But keeping intact the identity of the referent, and guaranteeing the ability to use names rigidly, clearly depend on the existential condition that these objects of reference fulfill. According to Kripke and Donnellan, a successful reference depends on a moment of "baptizing" when a name was attributed to an object. Only this initial dependency of a name on an existent guarantees subsequent successful uses of the name. A referential link is hence what constitutes naming; an inability to reconstruct a moment of baptizing creates a block in the referential chain and thus results in an unsuccessful naming. Existence is hence a necessary condition for reference, and it is by satisfying this condition that the linguistic practice of naming can be separated from epistemic considerations (such as knowledge and familiarity with the referent). Yet by preserving existence as a condition for reference, the applicability of these referential notions to propositions about Sherlock Holmes, is denied. Fictional propositions in the context of Donnellan's theory, truthful and sensible as they might be, cannot successfully carry the burden of reference and are bound to fail in this regard. For Donnellan and Kripke the motivation behind rejecting a name like "Raskolnikov" is logical rather than semantical: only existence can guarantee the fixity of a referent in possible and in counterfactual states of affairs.

Whereas philosophers continue to segregate fictional from actual reference, literary theorists on their part circumvent the existential condition in the interpretation they attribute to naming and to successful reference. Pavel (1979) shows that the new theory of reference is divided into two aspects: *structural* and *historical*. The structural aspect relates to the relativized and relaxed relation between a name, as a rigid designator, and definite descriptions considered properties of that name. This relativization holds both for actual and for fictional entities. Only the historical aspect of this theory concerns the distinction between the truth value of propositions that contain names of existents and those with names of nonexistents. By referring to the history of uses of a given name, the relation between the name and its referent can be validated: true reference depends on a causal chain of naming going back to the initial decision to attach a name to an entity. In this context, the difference between actual naming and fictional naming emerges: in the case of fictional entities the history of naming will end up in a block whereas the baptizing of an actual entity can, at least hypothetically, be traced back to its origins. Yet Pavel uses this analysis of the new theory of naming to support his contention that the ontological boundaries between reality, mythology, religion and mere fiction are often unclear, indeterminate, or fuzzy, and that in fact tracing a causal chain of naming an entity is an unlikely practice both in actual and fictional contexts. Many objects that we regard as real at one moment, might turn out to have a historical block at a later point. Such is the case with Greek gods, part of a real ontology in one historical moment, and nonexistents at the next. When the Greeks changed their beliefs, a block was introduced into the referential chain, cutting the name "Zeus" from any existent object. By showing that successful reference and semantical procedures of designation are independent of existential conditions Pavel shifts the very foundations of Kripke's model. Pavel succeeds however in dumping the existential condition while keeping the basic insights of the new theory of reference for a theory of fictional reference.

The difference between the segregationist orientation on the philosophical side and the integrationist orientation on the literary side is apparent. Philosophers continue to deal with fiction with relaxed concepts of reference and meaning in order to separate the logic of fiction from other logics, and literary theorists refer to philosophical concepts in the hope of incorporating fiction into a general semantic theory. Despite this discrepancy and despite the fact that each of the disciplines involved developed an interest in fictional reference for different reasons and as a result of changes undergone separately, *a domain of interdisciplinary exchange has been opened.* The distance between the two disciplines does not cancel the fact that the more flexible philosophical framework for reference can account for some important facts and features of fiction:

1 That fictional discourse can create or construct the objects to which it refers.
2 That fictional discourse can refer and construct incomplete but well-individuated objects (incompleteness does not contradict the self-identity of entities).
3 That fiction can construct impossible objects and other objects that clearly diverge from their counterparts in the actual world.

The new theory of reference allows us to include fictional entities in the class of semiotic objects produced by language and dependent, for their fictional existence and characteristics, on the power of language. Individuals are not compositions of essential properties, and concepts and names are not constellations of identifying descriptions. Reference is a discursive procedure dependent not on extralinguistic essences of objects but on the semiotic convention that discourse constructs objects.

The framework of possible worlds and the wider philosophical context in which it was developed, does not aim at a general logic and semantics for fiction. Yet, although the affinity between possible worlds and fictional worlds is far from obvious, new philosophical areas of theorizing (about possible worlds, counterfactuals and other non-actuals, about pragmatic notions of truth and about new theories of reference) demonstrate the relevance of possible worlds and related terms to the problem of fiction.

❖❖❖

2

The possibility of fictional worlds

❖❖❖

Possible worlds between the disciplines

The concept of *possible worlds* has, in recent years, served as an interdisciplinary metaphor representing a sphere of mutual fusion and interchange between philosophical logic, philosophy of science, literary theory, aesthetics and linguistics. This interdisciplinary interchange has been based on the presupposition of a common ground to which the various disciplines refer; that is, possible worlds serve as a common point of reference where problems raised by each discipline separately seem to converge. Yet this dialogue among the disciplines is more intricate than it seems, because talk about possible worlds turns out to be talk about different things in each particular discipline. This is due to the nature of the disciplines involved, which dictates a priori a unique set of problems to which possible worlds are applied, and a substantially different interpretation of the concept. Possible worlds present an intricate case whereby a concept originating in one discipline develops into an interdisciplinary tool, extending in the process its scope of application and undergoing substantial changes of meaning.

Possible worlds function as an exemplary case since the gradual metaphorization of a cross-border concept or paradigm is typical and inevitable. Each discipline has its own "self-referential" mechanism[1] necessitating such a change of meaning. Whereas the previous chapter dealt with the reasons underlying the cross-disciplinary interchange between philosophy and literary theory around the concept of *possible worlds*, in this chapter I shall concentrate on the unique and

---

1 Schmidt, Siegfried, J., 1984. "The Fiction is That Reality Exists: A Constructivist Model of Reality, Fiction, and Literature," *Poetics Today*, 5: 2, pp. 253–274. According to Schmidt's system theory, social systems, after the model of biological systems, are self-referential: "living systems are further characterized by their autonomy, identity, and closedness" (255).

incompatible interpretation attached to possible worlds by each discipline. Philosophical logic is the source discipline in which the concept of *possible worlds* was initially formulated and developed; literary theory is one of those target disciplines which has appropriated and applied possible worlds to its specific needs. I will attempt to portray the route by which possible worlds have proliferated in literary studies, while being subjected to literary theorists' own interpretation of the concept, an interpretation which diverges in specific ways from the original concept as developed in modal logic. I intend to explore the roots of this conceptual divergence by concentrating on two *productive dissimilarities* between the literary and the philosophical interpretations of possible worlds, dissimilarities that would ultimately illuminate some aspects of the complex of issues surrounding fictionality. The divergence in use of possible worlds can be manifested, I maintain, in the principles of *possibility* and *accessibility* embodied in the notion of possible worlds. I shall also attempt to explain this divergence of meaning in terms of the logic and object of study unique to each discipline. The philosophical application of possible worlds profoundly differs from that of literary theorists: philosophers, by constructing an ontological domain for categories of linguistics and logic, approach possible worlds as a model for substantiating these *abstract categories*. In literary (and art) theory possible worlds serve to name *concrete artistic phenomena*; that is, in the latter context possible worlds work as a lexicon destined to name and explicate a set of referential problems raised by fiction.

Possibility and actuality

The problem I address in this section relates to the place of possibility, necessity and impossibility in logical as opposed to literary possible worlds. I attempt to show that in logic, possibility refers to *abstract* logical probabilities of occurrence which exclude, by necessity, impossibilities; literary theorists interpret possibility and impossibility as alternative world-constructing conventions applied to concrete *worlds*.

The belief in possible worlds is based on the intuitive assumption that things might have been different and that one can describe alternative courses things might have taken. In logic the idea was to show that logical categories can be described in Leibnitzian terms, that is, by means of extensional systems. In other words, possible worlds served to ascribe a semantic interpretation and concrete ontological content to the modalities of necessity and possibility; possible worlds' semantics suggested that we should see modalized propositions as propositions about non-actual states of affairs and about alternative sets considered to be related or parallel *worlds*. Possible worlds hence turn abstract logical categories into concrete sets and states of affairs, thus tying "an exotic piece of metaphysical machinery" (Loux, 1979: 30) to the subject matter of modal logic, a link not all philosophers agree with. Nevertheless, most philosophers would appreciate the explanatory power this type of semantics implies for problems such as counterfactuals, modalities, reference as an aspect in a theory of meaning, and extensionalist discourse about properties, relations and propositions.

Despite the diverse interpretations given to possible worlds within philosophy (as surveyed in the previous chapter) and the difficulties emerging from each, it is fundamental to the idea of possible worlds that *possibility* is bound to the logic and probabilities of one world. That is, although philosophers may question the validity of talk about possible worlds, or ascribe a different degree of realism to possible worlds, they share the conviction that the position of alternative states of affairs as possible worlds is defined in relation to one reference world: the state of affairs being actualized. Generally speaking, from a philosophical point of view, different actual and possible states are part of a single world, of one continuous logical space: "the different possible worlds we talk about are usually all this single world under the different aspects of the ways it might be or have been" (Sanford, 1989: 162). At least the actualists among the logicians express this stand explicitly: for them possible worlds, together with the actual one, form part of one and the same world. Actualists go even further and insist that all possible states of affairs exist, although only one of them *obtains*. Yet the general idea that the plurality of worlds takes place within one world is true both for actualists and for philosophers who take possible worlds as abstract logical constructs. For the latter, possible worlds are not viewed as alternative parallel worlds, but rather as abstract possibilities orbiting the actual state of things. This is also true for modal realists like Lewis who regard possible worlds and the actual state of things as equally realized possibilities:

There is nothing so far away from us as not to be part of our world. Anything at any distance at all is to be included ... Maybe, as I myself think, the world is a big physical object ... But nothing is so alien in kind as not to be part of our world, provided only that it does exist at some distance and direction from here, or at some time before or after or simultaneous with now. (Lewis, 1986: 1)

Possible worlds are not perceived as independent, autonomous "worlds" (as "distant planets," to use Kripke's formulation) by philosophers; possibility is described relative to an abstract set (or relative to a concrete obtaining state of affairs, in the case of actualists) which, according to various principles of probability, is being actualized. That is, philosophers might argue about the ontological status, the concrete realism or the meaning of alternative states; they do concur however on the place of possibilities relative to an actual state of affairs (whatever the interpretation ascribed to that actuality). Even Goodman claims that discourse about possibles does not transgress the boundaries of the actual world, all being equally true descriptions of actuality. Hence, even from Goodman's perspective all possibilities are placed within the confines of one world: "all possible worlds lie within the actual one" (Goodman, 1983: 57).

These features of possible worlds' talk generated by modal logicians, as well as by aestheticians, might also explain why, despite the ontological content assumed by the framework of possible worlds (and handled in discussions of the "philosophy" and metaphysical implications behind possible worlds' semantics), ontological considerations regarding alternative worlds do not seem to occupy in themselves a central part in possible worlds' models for modal logic. Most philosophers, simply and bluntly, reject the idea of possible states of affairs as existing in some concrete space and time, and the idea that there are various modes of existence of worlds. The philosophical position also does not regard possible worlds primarily as a framework imposing ontological gradations on the world; possible worlds are incorporated, alongside an actual state of affairs, into one ontology.

Literary theorists, who adopt the concept of possible worlds in order to describe the status and structure of fictional worlds, detach the notion of possibility from any abstract idea of relative probability of occurrence as originally formulated in possible worlds' semantics. Literary worlds are possible not in the sense that they can be viewed as possible alternatives to the actual state of affairs, but in the sense that they *actualize a world* which is analogous with, derivative of, or contradictory to the world we live in. Literary theorists hence seem to be modal realists in their approach to fictional worlds; they attach a high degree of realism to the notion of worlds of fiction. This realism toward fictional worlds explains why in literary studies the notions of possibility and impossibility can be interpreted as alternative conventions for world construction. Before illustrating how this conception emerges from literary studies of fictionality, we should remind ourselves of the initial rationale for the adoption of possible worlds by literary theory. Literary theorists have adopted the possible worlds frame by arguing that, being non-actual states of affairs, fictional worlds form a subset of possible worlds. Yet the very rudiments of this analogy between possible and fictional worlds might seem problematic at the outset. The problems arising from this analogy have to do with the different ways in which the relations between the possible and the actual are perceived in the context of possible worlds on the one hand, and in the context of fictional worlds as possible worlds on the other. As sets of related objects, fictional worlds are, unlike possible worlds, not "total ways the world might have been, or states or histories of the entire world" (Kripke). It seems counter-intuitive to treat fictional worlds as non-actualized states of the world we actually inhabit, or as possible situations that did not take place. As will be shown below, literary theorists treat fictional worlds as possible worlds in the sense that fictional worlds are concrete constellations of states of affairs which, like possible worlds, are non-actualized in the world. Yet, it is obvious that possible worlds are indeed non-actualized but *actualizable* (an actualizability that explicate the very idea of possibility), whereas fictional worlds are non-actualized in the world but also *non-actualizable*, belonging to a different sphere of possibility and impossibility altogether. The possible construction of a fictional world has therefore nothing to do with abstract logical possibilities of occurrence. Instead of claiming that fictional worlds are possible situations that did not take place, it would make more sense to say that fictional states of affairs are actualized and actualizable in the fictional world, which reflects the different logico-ontological domain to which fiction belongs. That is, some fictional events (and situations) take place (Emma Bovary's suicide, Raskolnikov's act of murder) and some do not (Emma's living to old age, Roskolnikov's sweet temper getting the better of him). The thing about fictional events is that they do not take place in the world (and are not necessarily possible relative to the world), but they may take place in the world of fiction. Thus, even if philosophy could offer a straightforward way to treat non-actual worlds in terms of concrete ontologies (which intuitively could amount to a convenient solution for the fact that fiction constructs non-actual worlds), fictional worlds are not possible: they are not alternative ways the world might have been. The position of the fictional world relative to the world being actualized requires a different explanation from the one logic provides to account for the possibility of worlds. In fact, the "possibility" of fiction, and the nature of its position relative to the actual world, lies at the core of the very problem of fictionality and has nourished the two long literary traditions surrounding the problem of fictionality: the mimetic and the anti-referential. Literary theorists who use the analogy with possible worlds to solve the problem of fiction do not seem to find the fact that fictional worlds cannot be seen as alternative ways the world might have been disruptive to their pursuit. They seem to believe that the analogy with possible worlds solves the problematic position of the fictional world relative to the actual world, provided that due respect is paid to the fact that fictional worlds, relative to possible worlds, are in certain ways aberrant. Fictional worlds are aberrant because fiction assumes a different logic (of incompleteness, of inconsistency) or because fiction *actualizes in fiction* specific states of affairs that do not remain in the state of virtual occurrences (which would distinguish it from worlds of belief, desire and the like). By any literary explanation of fictionality in possible worlds' terms, the idea is that fiction is a possible world possessing an ontological autonomy not shared by other possibilities. A fictional world forms an independent modal system, and is, in this respect, less directly linked to the actual world than possible worlds. If using possible worlds in a theory of fictionality requires considerable modification of the concepts of possibility and actuality, can the analogy between possible and fictional worlds still be regarded as productive?

Whether the analogy is productive or not, it certainly relies on a diversion from the original philosophical notion of possibility. I would further claim that the analogy between possible worlds and fictional worlds is not only based on the specific interpretation of possibility given by literary theorists, but also on their interpretation of *actuality* and *necessity*. According to the philosophical conception of the possibility of possible worlds, the categories of "necessity" and "possibility" appear to have nothing to do with "actual" versus "possible" existence. That is, it is not the case that necessary predicates, entities, sets or states of affairs obtain in the actual world, whereas possible predicates and entities obtain in a possible world. In the context of philosophical logic, "necessity" refers to a state of affairs obtaining in all worlds, while "possibility" refers to a state of affairs obtaining in at least one possible world – both concern the likelihood of occurrence of a given state of things in possible worlds and not the question of whether this state of things actually occurs. Only in these terms can we understand why possible worlds have clarified some problems in philosophy regarding counterfactual conditionals (involving truth in all worlds closest or most similar to the actual state of things)[2] and naming (involving identity of rigid designators in every possible world). When the necessity of a proposition is explicated in possible worlds' terms (a necessary proposition obtains in all possible worlds), such an interpretation carries metaphysical overtones. Understanding necessity as truth in all possible worlds, claims Putnam assumes a Platonist totality of "all possible worlds," which might turn the "possible worlds" enterprise into a very dubious business altogether (Putnam, 1983: 66ff.). *Yet in no interpretation of possible worlds, neither one that admits to or disregards the metaphysical significance of this framework, do necessity and possibility distinguish between modes of existence, but only between probabilities of occurrence.* For philosophers then, although Nixon in the actual world is both a person and a (former) president, only his personhood may be considered a necessary property that could (according to some models of *essence*) be attributed to him in all worlds in which Nixon is included, whereas his presidentship is contingent.[3]

This interpretation of necessity and possibility with possible worlds is often re-interpreted in literary theory for obvious reasons. "Propositions about the real world fall under the modality of necessity. Propositions in fiction, by contrast, are governed by the modality of possibility; they require, in short, 'suspension of belief as well as of disbelief'" (McHale, 1987: 33). This interpretation of necessity and possibility as actuality versus fictionality is inevitable for theorists of fiction; by attributing fiction to the realm of the possible and the contingent, the capacity of fiction to actualize alternative or contingent

2 The most acute question regarding counterfactuals concerns the criteria for determining the truth value or validity of counterfactual situations (or of the conditionals representing them). Are counterfactuals validated by reference to logic, to material laws of probability, to circumstantial evidence or to any other factor (see Sanford, 1989)? The notion of actuality in this context or the sense in which counterfactuals are closest to the *actual* state of affairs, is hence open to interpretation.

3 Note that the distinction between necessary and contingent properties is far from straightforward since necessary properties involve questions of essence of the entity thus qualified.

properties (enabling Napoleon in fiction to diverge from Napoleon in history) can be explained. In this manner, fiction can be treated as a game with possibilities not actualized in our world. Yet the fact that fiction belongs to the domain of the possible does not make the notion of the necessary irrelevant to fiction. A similar maneuver of concepts involves the notion of necessity where the necessary in fiction signals what is actualized in the fictional world; fiction possesses its own necessity and possibility and the actuality of fiction is privileged with an essentiality of its own. By dissociating the notions of necessity and possibility in fiction from their logical counterparts, the sense of an internal logic unique to fiction is ratified:

Fictional necessity is an individuation principle. If John is fictionally the son of Tom, John must be always isolated as the son of Tom and Tom as the father of John. In Eco 1979 I called this kind of necessity an S-property, that is a property which is necessary inside a given PW by virtue of the mutual definition of the individuals in play. (Eco, 1989: 350)

Eco's interpretation of necessity as functional interdependence among properties, like other "literary" interpretations of necessity, equates necessity with actually obtaining properties and with essentiality relative to a given world. This interpretation reflects how fictional necessity differs from logical necessity. This is one obvious symptom of the discrepancy in use of possible worlds between logic and literary theory.

There is more to the notion of possible worlds than just demonstrating various ways things might have happened but did not: possible worlds are destined to distinguish non-actual but possible states of affairs from impossible ones. A possible world cannot include contradictions and it cannot violate the law of the excluded middle. To stress this point and to explain the logical notion of impossibility, let us take Kripke's well-known example of dice-throwing as a play of probabilities producing thirty-six possible worlds. The thirty-six possible states of the two dice are thirty-six possible worlds because in each state the dice's position is either $p1$ or $p2$ or ... $p36$; only one possibility holds in each state of the dice. The possible states of the dice are hence non-contradictory (in no state is the dice both in a position $p1$ and in $\sim p1$) and they exclude the middle (one of the possible states of the dice must hold). The notion of a possible world and the notion of a relation holding between different worlds, are taken to refer to and embody the abstract (empty) logical category of possibility. The thirty-six states of the dice hence ensure the range of possibilities and exclude impossibilities that either transcend this range, are self-contradictory or breach the law of the excluded middle.

One of the problems confronting many literary theorists who use possible worlds is indeed that of explaining impossible fictional worlds. It is not only that fictional worlds can include impossibilities, but violating the law of the excluded middle appears to have motivated a whole school of literary writing, namely that of postmodernism. Actually, postmodernist fiction constitutes the most ready literary corpus in the light of which possibility as a logical principle, applicable or inapplicable to literary fiction, can be examined. In the context of realist or modernist literature and criticism impossibility was considered a literary issue in quite a different sense. Impossibility referred to incompatibility between laws obtaining in fictional worlds that might include supernatural or improbable elements, objects and properties, and the natural laws and laws of probability obtaining in a given world encyclopedia. Although logically inconsistent states of affairs are not restricted to specific literary periods or genres, with postmodernism, impossibilities, in the logical sense, have become a central poetic device, which shows that contradictions in themselves do not collapse the coherence of a fictional world. In view of the range of impossibilities introduced by literature, literary theorists solve impossibility by calling the notion of possible worlds to their aid: by claiming that fictional worlds are in general incomplete (and hence being neither p nor $\sim$p does not violate logical possibility) (Doležel), or that impossibilities can be explained away by relativizing the incompatible possibilities to different propositional attitudes (Eco), to different epistemic or narrative domains (Pavel), or to different ontological levels (McHale). Since possible worlds represent states of affairs as ontic spheres, impossibilities can be neutralized relative to different spheres (one proposition does not contradict another − each is valid in another sub-world); and indeterminacies (p and $\sim$p) can be made valid when each interpretation of an indeterminate proposition obtains in a different ontic sphere. Eco proposes another solution for impossibilities: when possible worlds include impossibilities, that is properties that cannot be *constructed* because they violate our logical or epistemological habits, we will say that "these properties are simply *mentioned*, as it happens with the magic operators in fairy tales." Furthermore, "an impossible PW [possible world] does not mention something unconceivable. It builds up the very conditions of its own un-conceivability" (Eco, 1989: 353). Eco thus neutralizes the very basis of possible worlds in order to solve impossibility in fiction; instead of introducing the referential function of fiction in terms of extensional sets (possible worlds), the possible world of fiction is stripped of its extensional function.

Literary theorists, in order to explain impossible fictional worlds within a possible worlds semantics, take recourse either to different functions of language (construction vs. mention), to world-constructing mechanisms that reconcile such impossibilities (epistemic or narrative domains) or to a mode of thematizing such an impossibility (demonstrating the inconceivability of an impossible world) because for literary theorists the notion of possible worlds is taken literally: a fictional world is *a world* in the literal sense of the word and an impossible fictional world cannot be impossible because it is already out there in the ontic sphere of fictional existence. Hence for literary theorists the notions of possibility and impossibility have to do with alternative conventions of world-construction, and not with the prior question of the very possibility of construction. To prove the depth of this incompatibility between logic and fiction theory, it is sufficient to quote almost at random from any one of the literary discussions of possible worlds:

The set of fictional worlds is unlimited and maximally varied. If fictional worlds are interpreted as possible worlds, literature is not restricted to the imitations of the actual world ... To be sure, possible-worlds semantics does not exclude from its scope fictional worlds similar or analogous to the actual world; at the same time, it includes without difficulty the most fantastic worlds, far removed from, or contradictory to, "reality" ... It is well-known that Leibnitz imposed a restriction on possible worlds, but this restriction is purely logical: Possible worlds have to be free of contradictions ... Do we have to accept this restriction into fictional semantics? (Doležel, 1989: 231)

Doležel finds a solution to worlds containing contradictions within a possible worlds semantics by arguing that such worlds use narrative maneuvers as self-voiding devices: an impossible world is constructed but not authenticated; the authenticity of the fictional existence of impossible domains, is denied.[4] For literary authors, one might claim

4 The terms "authentic" and "authenticity" were introduced in Doležel (1980) as central concepts in a theory of fictional existence: motifs introduced into the narrative are determined as facts (authentic motifs) or as nonfacts (non-authentic motifs) according to the authority attributed to the source presenting these motifs.

along these lines, impossibility is not a restriction, but rather a new domain for exercising their creative powers. While this might shed light on fiction-writing, it certainly demonstrates that impossibility is interpreted as a convention of world-construction rather than as a logical criterion on the basis of which the whole edifice of the possible worlds frame was originally built. Doležel's formulation cited above further shows how he insists on developing from possible worlds semantics a theory for fiction. Doležel, like other literary theorists, relies on the premise that a semantics of fiction should emerge from a general semantics while transforming the latter to its specific needs.[5] In practice the theoretical leap from a general to a literary semantics entails a new set of premises, many of which go unnoticed (as reflected in the logical foundations of *possibility* that are subject, here as elsewhere, to reticent re-interpretations.) It should be acknowledged however that some of the solutions found for a semantics of fictional worlds are indeed not particular to fiction and pertain to other non-actual possibilities as well. After all, relativizing contradictions to different (epistemic or narrative) systems is not an invention unique to the case of fiction. Yet for literary theorists it is not that narrative or epistemic domains always reconcile impossibilities; moreover, it is not that these theorists necessarily *seek* to neutralize a contradictory state of affairs. Rather, impossibilities are accommodated by fictional worlds because they are interpreted as world-constructing devices for producing inauthentic worlds. Impossible domains in the fictional world are hence not viewed as violations of a possible worlds semantics.

Different interpretations of possibility in logic and in literary theory also result in different conceptions of *trans-world identity*. The notion of *trans-world identity* is another aspect of the possible world framework that welcomes and at the same time problematizes an analogy with the notion of fictionality. Trans-world identity involves criteria for identifying the same individual across world boundaries: is Nixon who is both a person and a president in a past state of the actual world the same Nixon as the one in an alternative course of events who retains only his personhood? By what criteria can different

---

5 This is part, in my view, of a wider attempt in literary studies to repair deeply rooted presuppositions which regard fictionality and literary language as deviations from standard logic and from norms of standard language use, respectively (see, for instance, Pratt, 1977).

occurrences of a name in different worlds with the same entity be identified? Trans-world identity is hence closely connected to the problem of naming in theories of reference. One may infer from theories of reference that identifying entities across worlds depends on the rigid designation carried out by proper names and descriptions. That is, trans-world identity raises the question of whether an entity can preserve its essential identity despite being characterized, located, or even named differently in different worlds. Can an entity be subject to trans-world identification when its name, its essential and/or contingent properties have been changed? What are, in other words, the minimal criteria for maintaining the individuality of an object or person across worlds? Possible worlds clearly pertain to these philosophical questions, and have been used in various ways to negotiate questions of essence and identity. Lewis, for instance, describes alternative worlds as parallel worlds which are necessarily autonomous; he consequently rejects trans-world identification as inconceivable and contradictory to the nature of being. In place of the misleading notion of trans-world identity he proposes a substitute in the form of *counterpart theory*.[6] Kripke on the other hand claims that possible worlds are kinds of mini-worlds describing the total ways things might have been (1972: 18). The set of entities composing the actual state of affairs and the set of entities composing alternative states are hence numerically (extensionally) overlapping. Trans-world identity is therefore maintainable across possible worlds.

In what sense can fictional entities entertain trans-world identity with entities in other worlds? First it is clear that trans-world identity or counterpart relations (to use Lewis's substitute for continuity of identity across worlds) only pertain to components of a fictional world with a historical counterpart and also to imaginary entities that inhabit more than one fictional world, like Sherlock Holmes, or Faust. Yet whereas counterpart theory in philosophy is destined to illuminate the

6 "The best thing to do, I think, is to escape the problems of transworld identity by insisting that there is nothing that inhabit more than one world" (Lewis, 1973: 39). Counterpart relation is a relation of similarity which enables Lewis to solve modality with standard logic; instead of creating modal operators in a nonextensional logic, Lewis makes an impasse by suggesting that if things are individuated as non-actualized possibles, just as they do in the actual world, we can say that things in different worlds are never identical and identity is no longer a problem (Lewis, 1983). The conclusion that nothing inhabits more than one world is hence both a working theorem and the rationale behind counterpart theory.

notion of essence and identity, models for counterpart relations between an extrafictional entity and its fictional embodiment center chiefly on whether the fictional entity can indeed be considered an extension of its extrafictional counterpart, or whether each is committed to an ontologically distinct sphere which cancels out counterpart relations (Doležel, 1988). In other words, the problem posed by Napoleon in fiction for a theory of fictionality is not whether his essence is maintained in its intra-fictional embodiment (according to any theory of trans-world or counterpart relations, there is enough similarity between the historical entity and its immigrant extension in fiction to ensure such a cross-world identification). The problem posed by the multi-occurrence of Napoleon relates to whether planting an extension of Napoleon in a fictional world imposes an ontological barrier between the historical Napoleon and his fictional counterpart, a barrier that excludes the possibility of cross-identification. Loux's (1979) discussion of trans-world identity indirectly touches on the sense in which identity across worlds can raise a problem for fiction. Loux shows that transworld relations do not just involve logical aspects of identity. Transworld identity in a logical interpretation is problematic on two accounts: (1) It involves standards of similarity between sets and similarity is obviously a relative, if not a diffuse notion; (2) It assumes that we have epistemic access to different possible worlds spread before us in their infinite details for some kind of investigation. Transworld identity also raises the problem of the prior constraints which render worlds and their inhabitants subject to such relations in the first place:

We say, for example, "Suppose Plato had lived ten years longer." In saying this we fasten on a world; but our very way of characterizing the world ensures that it is one in which Plato exists ... Transworld identity, then, presents a problem only if we think of worlds as things given us with the identities of their inhabitants as yet unsettled; worlds aren't given us; we stipulate just which world we mean to talk about, and our stipulation ensures that the individual we are concerned with is the object of our reference. (p. 44)

What we can learn from this formulation is that trans-world identity does not raise a problem when we treat all worlds relevant for cross-identification as if they were of the same logical order (cultural constructs or worlds we stipulate for various purposes). That is, trans-world identity is a relatively straightforward relation when questions concerning existence, identity, and epistemic access to things have already been settled or are not an issue. Trans-world identity does raise a problem in the context of worlds of different orders, worlds which do not belong to the same logical domain. Such is the case when we have a fictional construct on the one hand and the given world of our experience, on the other hand. Trans-world identity, which initially touches upon the notion of *compossibility* and of *rigid designation* across world-bounds, thus reflects again in its literary interpretations the difference between the way possibility functions in philosophical logic and in a literary theory of fictionality. The literary interpretation of trans-world identity focuses on the type and nature of the barrier between fiction and history.

The different interpretations given to *possibility* in philosophical logic and in literary theory, are also manifested in the *concreteness* attributed to worlds and their inhabitants within the literary discipline. For philosophical logicians possible worlds can be perceived as abstract constructs forming alternative world models. As such, possible worlds can allow for a world comprising only one or two entities, and even a world empty of entities or a world containing no language. The only restriction on constructing hypothetical world-models is imposed by logical possibility, and it is thus logically possible to have an empty world. It was shown above that logical possibility is not necessarily a valid criterion in the construction of fictional worlds; beyond that one may also claim that the abstract-hypothetical nature of possible worlds, which defines their *alternative-ness* to actuality and allows the possibility of emptiness, contradicts the way in which the very nature of fictionality is perceived by literary theorists and by readers of literature. Fictional worlds are "pregnant" worlds, concrete constellations of objects, and not abstract constructs:

A possible world is not a bare but an overfurnished set. We shall speak not of abstract types of possible worlds that do not contain a list of individuals but a "pregnant" world of which one must know all the acting individuals and their properties. (Eco, 1979: 218)

The "pregnancy" of fictional worlds implies that the possibility of fictional ontologies depends on the presence of *concrete fictional entities*; fictional worlds are worlds possessing some kind of concrete reality. The view of possible worlds as hypothetical abstract sets is inoperative in describing fictional worlds and it seems that the concept of *world* is used differently in each framework. Whereas in a philosophical framework a world has the status of a conceptual construct, in literary theory worlds are literally understood as constellations of concrete constructs.

The "pregnancy" of fictional worlds reflects another way in which literary theorists reject the abstract and hypothetical nature of possible worlds and introduce a changed concept of possibility into the literary discipline. The conclusion to be drawn from this is that since a fictional world manifests an ontic position distinct from the position of other worlds of non-actual existence, once such a specific ontic position or a distinct mode of existence is attributed to a world, this world has left the realm of the possible and it can no longer function as a variable of logical compossibility maintaining relations with worlds outside itself. The literary interpretation of possibility is hence bound to make use of possible world notions in a way that intensifies the autonomy of fictional worlds at the expense of doing justice to the logical meaning of possibility.

Accessibility

The question addressed in this section concerns the *reference world* assumed by accessibility relations. I will attempt to show that in logic, the reference world determining accessibility relations is essentially different from the reference world assumed in a theory of fiction; that in logic the notion of reference world is *relational* (any compossible state of affairs can serve as a reference world) whereas in literary theory the reference world is automatically identified with the actual world (whether "the actual world" is seen as a cultural construct constantly changing, or whether in identifying an "actual world" the theorist presupposes a stable epistemology enabling our un-problematic access to a "reality").

Although different philosophers ascribe different degrees of realism to possible worlds, they agree on some aspects of the interpretation of accessibility. Accessibility relations are defined in logic as *relative possibility*. That is, what determines the relation of one world being possible relative to another, and how is that relative possibility settled (relative to what criteria)? Accessibility obviously cannot be detached from the notion of possibility; in fact, Kripke introduces the two as equivalent concepts. Accessibility is destined to account for the truth values of modal and counterfactual propositions (for instance, is a counterfactual possible relative to an actual state of affairs?) Possibility ascribes a concrete content to relations of accessibility among sets, in that relative possibility determines inference in modal systems. Accessibility among worlds works as a restriction on the range of possible worlds; different models for accessibility define different formalizations for quantifying over accessible worlds, that is, not all possible worlds are compossible. Logic offers different models for defining accessibility, each proposing a different formalization for quantifying over accessible worlds, that is, each model places different restrictions on the accessibility relation. According to an m-model (model in the logical-mathematical sense of the interpretation given to categories of a formal language) accessibility relations are constrained and defined by reflexivity. According to a b-model accessibility in the modal system is restricted to reflexive and symmetrical relations; in an s-4 model accessibility is restricted to reflexive and transitive relations and in an s-5 model, accessibility is restricted to reflexive, symmetrical and transitive relations (see Kripke, 1963, Sanford, 1989: 72, Loux, 1979: 21–30). Whatever the relation that makes one world accessible from another, possibility is defined by a type of accessibility relation. A state of affairs is possible in one world (w1) only in case it is true in at least one world (w) accessible to w1. Once a world is relatively possible or accessible to another world, it means that every situation that obtains in the one is possible in the other. Without going into the details of these models for accessibility and into the exact place where possible worlds supply a concrete content or interpretation to the logical categories involved, it is first clear that possible worlds are not considered to be all on a par: a world can be subject to accessibility relations with another world (they are relatively possible) when they meet the conditions specified in that modal system and under which the one world could be realized instead of the other and hence seen as accessible to the other. Since different modal systems specify different accessibility relations, in each system "... only these genuine alternatives really count. Each statement has to be thought of as having been made in some "possible world"; and nothing can be said to be possible in such a world which would not have been true in some world realizable in its stead" (Hintikka, 1979: 67). In other words, accessibility defines the various conditions under which the compossibility of worlds is determined.

To explicate further the concept of accessibility as used by logicians, one can look at the problem of counterfactuals and at the principle of similarity with which counterfactuals are handled within the possible worlds paradigm. It should first be noted that counterfactuals are closely tied to the problem under discussion here because counterfactuals most acutely raise the problem of criteria of validation for non-actual situations. Counterfactuals obey standards of validation determined relative to some notion of "the (f)actual world" despite being *counterfactual,* and to explain the criteria of validation relevant to them some state of affairs external to them must be posited to serve as a reference point. Lewis's work on counterfactuals is an attempt to explain why the truth of a counterfactual cannot be determined from knowledge of the truth values of the antecedent or the consequent of a counterfactual ("if I drop the glass, it will break"). A counterfactual is true in a world in the event of the consequent being true at all the *nearest* possible worlds in which the antecedent is true. Problems of inference in non-actual situations are solved by Lewis, as by other possible worlds theorists, by referring to relevant similarities among sets which determine which other sets could have been realized. Lewis's treatment of counterfactuals, like Kripke's example of dice-throwing, shows that we can infer or determine the truth of propositions about possible worlds by relying on their similarity or closeness to the state of affairs actually realized. Two worlds are similar if moving from one to the other entails no change in the laws of probability or in the logic of the world:

It seems to me obvious that whatever is logically necessary here and now must also be logically necessary in all the logically possible states of affairs that could have been realized instead of the actual one ... Conversely, it also seems fairly clear that no new logical necessities can come about as the result of the realization of any logical possibility. (Lewis, 1973: 76)

This notion of similarity defines accessibility relations in counterfactual contexts and hence determines our ability to make inferences. Comparative similarity is something the frame of possible worlds has introduced into discussions of counterfactuals, induction, and so on. Note however that some philosophers deny possible worlds the ability to account for similarity between worlds. According to the view spelled out by Sanford (1989), for instance, possible worlds only introduce the notion of relevant similarity without solving or explicating the idea of sameness or near-sameness among worlds. In his approach, the weight placed by various treatments of possible worlds on comparative similarity between worlds suggests that some of the similarities are irrelevant. Yet once we can decide on the theoretical basis for distinguishing relevant from irrelevant similarities, there will be little further use for possible worlds in evaluating contingent conditionals.

Arguing over accessibility and similarity, however, neither Putnam, Hintikka nor Lewis (regardless of the very different interpretation each attaches to possible worlds) take the real universe to be a world of reference. For Hintikka, for instance, the whole idea of possible worlds theory is to enable us to talk about what is not *this* world, to enable logic to be different from zoology in its concern (that is, not with the real world but with its more general and abstract features). For modal logicians the real world is, at the most, an *optional* world of reference. This is also evident in the various systems of modal logic describing properties of the accessibility relation described above. A model for accessibility can represent reflexive relations, and/or symmetrical relations, and/or relations of transitivity, which means that the world with respect to which accessibility is measured changes according to the logical model for accessibility posited in a given context. Although for logicians the reference world is always the "center" of the system, a privileged member of the set of all worlds (whether this be "this world" or any other world), this center does not entail an ontological differentiation between the actual world and other worlds accessible to it. The changeability of the "actual" world is nevertheless apparent in logical interpretations of accessibility. For Lewis, as has become a commonplace, "actual" is an indexical term: it can be applied to possible worlds and to their inhabitants, depending on the zero point of reference. That is, "actual" depends for its reference on the circumstances of utterance.

Philosophers are predominantly preoccupied with questions of realism regarding possible worlds, but of a realism that has to do with the status of the theoretical paradigm and not with the ontologies of concrete worlds; that is, although they raise questions and discuss ontological issues, these issues concern the ontology of the model itself and the ontology of the entities the model introduces. Do the entities presupposed by the paradigmatic model for possible worlds (worlds, accessibility, identity) literally exist or are they just extravagant metaphors? Does our modal talk really assume the existence of alternative worlds? Are such alternative worlds indeed relevant to clarifying the problems at hand? Possible worlds carry ontological implications for philosophers only in a qualified sense. Possible worlds do not entail the existence of independent, autonomous ontological domains; the actual world relative to which states of affairs are regarded as possible is basically of the same ontological order as the order of these possibilities.

The fact that alternative possibilities to the one actually obtaining are of the same ontological order, is reflected in the definition of possible worlds as *maximal sets,* which presupposes that accessibility is determined by and dependent on regions of similarity and overlapping between possible worlds. When philosophers assume the occurrence of an alternative possible world, in which a different set of state-propositions obtains (in which, for instance, the dice fell differently, as in Kripke's example of a play in dice producing a number of possible worlds), all other domains of the actual world which were not contradicted by the occurrence of that possible world continue to obtain. The philosophical definition of possible worlds assumes that each world is presented by a *complete set of propositions* and not a partial world represented by those propositions explicitly asserted. This maximality of worlds is not unproblematic in itself: it implies that we can make a hypothetical local change in a world (in which the glass was situated safely elsewhere) and maximize an over-all similarity to the actual world, that is, we "tinker" with the actual world at one point and then let the laws of nature operate without further interference (Putnam, 1983: 6off.).

The metaphysical problem raised by maximality complicates both the idea of the world of reference (a world undergoing a local change that still allows maximizing over remaining domains) and the ontic differentiation between the reference world and worlds accessible to it (if all worlds are maximal, how does an ontic differentiation still persist?). Maximality also poses a more general difficulty for a possible worlds frame, that of determining the language-world relations presupposed by possible worlds. What is the status of "a complete set of propositions" relative to which accessibility is determined? Note that it is commonly agreed that though possible worlds are not *identified* with a set of propositions, they are nevertheless language-dependent; they are stipulated by the power of language. Yet, does the criterion of maximality allow for this interpretation of possible worlds-language relations? The maximality of a relevantly similar world is logically entailed by the mere notion of accessibility: a world is accessible only if all the propositions composing it are either true or false; that is, if in a world w_1 a proposition p is true, whereas p is indeterminate ("either true or false") in world w_2, w_2 cannot then entertain definite accessibility relations with w_1 (it cannot be determined, for instance, whether the accessibility relation between w_1 and w_2 is symmetrical — that the two worlds are numerically identical — or asymmetrical). In short, the accessibility relations among worlds with indeterminate domains, cannot be logically valued. Such a maximality of sets yet counteracts the interpretative capacity of possible worlds for logical relations, because on such a view of maximality the problem of world-language relations becomes central. Does maximality refer to the world being maximal or to the fact that all propositions that could be made about a possible world should be determinable? If we refer to the maximality of *worlds* it would mean that states of affairs are not separable from propositions representing them. For this reason some philosophers (Chisholm, Adams) claim that maximality forces us to identify possible worlds with sets of propositions, and that although sentences do not in themselves maintain logical relations, the possible worlds denoted by these sentences are identified with linguistic entities. With maximality, that is, possible worlds can be identified with linguistic entities, which again problematizes the notion of the reference world and of similarity among worlds. The question of whether possible worlds are "simply possible states of affairs relative to some fixed language" or whether they are "wholly independent of the linguistic frame we use to talk about possible states of affairs" (Putnam, 1983: 67), or, alternatively, that possible worlds are defined as linguistic entities, is one of the crucial areas of debate in the interpretation of possible worlds.[7] The link between the principle of maximality and the question of world-language relations as demonstrated in possible worlds interpretations, was explicitly stated in a recent paper by Hintikka. The idea that "possible worlds semantics somehow presupposes a Leibnitzian framework where the alternatives are entire grand universes ... is a hangover from the unspoken assumption of language as the universal medium," claims Hintikka.[8] For Hintikka the rationale behind possible

---

7 In contrast to Putnam's approach which vindicates the former view that possible worlds are related to a fixed langauge, Lewis advances the view that possible worlds are independent of the language used to denote them. Lewis claims that possible worlds are not to be identified with linguistic entities. His realism means that possible worlds are "respectable entities in their own right and are not to be reduced to something else" (1973: 85).

8 Hintikka distinguishes between the view of language as a universal medium and the view of language as calculus. According to the former we cannot in the final analysis escape our language and look at it and its logic from the outside; all semantic models are hence language again with no deeper philosophical significance than the language interpreted by a given model. According to the latter view we can re-interpret our language; "you can so to speak stop your language and step off ... you can discuss the semantics of your language and even vary systematically its interpretation" (1989: 54). Semantic models can hence supply interpretations which are not on a par with the interpreted.

worlds talk is that it provides an interpretation of our modal discourse and hence operates as a calculus. Our universe of discourse can therefore also be a "small world," that is, a short course of local events in some nook or corner of the actual world (ibid.). In other words, if we believe that possible worlds can explain accessibility relations among partial states of affairs, the maximality of worlds should be rejected. The rejection of maximality implies that possible worlds are separable from the linguistic entities used to represent them.

What the above discussion clearly shows is that in possible worlds semantics relevant similarity and logical accessibility have proven to be problematic enough, touching on metaphysical as well as logical problems. Accessibility is open to diverse interpretations because it can be determined relative to fixed probabilities or relative to a fixed language. Each interpretation of accessibility reflects on the reference world in relation to which accessibility relations can be established (both on the ontic status and on the degree of maximality of such a world). The fact that in using the notion of reference world we do not necessarily accept a straightforward and stable interpretation of relevance for accessibility relations is apparent in the case of worlds created by modal uses of language. Thus, McCawley (1981: 333) claims that in the case of epistemic worlds constructed by modal talk, we do not always depend directly on the real world. The desires, intentions and beliefs a person has and expresses have his *belief world* rather than the *actual world* as a reference world.

Thus despite apparent disagreement over possible worlds and over the way to interpret accessibility among worlds, no side of the debate claims that accessibility involves the relations between the real world and its branching inactualized possibilities. It is for this reason that possible worlds cannot guarantee the persistence of the ontology of one world behind a set of possible actualizations. In his interpretation of possible worlds Kuhn (1989) supplies a concrete demonstration of why accessibility relations and a similarity among worlds (for Kuhn each world represents a stage in the history of science, a scientific paradigm) presupposes a shared ontology. Once the presence of such a common ground is doubted, the history of science becomes a series of possible worlds with incommensurable lexicons. Kuhn shows that the notion of sameness is problematized when we move from one scientific paradigm to another even before new concepts are introduced into our scientific discourse. Two apparently identical scientific lexicons can present meaning incommensurabilities among their constitutive terms. That is, what seems like the same term in different states of our scientific discourse about the world, may prove to participate in different ontologies. When sometime between 1750 and 1950 chemical discovery pointed out that water obeyed the formula H_2O, the term "water" that was used before that discovery to refer to a *natural kind*, stopped being referential. After the formula for water was discovered, "water" started to refer to a chemical compound (H_2O). "Water" does indeed refer in both phases yet in each phase a different world is posited: the transition from one phase to another does not necessarily entail a change of members, but it can result in a lexical and hence conceptual incommensurability between the sets. Likewise, in comparing quantum physics with classical physics, the terms "electron," "position" and "velocity" are incommensurable; acknowledging this incommensurability places a different perspective on the continuity of the history of science.[9] The reference world of terms in use at various stages in the history of science is a product of the complete scientific paradigm within which the meaning of a term can be decided. The intricacy involved in establishing similarities among worlds is hence due both to a change of referents which comes about when one scientific paradigm is replaced by another, and to the interrelations among sets of entities composing a world; that is, similarity is problematic because the structure of a world is a result not only of the entities included in the set but also of the relative position and relations holding those entities together. Accessibility (or compatibility) among worlds, says Eco, involves *transformability among structures* (Eco, 1979: 224). Kuhn shows that relevant similarity cannot be decided in a vacuum. There is no point in describing the accessibility relations between two stages in the history of science because the two stages might imply a change of reference world. Likewise in comparing epistemic worlds, x's desires and y's desires each posit a different reference world in relation to which a relevant similarity is established: the belief world of each individual, rather than the actual world, will serve as a reference world in such contexts.

9 In arguing over the problem of natural kinds with Kuhn, Putnam criticizes the notion of meaning incommensurability because it disconnects the scientific term from a relevant theory and creates the misleading picture that we lack a common language. Putnam believes in an intuitive basis for theories of reference: within a given context or community of speakers, rational procedures are used for understanding theoretical terms that have changed their meaning. There is no uninterpretability among scientific lexicons (Putnam, 1990).

Although in philosophy itself discussions of accessibility transcend the boundaries of logic, accessibility is treated by philosophers as a relational concept which has nothing to do with the question of what actually exists in the real world. What bothers philosophers in connection with accessibility is whether the reference world is *a world*, a set of propositions, a stable set, a maximal set, is a continuity among possible worlds conceivable at all, and so on.

A very different interpretation of the nature of accessibility relations emerges from literary theories of fictionality which make use of possible worlds terminology. I will show that on the basis of a naive acceptance of accessibility (that is, by using possible worlds terminology only as a starting point), literary theorists ignore the problems accessibility involves in logic: literary theorists relate accessibility directly to a set of literary phenomena. In literary interpretations accessibility is viewed as involving the relations between what we know about the world and what fiction tells us. Some theorists of fictionality view the actual world as a stable ontology, some hold that the actual world is a (culturally) variable construct based on ideologically determined encyclopedias. Thus Ryan (1991) who represents the first view, supplies an elaborate analysis of accessibility relations between fiction and the actual world, relations which, according to her interpretation, exceed the limits of logic. Given that in her view the actual world is an unproblematic and stable reference world, we can regard the world of fiction as accessible or inaccessible to such a reference world according to a series of parameters: the identity of properties, the inventory of objects furnishing the world, chronological compatibility, compatibility of natural laws, world species, logical laws, analytical truths and language. One might say that by expanding the notion of accessibility to include a variety of parameters Ryan actually defines a particular set of conventions for world construction, thereby generating her typology of fictional worlds: each type of world diverges from a potential perfect compatibility with the actual world in one or more domains. Ryan does acknowledge that with certain world-types other worlds as worlds of reference can prove to be fruitful. The accessibility relations of fantastic texts, for instance, should be evaluated within the textual universe, selecting the textual actual world as reference world. This impasse does not contradict her basic idea that parameters of accessibility are valued with "good old reality" looming in the background, although this reality might change with the changing cultural-historical context within which literature is produced. In any case, a stability of the reference world is unavoidable in such an interpretation of accessibility.

Other literary theorists who do not share Ryan's relatively unproblematic view of the actual world as a stable reference world nevertheless do share her conception that accessibility has to do with a relation obtaining between fiction and the actual world, even if actuality is only equated with what one believes at a specific moment to be the actual world. Eco, for one, rejects a naively realist conception of reality. Accessibility, he claims, can only hold between two sets of a similar order. Rational constructs (that is, possible worlds) cannot be compared with something which is given, like the world of our experience. The world of reference, and not only possible worlds, therefore has to be postulated and dealt with as a cultural construct. The notion of the actual is hence replaced with that of propositional attitudes the sum total of which constitutes one's encyclopedia and hence one's ad hoc reference world. Therefore if A believes that p, it means that p is compatible with his encyclopedia. A's world of reference is therefore an encyclopedic construct (varying historically and culturally), a propositional attitude is dependent on the assumptions of a given encyclopedia and accessibility is a matter of formally and objectively comparing *two cultural constructs* (Eco, 1979: 222ff.)

We can summarize the difference between philosophers' and literary theorists' uses of accessibility relations by comparing Lewis's conception of similarity with Ryan's principle of minimal departure:[10]

The truth conditions for counterfactuals are fixed only within rough limits; like the relative importances of respects of comparison that underlie the

10 Note that the literary use of accessibility can be made commensurable with the philosophical use when accessibility is transferred from the relation of fiction to the actual world to the relation holding between various sub-worlds within the fictional universe. The fictional text is a system of embedded doxastic worlds introducing various propositional attitudes which are only partially compatible or accessible. Thus Eco shows the two worlds dominating *Oedipus Rex*: the world of the beliefs of Oedipus and the world of the knowledge of Tiresias, taken by Sophocles as the real world. Eco's conclusion is that "*Oedipus Rex* is the story of a tragic inaccessibility. Oedipus blinds himself because he was unable to see that he was living in a world that was not accessible to and from the real one" (1989: 351). Accessibility also works in a similar fashion in possible worlds' relations and between different but related fictional worlds. For instance, the world of *The Sound and the Fury* and the world of *Absalom, Absalom*; or between the world of *Hamlet* and the world of *Rosencrantz and Guildenstern Are Dead*.

comparative similarity of worlds, they are a highly volatile matter, varying with every shift of context and interest (Lewis, 1973: 92)

We construe the world of fiction and of counterfactuals as being the closest possible to the reality we know. This means that we will project upon the world of the statement everything we know about the real world, and that we will make only those adjustments which we cannot avoid (Ryan, 1980: 406)

The passages here cited demonstrate the difference in the definition of the reference world for accessibility relations in counterfactual (or other non-actual states of affairs) and in fictional contexts. Lewis, by acknowledging the variability in the reference world and hence the context-dependency of the truth value of counterfactuals, underlines the volatility of concepts such as similarity and comparison among worlds. Ryan, on the other hand, insists that similiarity is based on minimal departure from (what we know about) reality thus advancing the idea that the privileged reference world is identified with, in some sense at least, the real world. Note that I do not claim here that modal logicians hypothesize a context-relative reality from which the variability of the reference world is derived, whereas literary theorists promote a "naive" view of the real world. The difference between the two conceptions rather stems from the fact that the problematic ontological status of reality is not an issue either in the logical models for accessibility or in the literary ones, but in each case for different reasons. The ontological status of reality is not an issue for logicians because an actual world is another compossible system with no privileged status over other possibilities (the concept of the actual presupposes no ontological gradations among worlds). The ontological status of reality is not an issue for literary theorists because the actual world is identified with "a reality," and the latter is a privileged reference world ontologically distinguished from fiction, whether by "a reality" we refer to the physical real, to some version of it, or to a vague context-dependent notion of what we know about reality. In any case "a reality," of whatever ontological status, seems to be a presupposed belief behind talk about the fictionality of literary worlds.

Possible worlds between the disciplines, again

The diverging interpretations given to possible worlds *within philosophy itself* undermine any attempt to view a possible world as a clear, straightforward and unequivocal concept which the various disciplines can adopt for their own needs. Yet, although possible worlds do not cohere into a unified concept, the difference in approaches may explain how different disciplines attach such a variety of interpretations to possible worlds. We saw above, in chapter 1, how, for instance, the literary interpretation of possible worlds comes close to a modal-realist construal of the concept within philosophy.

The above discussion suggests that literary theory and logic differ in their use of *world*, of *possible worlds*, and of related concepts (such as possibility and accessibility) because of the cross-disciplinary movement of these concepts. That is, one could argue that logic represents the original literal interpretation of possible worlds whereas literary theory deviates from the philosophical use. This conclusion may be drawn from the difference in ontological density attached to possible worlds by the literary and philosophical discussions and from the way possible worlds are characterized in the literary versus the philosophical contexts. Thus, in the literary context possibility and impossibility are treated as alternative properties of fictional worlds and accessibility is interpreted as a device for comparing reality with non-actual ontologies. There are of course other differences and similarities between interpretations of possible worlds in literary theory and in logic. I chose to concentrate here on two productive dissimilarities which may illuminate a more profound divergence of interest exhibited by the two disciplines. On one level of analysis it may indeed seem that literary theory metaphorizes the notion of possible worlds by literally accepting possible worlds and their components as part of the literary object. But I would claim that the differences in the interpretations of possibility and accessibility discussed above are but symptoms, albeit telling symptoms, of a significant gap between the "logics" of the two disciplines in question.

In philosophy possible worlds suggest a framework for linking a metaphysical problem with a problem of language. More specifically, possible worlds' terminology supplies logical categories (such as necessity and possibility) with semantic content, and, conversely, possible worlds supply semantic and syntactic categories (such as tenses, modalities and conditionals) with logico-ontological content (see Bradley and Swartz, 1979: 62–65). Possible worlds can tie together two sets of problems and show how they interrelate (for instance, a conditional on the linguistic level can be described as constructing a counterfactual world). On this view possible worlds introduce *a new conceptual lexicon*: two sets of phenomena are interpreted by a common conceptual tool. Possible worlds hence work in philosophy as a theoretical model whose explanatory power results from its hosting and linking two sets of problems. It is only in these terms that one can understand why philosophers basically do not deal with the ontology of worlds but with the ontology of the entities posited by the possible worlds model. That is, philosophers either question or endorse the premise behind possible worlds that theoretical entities such as worlds really exist or that such entities, posited behind categories of logic and of language, can generate explanations for these categories. Philosophers investigate the question of whether categories of logic and semantics indeed carry ontological implications, whether possibility entails relations among alternative worlds and so on. Philosophers who promulgate possible worlds talk acknowledge the importance of these implications, whereas philosophers who reject the possible worlds framework deny the existence of theoretical entities like worlds and alternative states of affairs, thereby denying the explanatory power of these same entities. Notice that the fact that *possible worlds* is a framework suggesting a set of theoretical entities in terms of which logical and language categories can be related is also reflected in the metatheoretical debates regarding possible worlds. The central aspect of this debate focuses on the question of whether possible worlds should be identified with a language-model epistemology (whether possible worlds say something about the features of our language in its relation to the world) or with a language-model ontology (whether possible worlds say something about the structure of reality itself).[11] In other words, possible worlds talk in philosophy has come a full circle in a way, now

---

11 In the philosophy of science the debate over *possible worlds* indeed centers around the question of the productivity of a plurality of worlds theory in explaining physical phenomena. Bell (1989), for instance, questions the ability of a many-world interpretation in quantum physics to provide a coherent theoretical picture for visible events in our physical universe (like the image created by electrons on a television screen). The problem with a many-world interpretation, claims Bell, is that instead of providing a valid picture of physical events, it attempts to reconcile us with the fact that we cannot predict where an electron will scintillate on a screen; it aims to make us more comfortable about the unknowable existence of our own world. For this purpose, the many-world interpretation forwards a notion that is both extravagant and vague that all possible worlds actually exist: a dubious suggestion that misses its role as a theory. A many-world interpretation creates a romantic filter between the observer and the world rather than getting the observer closer to physical reality.

providing a new framework for discussing the perennial problem of the relation between language and world.

A significantly different conception of possible worlds is exemplified by literary theory of fiction. For literary theorists, and other art-theorists who employ possible worlds to account for fictional universes, possible worlds are not presented as a set of theoretical entities used to describe a hybrid of logical and linguistic phenomena, but are rather identified as an aspect of the object of study itself. Fictional worlds are regarded as possible worlds, and possible worlds hence involve the ontology of concrete artistic worlds. This explains why logical categories such as possibility, worlds, accessibility and identity across worlds are *literally* interpreted in the literary context. Possible worlds are not theoretical terms but rather descriptive concepts that work within a descriptive poetics. We can see why, whereas logic leaves the impression that possible worlds are empty, or thinly-populated if not abstract categories, in literary theories possible worlds are pregnant worlds that carry concrete ontological content and denote an ontological density epitomized in the idea of "a world."

This is indeed a substantial difference: in philosophy "possible worlds" is a label for a theoretical framework and for the abstract categories of a theoretical model; in literary theory possible worlds are treated as part of *the object* of theoretical scrutiny. This difference in meaning does not however mean that there is no translatability among the languages of the two disciplines. The fact that possible worlds have proved to be so productive a framework for the study of such diverse phenomena as logical relations on the one hand and fictional worlds on the other hand, derives from the productive basis of possible worlds which has provided both disciplines with a common point of departure. Possible worlds enable us to talk about the relationship between different states of affairs, to see worlds, whether necessary, actual or possible, as cultural constructs, and to relativize necessity and possibility to changing worlds of reference.

In literature and art theory, possible worlds have paved the way towards examining the ontology of worlds and for investigating the status of imaginary beings. Possible worlds have provided literary theory with the ideological legitimation for turning theoretical attention and energy back to referential questions. In the attempt to understand fiction in ways that were not possible before, and to substantiate previously held intuitions about fictionality, possible worlds provide a handy new terminological framework. Although I do not believe that possible worlds, in the way they are currently being interpreted by literary theorists, are indeed necessary or as illuminating for discussions of reference in fiction as might seem to be the case, they have certainly succeeded in creating a theoretical terrain where these problems can be legitimately addressed. The clearest manifestation of their productivity lies in the changes *possible worlds* have generated in the theoretical understanding of *fictionality*, which is the subject matter of the next chapter.

3

The fictionality of fictional worlds

Why is there a problem in defining fictionality?

Our world consists of a variety of world versions: worlds of physicists, worlds of common sense, ideological worlds, historical versions of the world and others. Included in this plurality of kinds of worlds is the class of fictional worlds which, not unlike world-classes of other ontological status, is both diffuse and constantly changing. In view of the history of culture, one could say that worlds projected by literary texts possess no absolute properties indicating their fictionality, and that fictionality cannot be identified either with cross-cultural or with meta-historical criteria. Texts originally written as history or as philosophy can be "fictionalized" (that is, converted into fiction) at a later point in cultural history; fictionality and actuality can be relativized to a cultural perspective (legends about Greek gods were presumably treated as versions of reality by people in ancient Greece). Moreover, it is not that fictional texts necessarily refer to imaginary beings: many fictions rely heavily on references to objects and events belonging to actual history. Fictional worlds hence constitute one set of world versions, which are delimited from other world versions according to time-specific or culture-specific determinations.

Apart from the fact that fictionality cannot be regarded as a stable property of texts and that the boundaries between fictional worlds and other world models in a culture can fluctuate, there is also a difficulty in trying to delineate any class of fictional texts produced and received as such in a given cultural context, because fictional aspects might also appear in texts claiming to be history, journalism or science. Any manipulation of facts (narrativization, selection, expansion and condensation of materials), a procedure which is in fact necessary for any communication, introduces the fictional into a text. The question of whether fictional texts can be said to possess their own set of distinctive features hence becomes especially problematic.[1]

Yet, despite problems incurred at the outset in any attempt to formulate a definite conception of fictionality, numerous attempts have been made to produce a universal model for fiction and indeed to describe what distinctive features distinguish a fictional text from other cultural products. All universal models of fiction are by definition segregationist in their approach to the relations between fiction and reality, promoting the view that fictional products can be segregated from other cultural products. Yet some of these models promote a *textual-taxonomic model*, while some are *logico-semantic* and *non-taxonomic*. To clarify this distinction let us first look at models of the former type.

Textual-taxonomic models of fictionality

Theorists have attempted to describe a set of linguistic features as indicators of fictionality: the epic preterite signaling the present of fiction (Hamburger, 1973) and free indirect discourse (Banfield, 1982). These are attempts "to arrive at the *differentia specifica* of narrative fiction in linguistic terms." Thus, according to Banfield, when a sentence representing consciousness occurs with a sentence of narration "they are a signal that we have entered the realm of fiction ..." (ibid.: 258–9).[2] In other words, the textual-taxonomic model is based on the assumption that it is empirically possible to enumerate a set of textual indicators of which at least one will appear to signal fictionality. Such textual features thus fulfill a meta-function of indicating fictionality; the presence or absence in a text of one of these fiction-indicators functions as a taxonomic means whereby fiction may be distinguished from nonfiction. A model similar in approach appears

1 Note that the notion of the *dominant,* formulated during late Formalism (Tynjanov, Jakobson), that is, the idea that in literary texts the poetic function dominates communication, cannot serve as a model for fictionality despite its inherent relativism. First, fictionality is not to be conflated with literariness since such a conflation is misleading, as will be discussed further. Second, the dominant poetic function, destined to define language use that is "literary" or "poetical" in essence, fails to account for all literary genres (see Ronen, 1986).

2 For a full survey of theories about free indirect discourse and for the way this phenomenon is treated as an index of literariness or as a characteristic of the fictional, see McHale, 1978: esp. 282–284.

in Genette's (1990) attempt to arrive at the difference between fictional and factual narrative in terms of a narratologically definable difference. Genette claims that he neither accepts that fictionality is textually marked, nor endorses what he terms the "Searlian" view that there is no textual property that will identify a text as a work of fiction. Genette opts for a third possibility, claiming that fiction is marked on the narratological level in the relations of non-identity holding between author and narrator. Genette, who is clearly attempting to establish an exhaustive distinction of fictional from factual narratives, is at least aware of the limitations of such an approach: "far from being always a manifest signal ... the relation A–N [author–narrator] can mostly be inferred from the sum total of the (other) characteristics of the narrative. It is undoubtedly the most elusive relation ... , and sometimes the most ambiguous ..." (ibid.: 25).

A model that advances the idea that the fictionality of texts is structured into the texts themselves, makes an implied claim for classification, and is hence taxonomic. Taxonomic models are of course not necessarily introduced as imposing a priori classification on texts: a class of fictional texts can be taken as a cultural given and fiction markers identified in that class. Yet once the properties of fictional texts have been identified and confirmed by a given group of texts, they are presumed able to work as classificatory tools for any group of texts. Fiction markers may even be expected to help us decide about borderline cases.

I will now take a look at the problems posed by a model of the taxonomic kind. Even if we agree that the fictional intention of an author is somehow registered in idiosyncratic or commonly recognizable textual markers, and that the fictionality of a text is reflected in its linguistic components (or, alternatively, on a higher level of narrative structuration), we can agree with Gregory Currie that "facts about style, narrative form, and plot structure may count as evidence that the work is fiction, but these are not the things that make it so" (1990: 2). There are at least three objections which may be brought forth against attempts to define fictionality in terms of a set of a priori given textual indicators:[3]

---

3 These objections obtain only in relation to textual taxonomies of fiction and nonfiction and not in relation to narratological taxonomies of the type Genette introduces. The latter's inadequacies have to do, as specified above, with the diffuse nature of narratological criteria and with their dependence, in many cases, on interpretational procedures and on the type of narrative theory put forward.

(1) Defining fictionality as immanently textual is methodologically cumbersome and conceptually unsatisfactory. Any textual indicator isolated as fictionality-marker is necessarily language-specific, genre-specific and medium-specific (Hamburger's epic preterite, for instance, is restricted to literary third person authoritative narration, and to specific European languages). In other words, even if, hypothetically, the conjunction of a complete set of fiction-indicators, might, in a specific cultural context, produce sufficient criteria for delineating the group of fictional texts by ostentation, such a set could amount to an endless list of fiction-indicators (each possibly indicating just a small sub-group within the class of fictional texts). Such an empirically observed but potentially limitless set of contingent features must hence be judged to be a poor solution for a theoretical definition of fictionality.

(2) Another motivation for denying the validity of linguistic indicators for fiction is that we acquire and employ only one language in order to understand and produce both fictional and nonfictional discourse. Linguistic markers of fiction are therefore not unique to fiction: usually they are only distributed differently or they produce a different effect in the context of fiction. It is only in rare cases that linguistic collocations which would seem ungrammatical outside fictional discourse will mark fictionality ("tomorrow was Christmas," to use Hamburger's example for "unspeakable sentences" in fiction). Identifying fiction with textual elements therefore depends on a prior pragmatic competence on the basis of which one reads and understands fiction, and not on the mere presence of these elements in a given text. That is, although reading literature requires the acquisition of rules and conventions that are not included in our regular linguistic competence, these are more likely to be of a pragmatic-conventional nature, rather than of a textual nature.

(3) Distinguishing fiction through a set of linguistic markers is a circular procedure that will only uncover fiction as a culturally marked category; it tells us, however, little about the nature of fiction. That is, the fact that we intuitively accept that language reflects in its structures certain consensual cultural distinctions (the aspect system, for instance, reflects our commonsensical distinction between a continuous and a punctual occurrence in time, deictic expressions mark the relations between a situation of utterance and the propositional content of that utterance), does not yet explicate the cultural category of fiction nor why this category should be distinguished from other

ontologies a given culture may construct. Linguistic indicators are hence only symptomatic of the deeply entrenched cultural belief that fiction forms a distinct cultural category; they do not inform us as to the logic behind these beliefs or their implications for our understanding of fiction. Thus the epic preterite indicates the way a here-and-now of occurrence is constructed in fiction, certain types of free indirect discourse may be viewed as unique to fiction — yet their occurrence does not explicate the essence of fiction.

In a way, even literary theorists who are fully aware of these problems do not reject or completely abandon the attempt to detect a linguistic basis for fictionality.[4] Somewhat speculatively, one may claim that this insistence is a result of a long tradition in literary studies that defines the literariness of texts in terms of the type of *language* literature employs (exemplified in the Formalist–Structuralist dichotomy of ordinary versus poetical uses of language). The approach to fictionality as textually marked reflects a similar orientation toward language-use distinctions. Moreover, this approach to fictionality derives directly from the way the literary is defined: the nature of fiction must lie on the level which is singular to literature itself, that is, the level of language-use. Here we touch on another aspect of the textual definition of fictionality: such a definition reflects a conflation of fictionality and literariness apparent in literary studies. This conflation is produced by a widely held, although only implicitly stated view in literary theory, a view that has its precedents in the work of Roman Jakobson, namely that it is the fictionality of texts that suspends the ordinary use of language for referring or asserting, thus allowing fictional texts to "focus on the message." In other words, fictionality, breaching the referential, communicative function of language is, implicitly at least, viewed as a prerequisite for exercising the poeticality of language. By claiming that poetical language deepens the basic dichotomy between signs and objects, Jakobson equates poeticality (attracting attention to the formal aspects of the message) with fictionality (noncommitment to a world of referents). Interest in fictionality, and hence in the textual markers of fictionality, is hence an outcome and a symptom of a deeply rooted impetus to

---

4 McHale, for instance, argues that despite the apparent ease with which counterexamples can be found for the claim that free indirect discourse is distinctive of literary writing, it can still be claimed that free indirect discourse is, if not exclusively literary, at least characteristic of the fictional.

show that the language of literature behaves differently from other uses of language. This very intuition is one that nourishes the whole domain of stylistics in the broad sense, including the various schools and methodologies of research into the language of literature. This domain is nourished by the idea that "artistic language is different in kind from 'ordinary' language, and that there is a sharp divide between the two types of discourse" (Toolan, 1990: 3). It goes without saying that locating the literary quality of texts in equivalence patterns and in stylistic markers represents attempts at a taxonomy of types of language use similar to the one discussed above regarding textual definitions of fictionality used to segregate fiction from nonfiction. It is hence no great surprise that literariness and fictionality tend to mingle in literary discussions; for a text to be fictional it needs to use language in a deviant, literary way. The effect of using language "abnormally" is a breach of the standard link between language and the world. A similar claim is made by Iser (1975) for instance: literary language selects a variety of social and cultural conventions; yet these assume no vertical relations with the real world, but only horizontal relations with each other. Fictional language is hence *depragmatized language*. Iser's argument demonstrates how an anti-referential approach to literature results in an overlap of literariness and fictionality to the point of conflation. Viewing fiction as a type of textuality emerges from the anti-referential orientation characteristic of literary studies mainly during the sixties and until the mid eighties. A prototypical example of this literary attitude can be found in Leech and Short (1981), who acknowledge that fictionality has to do with *what* is apprehended by the literary text whereas literariness has to do with *how* that world is apprehended. Yet, despite the fact that fictionality is put on the side of "content" whereas the style of fiction is placed on the side of "form and manner," "the two come together" almost indiscriminately in the scope of their book (ibid.: 150). The mingling of literariness with fictionality has resulted in attempts to identify where fictionality makes itself present in the text, as if this presence exhausts the problem of fiction. It has also led to a tendency to view fictionality as just another self-oriented mechanism organizing the literary text. Being subjected to a long-standing (and one might say, ideologically motivated) interest in inner-systemic modes of organization, fictionality has been perceived in literary studies as identical with literariness. It is in these terms, and against this tradition, that insistent attempts to identify symptoms of fictionality on a textual level of analysis can be comprehended, motivated and eventually deconstructed. This orientation toward inner-systemic literariness has neutralized the original sense of fiction (that being fictional refers to an object's relation to something else which is real, nonfictional or nonimaginary). The implications of this tendency to regard fictionality as referring to the self-focused, self-oriented nature of the literary system will be further examined in the context of the history of the concept of *world* in literary studies.

Non-taxonomic models for fictionality

In view of this tradition which transforms the fictional into a textual phenomenon and identifies it with the literary use of language, studies in the pragmatics of literature take an opposite approach. They attempt to prove that "literature is a context, too, not the absence of one" (Pratt, 1977: 99), and dedicate considerable critical energy to collapsing the correlation between fictionality and literariness. It is not very enlightening, claims Pratt, to view fictional, world-creating, self-focused discourse as identical with a distinct class of "abnormal" utterances; unpacking the bundle of literariness and fictionality is a necessary step toward a better understanding of what characterizes the literary speech situation. Although for Pratt fictionality is just a side-issue in her study of literary discourse, she does illustrate that fiction is not a stable category. I would claim that describing fluctuations of the fictional became possible in literary studies only when fictionality was regarded as discrete from the category of the literary. Fictionality has to do with the relation between a speech situation and its context, and with the degree and kind of commitment of the speaker to the content of his utterance. The literary is therefore not exhausted by fictionality and vice versa: a poem can be considered literary without the question of its portraying a fictional situation being raised at all (that is, the literariness of poetry does not seem to lie with fictionality); a speech situation can be fictional without its being part of the literary system. The interplay between fiction and literature opens up a variety of possibilities (some of which will be examined in the second part of this study); yet the two are not interchangeable.

An alternative perspective on the problems involved in defining fictionality would stress that the fictional by definition does not refer to an inner structure but to a type of relation: a relation maintained between what is contained within the literary text and what lies beyond its boundaries.[5]

The notion that the fictionality of texts emerges from an intrinsic value or that there is something in fictional texts that signals their fictionality is accepted by many members of the literary community despite the number of problems this raises. When examined meta-theoretically, a definition of fictionality in terms of linguistic markers is the only definition of fictionality destined to work as a taxonomic operator on texts. That is, linguistic markers are presumed to assist the reader in distinguishing, for instance, the biography of a real historical figure from an imagined biography of a nonexistent personage by the mere appearance of the texts involved. A non-taxonomic model for fiction, however, creates a universal logic or semantics for fictional texts without staking a claim for a classification that would tell fiction from nonfiction. The logic or semantics of fiction is described in texts already included in the category of fiction within a given culture. Such models for fiction present the logical, ontological or semantic laws and conventions by which fiction is produced or deciphered, but do not impose a priori criteria for distinguishing fictional from nonfictional texts. Non-taxonomic models for fiction – whether those constructing a semantics for fiction, or those addressing the logic or the cultural position characteristic of fictional texts – regard the class of fictional texts as a given. When fictionality is identified, for example, with a logical operator (Lewis), or located in the semantic property of incompleteness (Doležel, Howell), or when fictionality is defined as a certain freedom of interplay between time of statement and time of occurrence (Ricoeur), or as a degree of commitment on behalf of the speaker to the truth of the propositions (Searle, Walton) – each of these approaches to fiction analyzes its universal nature after the fact without bothering to deal with the question of how one identifies a fictional text in the first place, if at all. Most models of fiction consider texts as fictional or nonfictional regarding the two groups as determined by a cultural context. Such non-taxonomic models are contingent on the "official" status of the text and not on preceding procedures of identifying and isolating fictional from nonfictional propositions.

5 Currie (1990), for instance, suggests seeing fictionality as a relational property holding between the author's intention to produce an act of fiction-making and the attitude of make-believe the reader adopts toward the content of what he reads.

One of the claims I would make in this chapter is that a non-taxonomic definition of fictionality developed in literary studies is an offshoot of philosophical models for fiction. In a way, philosophical discourse has affected literary discourse by "liberating" it from a poeticality centered view of literature without throwing the baby of structural analysis out together with the bath-water of literariness. At the same time a pragmatic definition of fictionality as formulated in philosophical discourse and further developed in literary theory, is perfectly compatible with the view that literary texts manifest their own unique modes of inner organization.

How did the philosophical approach to fiction enable the development of non-taxonomic models for fiction in the domain of literary theory? By and large philosophers do not directly address the problem of how one distinguishes a fictional from a nonfictional proposition. Avoiding the problem of classification has to do with the fact that philosophy deals with *fictional propositions* rather than with fictionality as a general strategy of *texts*. Comparing "Sherlock Holmes lives on Baker Street" with "Mrs. Thatcher lives on 10 Downing Street," philosophers investigate the logical and ontological basis for determining the difference between two propositions that seem (syntactically and semantically) to be of a similar structure, yet only one describes an (past) actual state of affairs and refers to existents. Philosophers deal with fiction as part of the domain of a semantics or logic of propositions, and certainly not as part of text-theory.[6] The fact that philosophy deals with what might be called a micro-level fictionality also enables it to avoid the problem of fictional propositions that *do not* represent imaginary beings; propositions that do not refer to nonexistents are excluded from the realm of fiction (as in Searle, 1969). In short, philosophy can approach the problem of fiction without classificatory problems even being raised.

One of the main difficulties involved in defining literary fictionality has to do, however, with the fact that some works of fiction include both propositions about imaginary beings and propositions about historical entities. Moreover a definition of fictionality would count as

6 Note that even within the paradigm of literary text-theories no heed is paid to the problem of fictionality. Typical examples are both Greimas' semiotic model and Van Dijk's text grammar in which fictionality is of no consequence, is either side-lined or ignored altogether. Thus in Van Dijk (1972) the ontological and logical problems connected with the referential status of literary texts form only a minor issue within a literary text grammar, and are furthermore conflated with a concept of a different order, that is with *realism* (ibid. 336–337).

unsatisfactory if attached to a propositional calculus. Fictionality as understood by literary theorists is a property of *texts* and not of propositions. This difference of focus and interest between the philosophical and literary discussion of fictionality, calls for the semantic and logical solutions provided by philosophy for fictional propositions to be translated (rather than directly applied) into over all solutions for fictional texts.[7] It is in view of these reservations that the philosophical discussion of fiction should be subjected to the different interests of literary theory, a procedure never really undertaken in literary models of fiction, including those relying directly on philosophical concepts. It is necessary to analyze explicitly how fictionality becomes identified with a textual operator rather than with a quantifier over propositions. Once this procedure of reviewing the philosophical stand has been undertaken, a legitimate and coherent non-taxonomic view of fictionality can evolve in the literary context.

What can be surmised from the philosophical discussion on fiction is that the fictionality of a text may be described once the text has been classified as fiction (on grounds of various cultural considerations): it is at this stage that a semantics and/or logic of fiction become definable (Woods, 1974; Ihwe and Rieser, 1979). Granted then that logical and semantic tools developed in philosophy are extended to the scope of texts, the philosophical rationale can substantiate a literary pragmatic perspective on fictionality. Such a perspective allows one to skip procedures of classification, that is, to adopt a non-taxonomic model. From a literary point of view, omitting such classification is necessary in view of the fact that fictionality is a flexible dynamic property attached to texts on the basis of a variety of cultural criteria. Hence, only once the idea that fictional texts can be detected or identified by textual analysis is abandoned can a theory of fictionality develop with the aim of explaining the specific attitudes

---

7 This difference of focus has been noticed (although not explained) by literary theorists. Pavel (1986) goes to great pains in order to divide the literary theory on fiction from philosophers' discourse on fiction; the latter, according to him, "often examine fiction only indirectly, in passing, and in relation to other theoretical queries; in many cases their positions regarding fiction derive from philosophical concerns that are quite extraneous to literary interests" (12). Without going into the question of whether philosophers are respectful enough of the intricacy of literary concerns, it is clear that the mechanism of the influence of philosophy on literary discourse with regard to the problem of fictionality is in itself an intricate concern for methodology and theory and one of the side-interests of the present study.

elicited by the fictional text or the logical position assumed by the world projected by the fictional text. This seems to be the basic idea behind the work of pragmatists (such as Searle) and of aestheticians (such as Walton, Woods and others) who refer to the *make-believe* intention of a speaker or an author, or to the *say-so* (propositional content) of his sayings, without creating a new version of the intentional fallacy. The logic of *pretense* is a model for explaining the pragmatics of fiction and not the originary intentions behind fictional discourse. Indeed, if fictionality cannot be accounted for in terms of textual features, a plausible approach to the concept requires a *pragmatic definition*, and the logic of pretense presupposes such a definition.

It is not the purpose of this chapter to examine the various pragmatic models for fiction nor to analyze their pros and cons. Rather, I will analyze the very conceptual basis of a pragmatic definition of fictionality which, in one formulation or another, underlies all pragmatic models for fiction. In an informal definition of fictionality, which is also accepted in the present study, fictionality is viewed as a specific relationship holding between a writer and a reader of a text, a relationship reflected and manifested through the world this text projects or constructs. Following such a definition, fictionality can be explained in terms of a definite and universal logico-semantic model, a model which is perfectly compatible with attempts to account for processes of fictionalization or defictionalization of texts in a specific culture or at a specific historical moment (Pavel, 1986: 75–85) and for cases where fictions (as creations of the imagination) intermingle with actual states of affairs. That is, if fictionality is a pragmatically decided property of texts, such a property can be assessed even if states of affairs to which this property is attached are subject to change, and even if a fictional property is attributed to states of affairs composed of both imaginary and nonimaginary entities.[8] In short, this type of definition stems from the idea that the class of fictional texts, while not immanently dissimilar to nonfictional texts, is nevertheless founded on a separate set of logical rules, a set activated by the official cultural

8 It is true that Natasha will always remain fictional even if a historical enquiry were to reveal that a historical Natasha was identified by historians (Doležel, 1988). Napoleon however belongs to two different ontological contexts: to the fictional context of *War and Peace* where he is considered a fictionalized entity, and to a historical context where he represents his historical self – deciding between the possibilities of where to locate Napoleon is a matter of interpretation and depends on the type of theory one chooses to develop.

categorization of a text as fiction, and by the distinct horizon of reading attributed to it (rather than by textual features) once such a cultural categorization has been settled. It is by adopting such a pragmatic approach to fiction that a theory of fictionality could prove to be compatible with our intuitions regarding the distinct nature and status of fictional worlds despite cultural fluctuations, as well as our intuitions regarding the differences between the class of fictional texts and texts belonging to other categories of discourse and constructing other world-versions.

The pragmatics of fiction – its ontological, logical and epistemological distinctive features

The fictionality of a text is a type of relationship between writer and reader reflected in the world the text projects. Fictional texts project fictional worlds and it is the overall position of these worlds that enable us to regard them as forming a distinct class. The problem to be addressed in this section is how to determine the distinctive features of this class of worlds (how fictional worlds are distinguished from other world types) and to ascertain the classification of fictional worlds relative to other categories of worlds portraying possible but non-actual states of affairs. As shown in the second chapter, possible worlds as well as worlds of belief or desire, are tied to actuality in a manner different from the way in which fictional worlds are. Fictional worlds were shown there to differ from possible worlds in some of their most essential features. Whereas possible worlds are regarded as alternative possible but non-actualized courses of events, fictional worlds are subjected to other principles which allow their fictional actualization. Fictional worlds can be regarded as possible or impossible constellations of events and situations which are fictionally actualized or non-actualized. Thus, if a history book documents Napoleon dreaming about conquering the world at a certain point of his military career in the history of France, this hypothetical state of affairs can be defined as a possible situation that was never actualized in the world. The world of *War and Peace*, on the other hand, portrays and actualizes fictional (and sometimes historically deviant) situations in which Napoleon is engaged. These two states of affairs are hence attributed a different status in relation to the actualized states of the world. A fictional world is not a modal extension of the actual world, but rather a world with its own modal structure; once one is informed of the fictionality of Tolstoy's novel, the world projected by that novel is seen as belonging to an ontic sphere different from any historical narrative about the period and different also from the world projected by hypothetical documents registering Napoleon's imperialistic visions. The generic label attached to a state of affairs determines its ontological status relative to other possibilities. The flexibility and context-dependency of defining a text as fictional are manifested in two aspects of the relations between a text and its fictionality.

(1) The generic label attributing a given world to the realm of the fictional can be determined regardless of the degree of its resemblance to the actual world. The extent to which a fictional world is modeled on the actual world (in the present example, the degree to which the fictional world of *War and Peace* is modeled on a historical version of the actual world) is a problem separate from the fictionality or actuality of a world version.

(2) Since fictionality denotes an over-all type of ontology, a world can be deemed fictional whether it includes historical figures (like Napoleon), imaginary characters (like Natasha), or supernatural elements (like ghosts).

Since the fictionality of texts cannot be identified a priori with a concrete set of textual features or with a stable given group of texts, the way is open for a pragmatic definition of fictionality, which would take into consideration an integrated system of world-constructing conventions, cultural beliefs and reading procedures. This system, reflecting the diffuse boundaries of the class of fictional texts (otherwise fictionality would not have required a pragmatic approach), refers to a complex of ontological and logical features complemented by suppositions which orient one's attitude toward worlds of fiction and controlling the production and reception of such worlds. A fictional world has a different logical status from the world created by the historian or the physicist: fiction entails a different type of commitment to actual states of the world, objects inhabiting the fictional world are presumed to be of a specific nature, fiction requires a different conception of truth functionality, and so on. It is on these grounds that fictional worlds are treated as a separate class of worlds, and they are attributed a set of unique properties.

The following list of properties is nonexhaustive by its very nature. It is designed to give a sample of what an integration of various models of fiction can supply toward a pragmatic definition of fictionality. The list is also meant to indicate that conventions of reading literary worlds (fictional world reconstruction) are closely linked to the logico-ontology of fiction as formulated within the discourse of philosophy.

World-constructing conventions (the logic and ontology of fictional propositions)

(1) Fictional propositions assume a distinct fictional position of states of affairs relative to the actual world. A fictional proposition represents fictional states of affairs which make no direct claim about our actual world. The non-claim about reality is a general feature of the pragmatic position of fictional states of affairs, and this general observation can be rendered through a variety of models, each representing differently the way a fictional proposition is detached from a standard language/world relation and its truth value is suspended.[9] The fictional stand that propositions may assume is given a variety of interpretations. Fictional propositions can, for instance, be considered as actions of presenting states of affairs for the reader's consideration ("a fictioneer nothing affirms but something presents" – Wolterstorff, 1980: 234); or fictional propositions can be viewed as closed under a modal quantifier restricting their application only to the sum total of states of affairs they denote, as propositions "true in a game of make-believe" (Walton, 1990); or fictional propositions can be interpreted as being about nonexistents.

(2) Any set of fictional propositions is logically confined by its shared fictional property. However one defines this fictional property of a set of propositions, inferences drawn from such a set are restricted by that same property. Inferences drawn from: "it is fictional in the world of *Madame Bovary* that p" cannot be carried over to the set of propositions confined by a different fictional property "it is fictional in the world of *Crime and Punishment* that p." Inferring from one set of fictional propositions (which construct one fictional world) to another set of fictional propositions (which construct another world) is not a

9 In a standard language/world relation I do not assume that a pragmatic definition of fiction presupposes a positivist view on the way the world is related to language in nonfictional contexts or a naive-realist view on the way the world actually is. The world can be a relativized concept (relativized to our belief world, or to our encyclopedia) and fiction will be still regarded as uncommitted to the actual.

legitimate logical procedure. The fictional property of a set of propositions hence works as a type of modal quantifier operating on a given set, determining its logical structure and hence the possible inferences that can be drawn from it.[10]

(3) Fictional propositions might represent contradictory states of affairs (Walton, 1990: 64ff., Linde, 1989). A given set of fictional propositions assuming *a shared* fictional property does not necessarily follow requirements of logical possibility or logical consistency. In other words, a set of fictional propositions, although obeying structural requirements of consistency and coherence (as will be discussed in the following chapter), does not obey consistency requirements of a logical nature. A fictional state of affairs can include two inconsistent states each attributing a different color to the heroine's eyes, or a pictorial state of affairs can include two mutually exclusive perspectives. Impossibilities can be indicated directly or indirectly by the fictional utterances themselves or they can result from a semantic integration of the set of propositions.

(4) Fictional objects denoted by fictional propositions are in-determinate and incomplete. The nature of this incompleteness can be described in various terms and has given rise to alternative models, yet according to all interpretations every fictional set of propositions is not maximal: there are some properties with regard to which the question of whether p or $\sim$p holds is indeterminate.

(5) Fictional propositions represent both existents and non-existents: they intermingle denotations of imaginary beings with reference to historical entities. This blend has been subject to different theoretical representations: some relying on areas of fictionality or on degrees of actuality within a given fictional world, others claiming that all components of a fictional world are equally fictional.

(6) All properties of the fictional object are equally essential to it. Since all fictional objects (including the fictionalized versions of historical entities) are bound to the world of which they form part, one cannot separate components of the fictional world from each other; they are structurally bound together. In this respect all fictional propositions are equally necessary for the construction of a particular

10 In the context of philosophical suggestions as to how to solve the logico-semantical position of claims about fictional objects, some philosophers read such claims *de-dicto* while others suggest a *de-re* approach (see note 7 in chapter 1). For a full discussion of these two alternative understandings of the logico-semantic structure of fictional claims, see Howell, 1979.

fictional world. If, for instance, there were ten more real "Emma Woodhouses," writes Joseph Margolis, in addition to the one about whom Jane Austen wrote her novel, there should also exist real counterparts for every other element of the novel. "You cannot separate Emma from Highbury, her companions and the ball at the Crown. They all belong to the story" (Margolis, 1962: 183). A similar idea was advanced by Eco, some years later (1979: 239), when he remarked on the structural necessity of properties within a fictional universe. In a fictional world individuals are identified through their structurally necessary properties, by which they become textually interdependent. The essentiality of a property to any fictional entity is hence an outcome of the structural requirements of a story, and in this respect no property can be evaluated as inessential.

The above world-constructing conventions specify the logical and semantic constraints imposed on a set of propositions when this set is ascribed the property of fictionality. Note that some of these constraints are *restrictive* (fictional propositions make no claim to validity, they allow restricted inference), while others are *permissive* (fictional propositions can construct impossible states of affairs, indeterminate entities). A pragmatic definition of fiction is thereby shown to consist of a variety of constraints that determine the type of logical model that would be appropriate for fiction. Such a model would have to account for all these different factors which determine the nature of a fictional state of affairs.

World reconstructing conventions (the logic and ontology of propositions about fiction)

The set of world reconstructing conventions enumerated below specifies the constraints imposed on the process of understanding fiction. That is, what type of logic does the reader assume in the process of comprehending fiction, and how does this logic enable him to know certain things about the world fictional texts construct for him? Which rules are followed in reconstructing a fictional state of affairs from a set of fictional propositions? In other words, how do we know what the valid propositions are that can be made *about* a fictional world?

(1) The first overall convention controlling world reconstruction is that a fictional world is not a possible world *ramifying* from the actual state of affairs, but a world logically and ontologically *parallel* to the

actual world. Unlike the case of counterfactuals, fictional claims are not interpreted as referring to the ways the actual world could have been. Fictional claims construct an autonous world that only optionally, and according to varying degrees, can depart or stay proximate with the actual world.

(2)*a* In understanding a fictional text and in making propositions about a fictional world one assumes the presence of an author. The valid propositions made about a fictional world hence do not only refer to the beings denoted by fictional propositions and contained in the fictional universe, but also to the entity of an author, his properties and actions. The authorship of a fictional text reflects an understanding of fictionality as an intentional action (of world-projecting, of imagining, of belief-suspending).

b It is conventionally agreed that the ego of the biographical author of a fictional text is divided into an actual and a fictional part: the author as distinct from the narrator. By positing an author as a source of authority and control, one assumes that the fictional text is the only source of information about the world it constructs, which imposes specific constraints on the structure of the fictional universe.

c The fact that fictional texts have authors affects truth determinations regarding fictional propositions: only some fictional propositions come from an authorial source, whereas others come from a source to whom the power of narration has been delegated with different degrees of authorization (as demonstrated by the difference between an omniscient narrator, a person narrating about his younger self in the first person, and an unreliable narrator). The authorship of a fictional proposition is a world reconstructing convention which imposes a hierarchy of authenticity on the propositions that can be made about fiction.

(3) When assuming an author as a source of control, one also assumes that the author is a source or center of coherence for the fictional world. In this respect the author is identified with maximal coherence and integration to which understanding fiction should aspire. The process of reconstructing the fictional world is hence a process of maximal coherence-imposing. Propositions made about fiction are formulated in such a way as to show how fictional worlds obey structural requirements of coherence, continuity and organization. Fictional worlds are composed of meaningfully structured states of affairs and propositions made about fiction should reflect this meaningfulness. The author of a fictional text is hence not

only responsible for prefixing the text with the appropriate property (an author, Tolstoy for instance, technically marks the boundaries of the fictional world of *War and Peace*); he is also given the function of an organizing principle for that world.

When reconstructing a fictional world, the reader trying to understand follows the convention that a given world is not only characterized by what it contains, but also by specific modes of organization imposing order and coherence on the world-components.

(4) The coherence of fictional worlds does not collapse when a world of the fictional type contains inconsistencies or impossibilities. That is, the understander of fiction can make propositions about fiction that are either logically consistent or inconsistent. Consistency however has no consequence for the ability to reconstruct a world; neither does consistency bear on the extent to which the fictional world satisfies structural requirements assumed in fictional worlds. The fact that inconsistency can be detected in descriptions of Emma Bovary's eyes[11] does not make the world of *Madame Bovary* unreconstructible.

(5) In formulating propositions about fiction incompleteness is seen as an inherent property of fictional states and objects and not as a lack to be remedied. No completeness can or should be reconstructed for fictional entities, and fictional worlds only contain what is directly claimed or implied by the text. Conventions of world reconstruction might even attribute literary value to indeterminacies. Open-endedness or ambiguities can be considered a merit in texts.[12]

(6) Accessibility in fictional contexts is translated into two separate world-reconstructing conventions: the one stems from a literal understanding of accessibility; the other from the logical meaning of accessibility.

a Accessibility has to do with the position of the reader relative to the fictional world: propositions about fiction reflect the fact that while not being part of the fictional world, the understander of fiction is affected by that world. Propositions made about fiction show that fictional worlds are epistemologically accessible but physically

---

11 As analyzed by Julian Barnes, 1984: 74–81.

12 In this respect fictional states of affairs differ from absent states of affairs in that logically and ontologically speaking only the former are essentially incomplete. Claims to the contrary confuse psychological accessibility with logical possibility, i.e., we might not know all about an absent state of affairs, yet even absent domains of which we are ignorant are logically accessible to us. For a fuller discussion of incompleteness, see chapter 4 of this study.

inaccessible from the real world. In formulating propositions about fiction, this duality is variably expressed, evincing, on the one hand, the physical inaccessibility of fiction, and its psychological relevance to the world beyond fiction, on the other hand. In other words, the partial opaqueness of fictional worlds relative to the external reader determines the type and scope of propositions that can be made about a given fictional world. One could most likely say "Anna Karenina is unfortunate," but one could not claim that "Anna Karenina's complexion is exactly like my wife's" or "I will dissuade Anna Karenina from her suicidal plans." The intricacies of this world-reconstructing convention based on the type of contact fiction allows have been explored in Walton (1978, 1990: 191–196) who claims that one person can save (or kill, congratulate, handshake) another only if they live in the same world.

The psychological accessibility of fiction is also problematic in that it involves mixing ordinary emotions of admiration or distress with aesthetic desires and interests. That is, when alluding to Anna's unfortunate fate we mingle our psychological response with an aesthetic detachment, a kind of duality which the notion of *catharsis* so adroitly expresses: mixing pity and fear with pleasure and relief. This duality characterizes the nature of propositions made to account for the understander's response to fiction.

b Accessibility also refers to the possibility of a fictional state of affairs relative to accepted versions of actuality. In this sense the accessibility of fictional worlds to the real world is variable. First, not all parts of the fictional world are equally possible: since all fiction mixes references to historical beings with denotations of imaginary beings, judgments of accessibility might vary according to the domain in the fictional world whose relative possibility is described. Second, the actual state of affairs is not a stable point of reference: since a reader activates his beliefs and knowledge in deciphering any fictional segment, the distance of fictional worlds from the real world is open to interpretation and is relative to the position of the reader. The reader's relation to the fictional world, although it does not determine accessibility, affects the way fictional truths are described, emphasized, or de-emphasized, considered plausible, anomalous and so on, by the reader. Note also that the distance between fiction and actuality, or their relative possibility, is part of the rhetoric of a fictional text: the more a fictional world is presented as possible relative to actuality, the more the rhetoric of fiction will emphasize the great extent to which it draws on a world familiar to its readers. Accessibility is hence not just a matter of comparing two states of affairs, and reconstructing the accessibility of fiction reflects this.

(7) The set of fictional propositions and the set of truthful propositions about fiction are not identical sets. The proportion between the states of affairs directly denoted by fictional propositions and the fictional states of affairs implied or indirectly constructed by these same propositions, may vary. This lack of correlation is recognized in the fact that the world reconstructed from a text always includes more than what is explicitly indicated by the author. A fictional world contains both what is explicitly claimed by the author, as well as that which is implied in the integrated claims posited, and what is imposed on the text by readers' beliefs and thereby reflected in their understanding of that world. A complementary claim about world-reconstructing would point to the fact that no work is exhausted by the worlds it is satisfied with (a work includes segments which may contribute nothing to the construction of the fictional universe: stylistic elements, generalized claims, and so on). That is, such textual elements comprise fragments of fictional propositions, yet they are not translated into propositions pertaining to components of that world (they may however be translated into meaning-components or thematic structures, but not into parts of the fictional world as an ontological construct).

The logical and ontological laws activated by texts belonging to the distinct cultural category we term fiction determine the features of fiction and distinguish it from nonfiction. A complementary intuition equally necessary for the definition of fiction is that fictional worlds possess an *ontological autonomy* not shared by other possibilities or by other world versions. On the one hand the definition of fiction is dependent on other modes of being from which it distinguishes itself (whereby it is relatively possible or impossible, accessible or inaccessible). On the other hand fictional worlds are regarded as relatively autonomous in respect of these other modes of being. This ambivalent position manifests the intricate problem presented by fiction. Fictionality, as a pragmatic property, is wholly context-dependent, but at the same time fictional texts register their autonomy in relation to this very context.

Fictional worlds are autonomous in relation to nonfictional versions of actuality as demonstrated by the fact that such worlds are not likely to be treated as direct branches of, or divergences from, the actual world (fictional worlds are not, strictly speaking, possible worlds, as was shown in chapter 2). Yet the autonomy of a fictional world relative to the actual world does not circumvent possible affinities between the two world systems. As noted above, the autonomy of fiction is compatible with the extensive modeling of fiction on history. If one accepts a logical differentiation between fictional worlds and worlds that constitute versions of actuality, fiction can be shown to have a unique ontological status relative to other possible worlds. The autonomy of fictional worlds is of course a necessary tenet motivating the need for the construction of a logico-semantic model particular for the case of fiction. A logico-semantic model is however the only theoretical way to handle the incompatibility between the intuition that fictional worlds are a culturally marked class and the fact that this markedness is not textually indicated. The logico-semantic model proposed above, by reflecting this very duality of definition, allows the category of fiction to fluctuate.

The autonomy of fiction and the concept of *world*

What fictionally is the case is naturally thought of as being the case in a special realm, a "world," in a way in which what is claimed or believed or desired to be the case is not. (Walton, 1990: 206).

The pragmatic conception of fictional worlds both accepts their autonomy and considers this autonomy to be changeable and relative to other states of affairs (of a different ontological status). My aim in this section is to show that a pragmatic understanding of fictionality (an understanding that combines literary intuitions with philosophical insights regarding the nature of fiction) has permeated and has gradually affected theoretical usages of the concept of *world* in literary studies. I will show that unlike traditional literary interpretations of world, where the concept was employed to denote the closedness of the artistic system, "world" has more recently re-entered literary discourse as a different theoretical entity reflecting the inter-world perspective that has emerged from philosophical discussions. I will show that, unlike early uses of "world," the concept as currently used carries the ontological meanings we presently tend to associate with fictional worlds. The history of the concept of *world* in literary theory will be shown to reflect the influence of the interchange with philosophical concerns regarding non-actual, indeterminate ontologies and possible worlds.

Talking about "the world of Milton," "the world of Romance," "the world of *War and Peace*" and "the impossible world of Marques," is commonly accepted in discourse on literature, although presumably in each case we mean something different. The currency of the concept of *world* in literary studies and the way it is used illustrate a typical situation whereby a concept of a broad enough meaning, such as *model* or *structure*, serves as a convenient metaphor in diverse contexts and for diverse purposes. World, like any other concept, has a history, and I have chosen to address the case of world as a case in point since new developments in literary theory in general, and the incorporation of "possible worlds" talk into the discourse on literary fictionality in particular, have, at some point, caused terminological confusion. In many cases the different interpretations involved in each use of *world* seem to escape the attention of literary theorists, and in different contexts different uses of the concept can be shown to emerge from different conceptual frameworks and to carry different meanings. I will proceed to show that a fundamental difference lies between the way *world* was commonly interpreted by traditional mainstream literary theory – a structural definition of *world* – and the altogether new interpretation, proceeding from an ontological definition of world, imposed by a philosophical framework on our understanding of the worlds of literary texts. This new interpretation is also indicative of the more serious attempt on behalf of literary theorists in recent years to address the fictionality of texts.

To clarify this confusion and to pursue its sources, the following discussion will be devoted mainly to exploring the meaning of *world* in three readings of the concept: Ingarden's, Lotman's and Kripke's. Although the place of *world* and its centrality vary from one reading to the other, these three readings can be regarded as representing the main conceptual domains nourishing the various uses to which *world* is put in literary studies: the phenomenological domain, the semiotic–semantic domain and the logico-ontological domain. Ingarden and Lotman offer two typical interpretations of *world* as it is construed in literary studies, whereas Kripke represents the underlying philosophical tradition from which possible worlds concepts emerged, and have in recent years been adopted and applied to literary texts.

Ingarden provides an interpretation of *world* from a phenomenological perspective according to which imaginary worlds are perceived as products of the constitutive intentionalities of an aesthetic consciousness. To account for the constitution of such a unique aesthetic object, Ingarden describes the literary work of art as a stratified entity: from the first sound-stratum arises the second stratum of meaning units; these combine into syntagma of syntactic structures; out of the latter arises a third stratum of the *objects represented*. "The represented objects" says Ingarden "do not lie isolated and alien alongside one another but, thanks to the manifold ontic connections, unite into a uniform ontic sphere. In doing so they always constitute ... a segment of a still largely undetermined world" (218). Thus *world* is identified with a constellation of represented objects, with an ontic region constituted by the deliberate process of structuration carried out by a consciousness. Yet, as characteristic of represented objects, the world of a literary work has fuzzy boundaries and is pervaded by spots of indeterminacy. Ingarden emphasizes indeterminacy as the distinctive feature holding for all types of represented worlds. Worlds of literary works of art are further distinguished as worlds precluding an accurate and complete realization at any point. That is, whereas all representation leaves spots of indeterminacy, in literary worlds indeterminacies cannot be solved or wholly realized. In short, for Ingarden *world* in art stands for interrelated objects which are uniquely and by necessity indeterminate.

Second, the stage of interaction between text and reader at which *world* enters Ingarden's model for the literary work of art indicates how for him *world* is a purely *intensional* concept. The meaning content of propositions plays a central role in indicating those properties necessary for constructing states of affairs and hence worlds. In view of this conception, worlds are described as necessarily composed of objects "revealed," or "correlated with" rather than represented by states of affairs. Assuming that we accept that states of affairs are constructed by the meaning content of propositions, it is at the next stage, claims Ingarden, that the objects contained in the ontic range of the respective states of affairs are brought into existence. Note that the imaginary objects of art exist neither in physical-material reality nor are they bound to the subjective, ever-changing states of the mind – their ontological status is unique. For Ingarden, a world, being constituted by pseudo-propositions, can create a simulated illusion of reality. That is, Ingarden, qualifying the mode of existence of represented objects and showing how worlds arise from states of affairs, voices a clearly nonmimetic interpretation of *world* as the composite meaning and meaning-relations generating a representation. Ingarden assigns an interpretation to *world* which insists on the metaphorical meaning of the concept in the context of art. Worlds of art are not made to exist anywhere (not even in mental existence) and they remain inherently indeterminate. Their state of being is confined to what meaning-units of the text reveal; they are confined to an intensional realm of being.

The concept of *world* has a predominant place in Lotman's semiotics of artistic texts and, at least on the surface, it diverges radically from Ingarden's view. *World* here represents the stratified system of artistic composition on the one hand, and on the other, the relations between the concrete modeling carried out by a text and the infinite object (reality) to which the artistic system gives form. Lotman adduces the concept of world to explain how the artistic work models an infinite universe through its spatially limited system. This modeling of an infinite object by means of a finite text is theoretically explained by the relations established between the space of a modeling artistic world and the infinite space of a modeled reality. Thus *world* has a double status: the world, or reality as a whole, the whole picture of which is somehow reflected in the artistic text, and the limited world which is the product of artistic modeling. The latter's relations to the former are established through the operation of space, plot, persona and boundaries creating a semiotic system used to transmit information about cultural models. Features of the artistic work operate to organize contents and materials of a nonartistic nature. The world of the artistic text acquires this modeling capacity through two aspects of its particular nature:

(A) Specific features of the text-structure actualize and reflect models of a more general type. Every text functions within a cultural semantic field, or is projected against semantic structures basically defined as models of culture (a romantic model of the subject, a model of religious ethics). The artistic text, being the sum of historically determined codes, models the universe in its general categories, thus linking through its world the textual with the extratextual.

(B) Artistic rules create a world by systematizing the extraartistic, nonsystemic reality: "literature imitates reality; it creates a model of the extrasystemic out of its own inherently systemic material" (59). The artistic text manifests an interaction among levels, which is more vigorous than in nonartistic structures. Art is capable of simultaneously activating diverse semantic structures through the intersection of many (sometimes contrasting) stylistic layers. Each textual element can be translated at the same time as an element in different textual "grammars." It is by this very system of complex rules of composition that the artistic text transforms the structurally unorganized material of "reality." The closed world of art reflects the outside world not by being correlated with the parts of the latter, but by being its model, which points at the *semiotic* (rather than *mimetic*) interaction between art and extra-art.

The place of *world* in Lotman's model indicates two substantial features reflecting what the concept denotes. First, *world* stands for the set of components of the artistic universe *and* for the specific rules composing the artistic system: repetitions and oppositions, integration of conflicting styles and grammars, multilayered transmission of information, and so on. Second, the point at which *world* enters Lotman's model indicates that the concept denotes an advanced stage in the processing of the artistic text at which semantic and linguistic materials have been fully integrated.

The interpretations of *world* proposed by Lotman and Ingarden seem to diverge considerably. Whereas Ingarden introduces the concept within a purely phenomenological framework where *world* stands for a certain outcome of a mental act of understanding or imagining, Lotman interprets *world* within a structural–semiotic framework where the orientation is totally toward the object. Each conceptual framework, as shown above, formally imposes a different reading of the concept of *world*. To mention one example, while both Ingarden and Lotman underscore the stratification of literary structures as prerequisites for the construction of worlds, Ingarden emphasizes this point in a way that shows the nonreferential being of art (the representational intention behind the literary work of art is defined as emerging, in an elaborated constitutive process, from a sound stratum). Lotman on the other hand, indicates by the multilayeredness of the artistic text the "universal integrality" by which the artistic universe can reflect the outside universe.

Yet the similarity in the use of *world* is no less instructive than its differences. Not only is the "world of art" used in both cases to indicate that art is cut off from nonartistic reality, but there is also a similarity in the scope of meaning covered by the term "world" in its different interpretations. For both Ingarden and Lotman *world* apparently denotes a *certain mode of representing or organizing knowledge*. For both, a world is primarily a set of objects and participants located in time and space, to which a component transforming this set of elements *into a world of an artistic nature* is added. Ingarden refers to states of affairs and unrealized spots of indeterminacy as the components defining the "worldliness" specific to art, whereas Lotman refers to world-components (characters, plot, space) and to the semiotic rules specific to the artistic system in order to define artistic worlds. In this respect, both intuitively refer to *world* at that point in their account of artistic composition where the need arises for describing a stage of semantic integration in the understanding of art, although in each model the concept of *world* stands for a different set of semantic or grammatical rules perceived as specific to art.

The crucial point is that, despite apparent differences between Lotman and Ingarden, revealed not only through the very different conceptual system within which each develops their arguments about artistic worlds, as well as through the different components *world* stands for in their respective models, there is a striking conceptual affinity between them. In fact, both theorists refer to the concept of *world* in order to identify *the value added to a set of objects by virtue of which that set becomes a domain, an integrated system*. It is by virtue of this added value that art can represent a world for us. In view of the above, I suggest regarding Lotman and Ingarden as two exemplary cases illustrating the way *world* was typically and traditionally interpreted in mainstream literary studies, reflecting what can be described as a centrifugal tendency of the discipline at large. Pointing out Lotman and Ingarden's models as test-cases, I would claim that *world* is used as a means to refer to a specific stage in the interpretative integration of the literary text, and as such *world* stands for an internal principle of organization of textual materials. *World*, in other words, introduces in each model a specific interpretative stage and a specific step in the process of understanding the semantics and syntax of artistic composition. Lotman refers to *world* at a more advanced stage in the semantic–syntactic processing of a text than Ingarden. In Lotman's model the intersecting of the space of the literary text by cultural models is indispensable for the conception of artistic worlds. For Ingarden the filling-out of schemata depends, rather early on, not on the object itself but on various factors of a subjective nature which vary from reader to reader. That is, Lotman refers to intersubjective shared forms of intelligibility, whereas Ingarden points to individual, basically subjective concretizations.

In one respect Kripke's use of *world* converges with Lotman and Ingarden's. A world is assigned a set of objects, and these sets are called the domains for various possible worlds. That is, for Kripke a world consists only of the first level of objects, a level to which Lotman and Ingarden added a secondary level of elements and rules distinguishing art from nonart, representation from nonrepresentation. The first, most apparent difference between Kripke and the other readers of *world* hence lies in the fact that in Kripke *world* does not constitute a step in accounting for *artistic* world construction; it rather appears within the context of a general semantic model for modal logic. Kripke, like other philosophers addressing the concept of possible worlds, has no direct interest in the problem of art but aims to solve a logical problem.[13] The concept of *world* fulfills a clear function in the context of a model like Kripke's: it provides a way of investing our possibility claims in nonphilosophical discourse with concrete semantical content. Possible worlds semantics interprets modalities as quantification over accessible worlds. The Leibnitzian picture behind Kripke's semantics explains to us what modal systems in logic *are about*: they are about worlds. It is in this sense, as part of the attempt to talk about modalities as propositions about worlds to which no actuality is attributed, that *world* is construed by Kripke. Kripke's position within the philosophical debate about possible worlds reflects an attempt to link a formal modal theory with one's intuitive conceptions of non-actual states of affairs. Kripke denies however most ontological implications for possible worlds, as shown at an earlier stage of this study:

"I argued against those misuses of the concept that regard possible worlds as something like distant planets, like our own surroundings but somehow existing in a different dimension" (15). For Kripke, other, non-actual possibilities are abstract states or objects that we need not posit as other entities, existent in some never-never land that corresponds to the physical one before us. Kripke argues against taking the concept of world in this context too far. Within semantic

13 Kripke does however refer to the problem of fiction in his classical paper on possible worlds semantics (1963). The case of "Sherlock Holmes lives on Baker Street" poses a problem for a semantician of modal logic like Kripke because his model attempts to establish the conditions determining validity for modal propositions. "Holmes" presents a free variable to which only a nonexistent can be assigned. The problem Kripke faces in his semantic model for modalities is whether having a domain which does not overlap with the actual world (Holmes does not exist, but he would have existed had another world, his own, been actualized) forces us to change our logic to decide alternative truth conditions for such contexts.

logic *world* is explicated first as an intensional concept given by the descriptive conditions we associate with it. World does not exist as "a distant country that we are coming across, or viewing through a telescope." Possible worlds are "stipulated not discovered by powerful telescopes" (44). Kripke's phrasings partly cited above show how possible worlds enable us to see worlds as semiotic models, as language dependent constructs, optionally carrying ontological significance.

Yet it should be noted that the main difference between Kripke's interpretation and the literary interpretations of worlds lies in the fact that within the context of a philosophical discussion about the logical–ontological significance of a possible world, *world* is employed to account for the closure of a modalized set of propositions representing one state of affairs, or one world relative to other sets. This is a striking divergence from Ingarden and Lotman who, as we saw, employ *world* in order to systematize the structure of the work of art from within, referring to *world* from an inner perspective looking at the outermost limit (the horizon) of the artistic system; Kripke, on the other hand, refers to *world* relative to other possibilities, addressing the relations between possible worlds and worlds constituted by other modalities. Hence, for Kripke, the difference between worlds does not lie in what they include, or in the rules organizing and interrelating their constituents, but in the position of a set of objects or a set of states of affairs in relation to what lies *beyond* the set boundaries. In this sense Kripke is closest to our commonsensical understanding of what a world is, in that he refers to a domain of objects to which we assign, by different criteria, the label of *world* (the criteria for differentiating worlds vary: they can be related to principles of cross-identity, to the logic that excludes impossible states of affairs beyond the world's boundaries).

In Kripke's interpretation *world* implies ontological differentiations (between what is actualized and what could hypothetically be actualized) making it an appropriate metaphor for worlds of various orders and kinds. The modal differentiations imposed by the ontological content given to the concept of world explain the unlikelihood of us meeting Raskolnikov in our world, and the impossibility of Raskolnikov's rescuing Anna Karenina from under the train. Every world posits its own sphere of existence, and transworld traveling becomes by necessity limited to mental traveling. It is for this reason that more recent literary interpretations of *world*, in response to philo-

sophical modal concepts, have begun by describing the fictionality
of worlds of artistic texts prior to any account of the internal modes
of organization exhibited by such worlds, since it is precisely the
worldliness of a world that stipulates and enables such an inner
organization. The fact that the fictionality of a world operates over all
the domains constituting that world must affect the world's inner
structure. In this respect the fictional property of a text must precede
a study of a text's inner organization.

The effect on literary studies of interpreting *world* as a global
ontological organization, rather than merely as an inner type of
coherence, is apparent. Not only has the concept of *possible worlds*
become a productive and a popular source for theorizing on literature
in recent years, but, moreover, many literary theories which only
indirectly lean on this philosophical framework, reflect the effect of the
philosophical interpretation of *world* in their approach to the
problem of fiction. I would claim that recent theories of fiction within
the literary discipline, represent the duality inherent to fictionality
described above, a duality for which the philosophical discourse has
supplied means of expression. Fictionality no longer refers either to
issues foreign to literary concerns or to the inner organization of the
artistic system; structural considerations developed around the
concept of *world* (as advanced and formulated by traditional theorists
such as Ingarden and Lotman),[14] are now combined with considerations of inter-world relations that fiction maintains with other
ontological systems, thus drawing on insights developed along the
philosophical line of thought (as exemplified in Kripke's case).

In his 1984 study, Hrushovski clearly represents this hybrid
conceptualization. In his model for a semiotics of fiction the concept of
an Internal Field of Reference serves to distinguish fiction from
nonfiction. In a text with an internal field of reference at least some of
the referents are unique to that text "and make no claim for external,
factual existence" (1984: 235). Since the language of fiction is no
different from the language of extrafictional situations, the peculiar
nature of fiction is shown to lie in the field of reference pertaining to
the literary text. With the concept of an internal field of reference

14 "... the novelist offers ... a world. The great novelists all have such a world –
recognizable as overlapping the empirical world but distinct in its self-coherent
intelligibility" claim Wellek and Warren (1963: 214) who go on to examine the
stratum of "world" by looking at its self-coherent intelligibility which relies solely
on artistic devices such as characterization, story and setting formations.

Hrushovski combines the traditional intuition that the artistic world has an inner mode of coherence and organization, with the idea that referential considerations are of prior importance for describing artistic worlds. The forging of a model for fiction which reflects the incorporation of the philosophical discourse on worlds is also manifest in Pavel (1986). Unlike Hrushovski, whose concepts are explicitly derived from an immanently literary semantics, Pavel's work on fictional worlds forms a paradigmatic example for cross-disciplinary fertilization in that it bears heavily on the philosophical discourse on the logic of fiction. Pavel raises as a central issue the problem of distinguishing fictional states and beings from other nonempirical beings. It is made clear throughout his work that objects of fiction are attributed their specific features (a degree of completeness, a distance from reality) on the basis of the global ontological stance to which the text in question belongs. Thus, when Pavel describes the fictional and nonfictional activities of ontological landscaping and planning in a culture he points out that the concrete content of fictional ontologies counts less than their position within the functional organization of that culture. Since fictionality, like possibility and actuality, is a global constraint on worlds as sets of objects, the ontological status of a given set is logically considered the primary step in describing the world of fiction. Likewise Doležel (1976), in a paper inspired by the logical semantics of Hintikka, claims that a world system accounts both for the logical status of certain narrative worlds, and for the global constraints establishing a story's coherence; its macro and micro levels of coherence.

The literary interpretation of *world* after the modal logic of Kripke and other philosophers, hence reflects a dual meaning attributed to the concept. The concept of *world* is first made to signify an ontologically distinct set of entities; a set can justifiably be denoted by the term *world*, when components of the set are united by a common modality, when members of the set belong to a shared ontological order. A fictional text hence constructs a world because the system it projects is ontologically distinct (as a set of nonexistent, incomplete, uncommitted to truth objects). This aspect of the recent literary conceptualization of *world* is in line with the tradition which attributed structural qualities to world-like organization. The second aspect of the current state of *world* in literary studies is evidenced by talk about possible worlds the results of which were described in the previous chapter. In general, possible worlds' jargon enables literary theorists to see fictionality as the outcome of the relationship holding between the literary text and external reality: between the world constructed by the literary text and what we know about the actual world that surrounds us as readers, between an author and his "actual" surrounding, and the sequence of propositions he produces and whose status in relation to "actuality" varies.

Modern literary theory regards the mimetic view, namely that literature is a mode for directly representing or even reflecting the real world, as obsolete. In a nonmimetic framework fiction is granted a direct position in relation to which the real world has no privileged position, a framework within which the subtleties of literary representation can be fully appreciated. Adopting parts of the possible world framework and specifying the ontic position of fictional worlds does not result either in a mimetic or an anti-mimetic stand: it combines structural concerns with referential considerations. The theoretical scope covered by the concept of world hence relates to three areas:

(1) Each world is defined by its unique ontic position relative to worlds of other ontic determinations. A fictional world has a distinct ontic property distinguishing it from other worlds and their beings.

(2) Each world is a domain subjected to one modality that ensures its distinctness from other worlds and secures its autonomy. As the current place of the concept of *world* within literary studies demonstrates, the autonomy of fiction relative to reality is in line with traditional views of the worlds of literary texts as hermetic or partially closed artistic systems.

(3) A definition of a world does not require the existence of a stable ontology, neither within the world concerned nor as an external background. The world of fiction has no stable actuality as its reference point. Modes and degrees of reliance of fictional worlds on the real world reflect different representational conventions and not a fixed similarity. The concept of a *world* hence eludes the question of mimeticism in the relations between the fictional and the actual.

The concept of *world* as developed in philosophical logic and adopted by recent literary theory of fiction epitomizes the interface between inward and outward organization in the domain of fiction. A world is a constellation of entities whose composition results from their ontic position relative to other similar and dissimilar systems. Grasping the meaning of the fictionality of fictional worlds hence relies on an exploration of two components: the property of "being fictional" and the concept of *world*. After a close examination in the earlier parts of this chapter of what the logico-semantic properties that constitute the property of "being fictional" are, the concept of *world* was presented in this section, its history and current use in literary studies explored in order to reveal the conceptual meaning of this second component in the collocation *fictional worlds*.

4

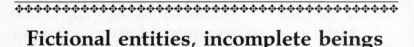

Fictional entities, incomplete beings

Existence and fictional existence

Every literary work is in principle incomplete and always in need of further supplementation; in terms of the text, however, this supplementation can never be completed. (Ingarden, 1973: 251)

Ingarden's definitive statement on the nature of the represented objects intended by a literary work summarizes the three basic facets revealed in the mode of existence of fictional entities:

1 represented objects are never fully determined in all their aspects;

2 spots of indeterminacy are never totally absent from fictional objects;

3 while reading a literary work we are seldom aware of any gaps or spots of indeterminacy.

These three facets of fictional existence represent in fact the complex of logical, semantic and rhetorical considerations (respectively) involved in the attempt to clarify the mode of being of fictional entities. Taking Ingarden's early formulations as a point of departure, together with later models for fictional existence and the approach to the problem of fiction developed in the previous chapters of the present study, an explication of some of the intricacies involved in a description of the fictional domain of objects will be attempted.

The domain of fictional entities poses the most obvious problem for the view of fiction portrayed in previous chapters. Fictional entities seem to deny a pragmatic definition of fictionality because they simply do not exist. However radical the degree of relativism one might adopt regarding the status of fiction vis à vis reality, it cannot change the fact that Natasha in *War and Peace*, with whom we share the most intimate thoughts, is a nonexistent, whereas a Natasha in the remotest Russian village, about whom we know practically nothing, does exist. In other words, granted one accepts that a fictional world is constituted by well-individuated entities interacting through concrete relations, these states of affairs appear to diverge a priori from nonfictional ones since they present *the relations among nonexistents*.

Yet the logico-ontological differentiation between fictional states of affairs and actual ones that derives from the nonexistence of the former, turns out to be far from straightforward. First, not all entities included in fictional states of affairs are equally fictional: fictional worlds might include counterparts of historical beings. Besides, although it is true that fictional entities (like the character of Raskolnikov, the event of Emma Bovary's suicide and the place of Rastignac's residence in Paris)[1] do not exist in the actual world, they might be claimed to exist in the logico-ontological spheres of their respective fictional worlds. Their existence in an alternative ontic sphere is suggested by the fact that they can be abstracted from their textual presentation, that they can be referred to and qualified. The mode of existence of fictional entities in an alternative sphere is implied in a fiction operator or in any other demarcator of the boundaries of fiction ensuring the autonomy of the fictional sphere of existence, that is of a fictional *context* (see Fine, 1982). Yet the problem of fictional entities has further implications which reflect the intricate mode of being of fictional worlds. Fictional entities are beings which are commonly claimed to be *incomplete*: fictional entities can have the property "p and ~p" because there is no referent in relation to which either p or ~p can be determined. Yet, if fictional entities are regarded as existents in an alternative and parallel ontic sphere, how can they possibly violate the fundamental logical law of the excluded middle? That is, granted that fictional entities exist in an alternative ontic space, they are logically bound to be *complete* in that alternative universe they inhabit and their alternative completeness thus effaces the distinction between fictional and actual entities. Conversely, if one claims that fictional entities are *non*existents (and are hence un-constrained by the law of the excluded middle), their distinctness relative to actual existents is kept yet other philosophical problems emerge. One problem is, how can well-individuated entities be constructed without existence being ascribed to them, and how can nonexistents be referred to, characterized and abstracted from their textual presentation ("Emma Bovary was dark-haired," "Raskolnikov repented," and so on). "Something funny is going on in fiction,

---

1 These examples illustrate the difference between first-order entities (characters, objects) and second-order entities (events, places).

however we look at it," writes Walton (1990: 387), and right he is. Fictional entities, their incompleteness, and the problems ensuing from their nonexistence, deserve some serious consideration.

Incompleteness, it should be stressed, is regarded in the context of modal logic and the philosophy of logic, as the feature distinguishing between types of existents (that is, between modes of being). I would claim that varieties in the attitude toward incompleteness reflect the difference between diverse philosophical views on the type of line dividing real objects from non-actual ones. Thus, completeness is a strict logical criterion when a clear distinction between real and non-actual objects is maintained and a maximal set of properties is assigned to the former but not to the latter; when, however, the context is that of a relativist approach, where what is emphasized is the epistemic inaccessibility of reality, existents and nonexistents are presented as commensurable. Within such a context incompleteness is interpreted as a semantic criterion where types of existents allow various degrees of semantic accessibility and exploration. Looking at the various ways in which incompleteness is related to fictional beings, it might generally be claimed that the less philosophers insist on the derivative nature of a logic of fiction, the less radical the interpretation likely to be given to incompleteness. When incompleteness ceases to be the distinctive feature of fictional entities, the distinctness of fictional existence and of the logico-semantics attached to fiction tends to be played down. Why is it that when relativized notions of fictionality and actuality are accepted incompleteness is no longer regarded as a distinctive feature of fictional existence?

Before this question can be examined it can be surmised from the discussion above that fictional entities posit a somewhat different problem for philosophers than for literary theorists and aestheticians. This difference is reflected not just in the initial motivation behind the interest in fictional existence, but in the place assumed by *existence* in philosophical versus literary discussions. From the point of view of philosophers, as shown above, existence is the distinctive feature of reality, and nonexistence is a distinctive feature of some non-actual (imaginary) beings. The question of existence remains a central issue in the philosophical domain, although in the last ten years or so, logicians, aestheticians and philosophers of language have devised and presented logical models for imaginary states of affairs, thus demonstrating that existence does not stipulate all logico-semantic procedures. As described in chapter 1, the possibility of devising a logical model for fiction in philosophy is connected to a relaxation of logical concepts and to a consideration of the power of language to refer and construct entities of discourse. Both in models of fiction that assume that "novels are just words, after all" and assign no extraordinary logical status to fiction, (for example, Heintz, 1979: 98), in models that take nonexistent beings literally and treat them realistically (Parsons, 1980) and in models that consider a separate logico-semantics for fiction – the solution for incompleteness proposed in philosophical contexts is always subordinated to the notion of existence associated with a given model. In other words, all philosophical models for nonexistents take the mode of being of nonexistents as prior to any semantic consideration involved in fictional (or other non-actual) referring or asserting. These models differ only in the type of logical implications they attribute to the problem of nonexistence.

Yet the philosophical implications drawn from assuming or denying fictional entities an existence do not appear to occupy a central place or even to be relevant to the ways in which literary theorists deal with fiction. In other words, the question regarding whether fictional entities exist and how seems marginal to the literary discussion of fictional characters and objects. The point here is that incompleteness is presented and resolved differently by literary theorists since in the literary context incompleteness is not part of a general theory of non-actual existence, but part of a general semantics for literary texts. A telling example could be Margolin's theory of characters (1991) which presents the most definitive and comprehensive model for fictional characters so far, combining the insight supplied by possible worlds logic and semantics with literary intuitions regarding fictional beings. Margolin shows how the referring and attributive functions of literary discourse work to establish the four conditions necessary for a fictional individual to be postulated: the conditions of *existence, individuality, uniqueness or singularity,* and the *unity of features under a given category.* Nowhere does Margolin imply that the ontological status of fictional and actual individuals is the same; quite the contrary: to his mind fictional entities are no more than conceptual constructs (only characters in fiction that are actuality-variants, are genuine possibles). Yet the question of the different logic assumed by fictional existence is not addressed at all. Within the model he proposes, which relies on assumptions about the constructivist functions of language, existence, individuality and the like can be stipulated to guarantee the creation of a fictional individual without the notion of fictional existence vs. actual existence being raised as a pertinent issue. Existence is regarded as a logically necessary condition for constituting an individual in fiction. Yet a model for the fictional construction of characters can be formulated independently of the logic of nonfictional existence and nonfictional individuality. For Margolin, who for the present purposes can serve as a representative of the literary discourse on nonexistence, existence is a matter of rhetoric and hence relates to the semantics of a given text. Existence can be established or undermined by a text (the existence condition is satisfied by realistic literature, but is hardly respected in postmodernism).

In view of this model of fictional characters, the point to be made is that for literary theorists, including those fully aware of the specific logico-ontological considerations raised by fictional worlds, the distinctive feature of fiction is the total dependence of its constructs on the world-constructing act of a narrator or any other constituting agent. In line with this view incompleteness is presented as part of a model for the rhetorical strategies in fictional world construction. The logico-semantics for fiction is therefore hardly affected by the corresponding breach of the logical law of the excluded middle. For philosophers, however, incompleteness is either stressed as a permanent obstacle in the way of any attempt to incorporate fiction into a general logic, or else it is granted a place within such a logic. In any case, the difference in emphasis between the literary and philosophical discussions of issues such as fictional existence, incompleteness, referring expressions in fictional discourses, and so on, explain, I would maintain, why in the literary context incompleteness is presented, in many respects, as a rhetorical issue. For literary theorists, the problem of fictional existence and the incompleteness of fictional entities is transformed from a problem of a *logical* order into a problem of a *rhetorical* order. This point is already illustrated in Ingarden for whom the cardinal difference lies between "real" objects and represented objects rather than between real and fictional represented objects. The latter distinction is presented as derived from or secondary to the former. Therefore, I would claim, that the major difference between the philosophical and literary discussions of fictional existence is that the former concentrates on the logical aspects of fictional being whereas the latter reflects in its arguments the rhetorical aspect involved in the construction of fictional beings through the power of language.

This claim has some further implications regarding the status of the discourse of literary theory: when literary theorists adopt an integrationist approach (collapsing the differentiation between imaginary and real existence), this does not reflect an a priori tendency on their part to accept a radical relativism of the kind Goodman promotes (presenting fiction and nonfiction as alternative versions of a world, the reality of which remains equally inaccessible to both) or to accept any other specific epistemology for that matter. Rather, for literary theorists the question of the ontological status of reality is not an issue, and theories of fictionality are formulated with no necessary metaphysical or epistemological presuppositions behind them and they contain no particular commitment to the ontological status of reality itself. This is not owing to a blindness on the part of literary theorists but to the different object of theorizing characteristic of the respective disciplines. Having fiction as its primary object of study, literary theory can regard fictional beings and deal with the problem of reference in fiction in a way that might suggest a conflation between the fictional and the real, but this conflation does not emerge necessarily from any clear notion of what *the real* is like. The position of literary theorists does not presuppose a philosophical stand on the ontological status of reality. Not all literary theorists are like Goodman in their views, one might say, and if they are, their metaphysical notions about reality are not directly relevant to their theory of fiction, even if their theory makes ontological considerations its prime business (as is the case with Margolin). More than that, unlike the position of literary theorists of fiction, relativism or absolutism regarding "the real world" is the business of philosophers obliged to take a stand in this regard even when addressing, as a central issue, the problem of truth and reference in fiction. Having existence or standard reference as their primary object, philosophers cannot solve the problem of fiction except by juxtaposing it to some view concerning the existence of "real" things and reference to existents. The business of literary theorists, however, has to do with the specific attitudes that literary texts manifest toward the "reality" they present, regardless of how this reality differs from "real" reality. This difference might serve to explain an apparent difference of emphasis in the way philosophers and literary theorists address the problem of nonexistence. In each discipline nonexistence raises a different set of issues relevant to the corresponding disciplinary general line of pursuit.

The way fictional worlds and fictional entities are approached by philosophers as opposed to literary theorists is an important lead toward a fuller understanding of the pragmatics of fiction. That is, although fictional entities do not exist from a logical point of view (there is no text-independent referent in the strict sense of the word for most fictional individuals), they do exist in our cultural practice (where one can refer to Don Quixote's properties), and they do exist in the theories made to account for the nature of fiction. The "reality" literature possesses for its readers and interpreters motivates the way literary theorists detach ontological problems of existence from the textual practice of referring and individuating objects regardless of whether the objects concerned exist or not. Turning the problem of nonexistence into a problem of semantics and of rhetoric satisfied or unsettled by textual practice is revealed in the tendency of literary theory to take theoretical notions literally or to subject the authority behind philosophical concepts to radical interpretations and circumventions.

Without, then, addressing directly the question of whether reality and fiction exist equally, or whether the facts of fiction are dependent or independent of our world versions, it should be clear that theories about fiction, be they formulated by philosophers or literary theorists, reflect in different ways the problems posed by fictional entities. Being part of the theoretical discourse on literary fiction, this study adopts the literary stand and avoids taking metaphysical questions of existence as a relevant object of argumentation.

The incompleteness of fictional entities

Fictional entities are inherently incomplete. Their incompleteness is primarily logical and secondly semantic. Fictional entities are *logically* incomplete because many conceivable statements about a fictional entity are undecidable. A fictional entity is *semantically* incomplete because, being constructed by language, characteristics and relations of the fictional object cannot be specified in every detail. These are the two facets of the incompleteness of fictional entities: the absence of a complete referent behind what is stated (directly or indirectly) about a given fictional entity entails indeterminate areas, and the impossibility of verifying properties of the fictional entity not attributed to it by the fictional text itself. This absence of a complete referent underlying the fictional construct leaves many propositions ascribable to the fictional world indeterminable. In reality, as opposed to fiction, we assume that there are no gaps and that gaps in representation can be filled by reference to a complete, fully detailed and, at least in principle, available object. Incompleteness is thus the formal manifestation of a difference between reality and fiction, between an extraliterary real object and a fictional construct. Incompleteness reflects on both logical and semantic aspects of fictionality: it has to do with the essential status of fictional objects and with the verbal mode of their construction.

The ongoing debate over the completeness or incompleteness of fictional entities takes place mainly in the philosophical domain. The problem of incompleteness, as observed above, is related both to the mode of existence of fictional entities and to their degree of individuation. That is, the problem with fictional entities is related to whether the logical and semantic property of incompleteness counteracts the *particularity* of these entities and whether incompleteness is the distinctive feature of the fictional mode of being. Note that completeness and individuation are two separate but related dimensions of *textual* existence. Anna Karenina can be incomplete but well-individuated whereas people she passes by in the train station are neither complete nor individuated (in fact the problem of completeness is less acute when it comes to collective nouns that denote non-particulars or entities that are, by definition, not maximally propertied). Generally speaking, from a philosophical point of view fictional entities are either viewed as entities that *exist in fiction* (in the context of a story or film), and what distinguishes them from entities existing outside fiction is their incompleteness, or fictional entities can be viewed as *nonexistents,* and expressions referring to them as empty. If the fictional entity is claimed to exist somewhere, even if in another logical sphere, such as a universe of discourse, this could neutralize any substantial differences between the way we perceive fictional entities and the way we perceive any other entity, directly or indirectly accessible to us. By attributing alternative modes of being to fictional entities, the problem of incompleteness can be circumvented and the difference in ontological status separated from the problem of individuation. When the individuation and the logic of fictional existence are viewed as similar to the individuation and mode of existence of actuals, fiction is no longer excluded from the realms of standard logic and general semantics. One can claim that although, logically speaking, fictional entities are incomplete, they are no different from actual but absent entities or any other entity about which our knowledge is limited and to which our access is restricted.

As in other cases where logical concepts are incorporated into the literary discussion, there is a discrepancy between logicians and literary theorists concerning their interpretation of incompleteness. It is common among the former to stress the logical status of fictional objects, and their incomplete mode of being: "two features of fiction that put it beyond the reach of most going semantical theories, [are] namely possible inconsistency and invariable incompleteness" (Routley, 1979: 6). Literary theorists address the incompleteness of fictional entities by claiming that although the constituents of fictional worlds are inherently incomplete, they are not necessarily grasped as such; incompleteness is hence rhetorically neutralized. Before moving on to describe one specific way in which the incompleteness of fictional objects can be explained away (on p. 136ff., of this book), I will first present the range of possible approaches to incompleteness and to its far-reaching consequences for the nature of fictional entities, and the way incompleteness is explained by various trains of thought and by a variety of logical, semantic and rhetorical claims about fiction. Following are four ways to approach the problem of the incompleteness of fictional entities and to explain the mode of existence of incomplete entities: the first three relate the variety of philosophical approaches to this notion; the fourth presents the typical literary maneuvers carried out in relation to incompleteness.

(1) Incompleteness can be explained away by appealing to *an actualist approach*. According to the actualist view existence is a condition for reference; thus, one cannot refer to what does not exist. Any state of affairs that could have existed does in fact exist or there is simply no such state of affairs. In an actualist framework existence is an essential property of objects and whatever exists has a correlative set of properties. An object correlated with a set of properties is hence necessarily well-individuated and distinct from all other objects. An object that exists can even be correlated with a set of properties that contains a contradiction or an inconsistency; it can be associated with the property of "being a square circle" and with that of "having a mole on the left shoulder and not having a mole on the left shoulder." In an actualist framework such as the one in which Plantinga (1974, 1979) works, every object that possibly exists, does exist, and whatever exists has a maximal set of propositions attached to it. For Plantinga, fiction cannot be about fictional nonexistents with in-

complete sets of properties. Rather "stories are about nothing at all and the names they contain denote neither actual nor possible objects" (1974: 163). Propositions about Hamlet are therefore true in some of the Hamlet Situations; contradictory propositions are true in different Hamlet Situations; indeterminate propositions about him are neither true nor false in any Hamlet Situation (1974: 153–159). Plantinga, in other words, rejects any attempt to associate existence or possibility with fictional beings; incompleteness is thus not raised as a problem for actualist logic. In a quasi-actualist framework, such as Parsons' (1974, 1980), actualism is not exercised through the rejection of nonexistents: fictional objects are presented as distinct and genuine objects which differ from real ones only in terms of the set of the *extranuclear* properties associated with them, a set which includes ontological properties (about the mode of existence of the objects concerned), characterization of their modal status (the possibility or impossibility of objects), and technical properties like completeness. On this actualist view, existence and nonexistence are alternative characterizations of an entity and do not stipulate the individuation and distinctness of the objects concerned. Parsons thus illustrates how the actualism of objects is not necessarily undermined by their nonexistence, a stipulation enabled by treating existence, as well as incompleteness, as two of the properties that could be attached to an object.[2]

(2) Incompleteness can be explained away by hypothesizing *various modes or degrees of being*. Within such a mode of explanation for fictional entities two directions can be detected: in one direction nonexistence is separated from a referring capacity; it is assumed that a universe of discourse supplies sufficient grounds for exercising the referential and descriptive functions of language, regardless of whether the referent of discourse satisfies the criterion of existence. That is, although fictional entities lack the property of existence, they are things to which one can refer, which one can imagine, characterize and qualify. In the other direction, fictional entities are viewed as kinds or as instantiations of fictional types and therefore as entities to which existence cannot be applied.

Pavel (1986), who represents the first direction, claims that the notion of ontological commitment to imaginary or fictional entities

---

2 Likewise, Fine (1982) proposes to distinguish actuals from possibles, and among the actuals, makes a further subdivision into existents and nonexistents.

touches on the essence of our way of understanding fiction. Yet, claims Pavel, our ontological models should allow degrees of being that will distinguish different grades of ontological commitment.

An extension of ontology to realms beyond the borders of tangible reality requires a differential model ... To be existent without existing is a sophisticated property equally shared by mathematical entities, unfinanced architectural monuments ... We do not however, want to see all nonempirical beings granted the same status ... (ibid.: 31)

Pavel proposes to differentiate degrees of being and gradations of ontological commitment. In this manner the incompleteness of fictional entities is interpreted as a reflection of the ontological commitment these entities entail, a commitment which does not necessitate "absolute" existence. Fictional entities are only ascribed a selective set of properties as a symptom of their being existent without existing. Instead of allowing a dichotomy between complete (actual) entities and incomplete (fictional) ones, completeness becomes a matter of degree reflecting the type of commitment one makes in introducing an entity. Proposing grades of being is hence one possible solution for the problem of fictional entities. The idea that non-actual ontological realms (represented in different domains of discourse) do not contradict the ordinary laws of logico-semantics for reference and inference is an important philosophical move that will come up again later in this chapter in the context of theories of naming. When fiction is regarded as an alternative domain of discourse, the problem of existence can be separated from that of individuation, and the problem of ontology from that of language-practice. In the fictional domain the information about a given entity is always partial, yet partial information does not necessarily inhibit individuation: what authors fail to tell us about the entities they write about, either explicitly or by implication, simply does not exist. Being constrained by the describing capacity of language, incompleteness in the logical sense (deriving from lack of existence) is camouflaged. Real or fictional entities might require different means of checking the truth of statements: in the latter case what is available to us is the information provided by the statements of the author and what is not provided thereby remains nonexistent.[3] Things can be referred to although these things lack the property of existence because things can be products of imagination and of discourse and not only of perception. The problem that still remains open to discussion within such an approach is whether

3 Heintz, 1979, provides an argument along these lines.

nonexistents fail the uniqueness requirement of things. According to Zemach (forthcoming) and Heintz (1979) the uniqueness of non-existents is assumed and not discovered and there is therefore no reason to deny nonexistents a uniqueness of being in a fictional world. Hence the first solution for nonexistents works by showing the semantic (if not) logical commensurability between existents and nonexistents.

The other solution for the incompleteness of fictional entities which also employs an ontologic-semantic type of argument is the one that compromises the *particularity* of such beings. Wolterstorff (1980), for instance, introduces a theory of *kinds*: since it does not make sense to attribute properties to things that have never existed, he suggests that when Gogol used the name "Chichikov," he was not using it to refer to someone specific; by using it he was delineating for us a certain kind of person – the Chichikov in *Dead Souls* kind. By construing characters as kinds the problems of fictional existence and of incompleteness are resolved since kinds themselves are complete entities, although not always determinate. The problem of fictional existence is hence solved: "If a work's world is possible, then a character in such a world is a person-kind which is a maximal component of that world" (Wolterstorff, 1980: 155). A solution in the same direction is proposed by Inwagen (1977) in the form of the following impasse: creatures of fiction are creatures that exist and are referred to in the propositions we make *about* fiction (fictional propositions in themselves are about nothing). The extensions of the propositions we use when talking about fiction "belong to the broader category of things I shall call *theoretical entities of literary criticism*, a category that also includes plots, subplots, novels ... " (ibid.: 302–303). Such entities are things we can refer to without taking on ourselves the weight of ontological responsibility that a strict use of "exist" entails. The problematics of the indeterminate nonexistence of fictional entities is thus solved by Inwagen through the introduction of an alternative mode of being of what he names "theoretical entities."

(3) Explaining the incompleteness of fictional entities in terms of their *mode of construction*. This philosophical approach to the logical problems raised by fictional entities takes the route of showing that although some propositions made about a fictional entity are indeterminate, these indeterminacies are not constructed/marked as such in the act of their construction. Howell's (1979) criticism of Parsons' treatment of fictional objects illustrates this direction. Howell

claims that on Parsons' interpretation of incompleteness, all fictional objects are presented as *radically incomplete*, although in fact except in rare cases fictional entities are only *nonradically incomplete*. Unless the author explicitly attributes both the property of "being right-handed" and of "not being right-handed" (which happens only in rare cases), most novels will only arrive at the situation where the characters of the fictional world either have or lack the infinite number of properties that would belong to a maximal set. In other words, there is nothing logically deviational in attributing the one property "either being right-handed or not being right-handed" to an entity. In such a framework incompleteness is not viewed as a radical logical deviation of the type usually described by philosophers, and the nonexistence of fictional entities is not presented as a central factor in our understanding of the nature of fiction. Howell himself suggests that Anna Karenina is part of Tolstoy's imaginative worlds where, before her inventor's mind's eye, she is an individuated entity. Tolstoy nevertheless selected from the properties of the complete Anna in his mind and associated her with only a limited number of properties in *Anna Karenina*. Following such a rationale, fictional entities are basically viewed as very similar to real ones, except that in the case of the fictional we happen to know less about them. Castañeda, for instance, presents an extreme formulation for blurring the distinction between fictional and real entities. According to him both fictional and real entities are composed of atoms of identification that draw from the same stock.

The difference between fictional characters and ordinary objects does not, therefore, lie in their building blocks, or in their properties, but in the way those building blocks are put together ... (Castañeda, 1979: 53)

Because one assumes the completeness of real objects, the contingent building blocks of a real object are viewed as part of an infinity of properties and any real object is "infinitely propertied." When, however, an individual is believed to be unreal, no further beliefs about the nonexisting individual than the finite set of individuating properties grouped around that individual are forwarded. Incompleteness is equated with an ontological isolation from an infinite set of individual guises. Likewise, Walton (1990) assumes that fictitious entities are products of pretense or make-believe. When using a name the speaker only pretends to refer to something or alludes to a kind of pretending-to-refer. In other words, Walton solves the problem of fictional entities by claiming that we describe fictions as we would ordinary concrete particulars. By talking about fictional or nonexistent entities we do not yet solve the metaphysical and semantic problems involved in fiction. The key to understanding assertive uses of sentences appearing to make reference to fictional entities is to take as primary their use in pretense.

Underlying all these very different propositions is the view that fictional entities are products of acts of composition; their mode of being and their incompleteness are an outcome of their being *composed* constructs. Neither Castañeda, nor Howell or Walton need to posit a radical logic to account for the case of fictional existence.

(4) The interpretation of incompleteness given by many literary theorists is that of explaining incompleteness by transforming it into an *object of aesthetic considerations* and a product of rhetorical manipulations: "If incompleteness is a logical 'deficiency' of fictional worlds, it is an important factor of their aesthetic efficiency. Empty domains are constituents of the fictional world no less than 'filled' domains" (Doležel, 1988: 486). The rhetorical effectiveness of incompleteness is based on the idea, recurrent in literary theory, that what the story chooses not to tell is as significant as what it chooses to recount.[4] "Faced with the unavoidable incompleteness of fictional worlds, authors and cultures have the choice of maximizing or minimizing it" (Pavel, 1986: 108). By claiming that the thematization or repression of incompleteness is optional, the immanence of incompleteness in formal terms is played down in the literary context. Incompleteness does not count as a logical deviation (unless the author chooses to mark it as such) but as a potential device for attaining thematic effects.

Another complementary mode of confronting an incomplete world is by denying the relevance of maximality to fiction. In reconstructing a fictional world one does not assume that a maximal set of propositions is implied but not stated. The sufficiency of information is a prevalent aesthetic norm advanced by theoretical discourse about literary texts. What the text chooses to present is sufficient for the reader "to place himself correctly against the world constructed before him" (Goffman, 1974: 149). In teleological terms, areas of indeterminacy are irrelevant to the fictional world. The Shakespearean text does not tell how many children Lady Macbeth had because this is an

---

4 See Prince, 1988, about the "disnarrated."

indifferent detail with respect to the unfolding events of the drama. The indeterminacy regarding this property of Lady Macbeth does not entail an incomplete character. The sense of completeness of fictional worlds, which is not less than the completeness effectuated by versions of reality, is not regarded as a trivial fact by literary theorists for whom the reality of fiction is to be detached from the rigid laws of logic. Against the philosophical view, the absence of a complete referent in the background, the extensional emptiness behind imaginary beings, does not prevent a sense of completeness being left by fictional worlds. The absence of a pre-existing complete referent with respect to which the limited set of characteristics actually attributed to the fictional entity can be regarded as incomplete, is a telling absence in this respect. This absence indicates that fictional worlds are limited to what is described, implied or alluded to in the text (Pavel, 1983: 50), whereas other entailed gaps, in the logical sense, are not pertinent to the construction of fictional entities. Literary theorists tend to confirm that the fictional entity is, in principle, a whole composed of those properties actually attributed to it in the course of the narrative. Manifestations of incompleteness are a matter of choice: literary texts may either accentuate an incomplete quality of the worlds they project or they can overcome or suppress it.[5]

In this section interpretations of incompleteness by philosophers have been shown to be linked to their presuppositions regarding the actual existence of things, and to be linked as well, in the case of philosophers and of literary theorists alike, to the object of study of the respective disciplines of research. The interpretation of incompleteness is thus always motivated by an overall view of what fictional existence in general entails.

Are fictional entities equally incomplete?

The autonomy of a fictional world resides in the fact that the entire fictional domain shares an ontological perspective (Pavel, 1975: 172–175). Positing a common ontological position to the different

---

5 It is against this background that literary theorists have developed the notion of functional gaps in the reading process. Ingarden, Sternberg and Perry and others, have claimed that some information missing from the text looms large in the overall meaning-structure of the literary text concerned. When indeterminacies are viewed as gaps, they are interpreted as contributing to the very foundations of the text's meaning.

domains of the fictional universe is a view adopted by models tagged "integrationist" in Pavel's later study (1986), since within such models different types of objects can serve the same cultural function. Integrationist models therefore give up on the categorical differentiation between propositions about fictionals and propositions about actuals, and all types of objects represented by language are accepted as cultural constructs of similar nature. Yet, even if one has relaxed the notions of existence and reference to produce more flexible relations between fictionals and actuals, there is still a problematic aspect to any attempt to adopt this view in relation to fiction because fiction itself seems to counteract any attempt to treat all objects constructed in it as of an equal fictional status. Can we indeed claim that the entire fictional domain shares a single ontological perspective? Fiction admits individuals that are unique to a given fictional world but also individuals that have been borrowed from reality. Within the fictional universe one can distinguish between totally imaginary entities (Natasha's personality and Anna Karenina's suicide in Tolstoy's novels) and entities that have their counterparts outside the fictional universe in the actual world (Napoleon in *War and Peace*, Paris in Balzac's works and the French revolution in Dickens' *A Tale of Two Cities*) or in another fictional universe (Madame Bovary in Flaubert's novel and in "The Kuglemass Affair" by Woody Allen; Shakespeare's Hamlet and the Hamlet of Stoppard's "Rosencrantz and Guilderstern Are Dead").

The fact that fictional texts mingle entities of both types casts doubt on the overall fictionality of literary worlds. When the literary text names an object that has a correlate in the actual world the autonomy of fictional worlds that resides in their global fictionality is breached.

He had been to Amsterdam, Mr. Bankes was saying as he strolled across the lawn with Lily Briscoe. He had seen the Rembrandts. He had been to Madrid. Unfortunately it was Good Friday and the Prado was shut. He had been to Rome. Had Miss Briscoe been to Rome? Oh, she should – it would be a wonderful experience for her – the Sistine Chapel; Michael Angelo; and Padua, with its Giottos. (*To the Lighthouse*: 68)

The constant mixing of fact with fiction, the intermittent use of names designating referents and names referring to nothing is a feature of the fictional construction of worlds, a feature which has been subject to two incompatible views:

(1) The view that Amsterdam and the Ramsays' lawn, Napoleon and Prince Andrei are categorically different entities within fiction.

(2) The view that despite logical considerations, all entities concerned are equally part of the fictional sphere of objects.

The former view is the one held by Parsons (1980) for instance, who distinguishes between objects *native* to the story and objects *immigrant* to the story. The former are constituted by constellations of properties that are unique to that fictional world; the latter are correlated with properties that also appear outside fiction. Parsons grounds this distinction in specific "extranuclear" properties that characterize native objects as incomplete and nonexistent, whereas immigrant objects are complete and existent. Incomplete fictional objects carry only those attributes ascribed to them in the course of the story. Immigrant objects are however correlated with real entities and are hence complete. Parsons qualifies his argument by introducing an additional category of *surrogate* objects:

Now there are those who think that the real London does not appear in those stories but rather that another object does; it is a fictional object called "London" in the story and it is different from the real London. It, like Holmes, is an object that is native to the story; it is a city "created" by Doyle (with the aid of our common understanding of the real London). So the London of the novels will be an incomplete object, and will also be a nonexistent object. (ibid. 57–58)

Parsons, wavering between the two positions (of seeing London as an immigrant and seeing it as a surrogate entity), favours the view that the London in fiction directly refers to London in reality despite the fact that he acknowledges a possible difference between a fictional London and the real London. A surrogate London, he claims, does not appear in the story as such; it only emerges when, standing outside fiction, we refer to "the London of Conan Doyle's novels" which is a specific version, created in fiction, of the real London. In other words, when considering the logical status of fictional propositions, and the status of naming in fiction, there is a difference in kind between propositions in fiction that refer to imaginary entities, and propositions in fiction that refer to real entities. However, in the re-construction of propositions *about fiction*, the mediating category of a surrogate object that created a logical sphere *within ficiton* for immigrant entities, now subsumes immigrant entities into the fictional domain. In other words, in talking about fiction, both London in Conan Doyle's novels and the imaginary Sherlock Holmes are part of one and the same domain.[6]

6 Rescher and Margolin, along similar lines, distinguish between the *actuality variant* type of individual and the *supernumerary*. The former possess actual world

In a similar manner, other philosophers also differentiate between different propositions in fiction and their distinct logical status: "a fictional hero is not merely ... a real hero deprived of specific and particularized properties or features. Fictional objects remain wholly unreal, in a segregated realm of their own. The difference between the real and the fictional realms is abysmal" (Castañeda, 1979: 35). Searle (1979) also argues that Conan Doyle's reference to London is an example of a nonfictional element within a work of fiction. In such cases, maintains Searle, the author has a nonfictional commitment as in any real act of referring (ibid.: 72). When describing Sherlock Holmes however, Conan Doyle only *pretends* to be referring to a character who is in fact the creation of a fictional act.

If Sherlock Holmes and Watson go from Baker Street to Paddington Station by a route which is geographically impossible, we will know that Conan Doyle blundered even though he has not blundered if there never was a veteran of the Afghan campaign answering to the description of John Watson, MD. (ibid.)

In a similar vein, Wolterstorff (1980) claims that "the entities to be found 'in' the worlds of works of art are not all fictitious entities" (141). Wolterstorff distinguishes between different uses of names: naming with rigid designators used in order to refer to the same element in any possible world ("Russia" in *Dead Souls*) and naming characters of fiction ("Chichikov" in *Dead Souls*) which is naming with no intention of referring. From a philosophical point of view, not all propositions in a fictional text have the same logical status and not all seemingly referring expressions refer in the same way.

Names and expressions like "Amsterdam," "Baker Street" and "the city of Sherlock Holmes' residence," can therefore undermine the view of fictionality as a global strategy of fictional texts and hence the ontological autonomy of fictional worlds. If expressions of the type given above are real acts of referring, entailing commitment to actuality on the speaker's part, fictional worlds can be claimed to be only partially fictional. If one treats such cases as "islands" of nonfictionality within the fictional domain and as direct references to complete objects in the actual world, it becomes practically impossible

singular prototypes of which it is a variation, whereas the latter is a purely conceptual construct added to the furniture of the universe. Rescher's distinction is different from Parsons' in that it specifies the exact logical relations holding between an actuality variant and its real prototype and the logical criteria satisfied by each type of construct.

to speak of the autonomy of fictional worlds in relation to the actual world. The division of literary worlds into real and fictional domains therefore has an obvious implication for one's understanding of the incompleteness of fictional constructs. The actual world to which some of the propositions in fiction refer imposes a differentiation between objects with a complete counterpart in reality and fictional constructs that lack such a counterpart. The segregationist approach of such philosophical models of fictional existence thus culminates in the attempt to impose divisions on the fictional world itself. The demand to make logical distinctions between propositions about existents and propositions about nonexistents affects the way in which fictional worlds are described by philosophers. Fictional universes that mingle facts with fictions present heterogeneous ontologies; these ontologies are represented by a mixture of fictional propositions and of propositions committed to the actual state of affairs, of referring expressions and of nonreferring names.

The distinction within a literary work between the fictional and the nonfictional also implies that only propositional acts that tie themselves to actual states of affairs fulfill the "normal" functions of language. Parsons, Wolterstorff and Searle in various ways privilege the real world over fictional worlds since only the former enables the operation of the normal functions of a language. This privileging is either expressed in terms of referential power or in terms of completeness: facts of the actual world stipulate the truth value or the logico-semantic status of propositions about fictional entities, thus constraining the representation of these facts in fiction.[7] Basically, according to such views, fictional objects with a correlate in reality are completed by reference to a familiar and complete set of attributes associated with the object in reality. This explains the required truthfulness-to-life in their literary representation. When compared with objects in reality and with existent objects that have counterparts in fiction, native fictional objects are considered incomplete.

What is the solution for entities that exist across worlds? Do they make the overall fictionality of a world doubtful? The case of Paris as

7 Although the various philosophers differ in the weight they assign to the overlap between fictional worlds and the actual world, they share the view that this overlap is necessary. Parsons claims that all fictions mingle entities of both native and immigrant kind; Wolterstorff employs the notion of *anchoring* to describe this overlap. According to him existing entities supply the very foundations for a fictional world construction and a world of a work of art is anchored in existing entities, even if these entities are not referred to.

constructed in fiction will serve to demonstrate the twofold difficulty in trying to relate objects constructed in fiction directly with their counterparts in reality: (1) it is impossible to demarcate essential properties of Paris which do (or should) recur in each of its literary constructions; (2) diverse descriptive sets can be attributed to the same name in different fictional worlds and therefore descriptions that replace a name in one particular fictional world cannot be transferred or applied to other possible worlds.

One morning in December, on his way to attend a lecture on procedure, he thought he noticed more animation than usual in the Rue Saint-Jacques. Students were rushing out of the cafes or calling to each other from house to house through the open windows; the shopkeepers were standing in the middle of the pavement, watching uneasily; and when he reached the Rue Soufflot he saw a large crowd assembled round the Pantheon (*Sentimental Education*: 38).

This is a typical description of Paris in Flaubert's novel. It follows our common world knowledge according to which Paris, as an urban center, "contains" places such as streets, cafes, public halls, squares — all belonging to the paradigm of a city. Moreover, specific places in Paris (such as Rue Saint-Jacques and Rue Soufflot) are mentioned and serve to locate the actions of the agent and the situations he encounters on his way. Such cases of anchoring fictional events in real places, are the cases that seem to necessitate a nonfictional commitment on behalf of the speaker. It is not only that Paris serves to denote city-life in general as the setting for fictional events; in the present case Paris could not be replaced by another urban environment: what is specifically known about Paris outside fiction is duplicated in the counterpart existence of Paris in the world of *L'Education sentimentale*.

Yet, other fictional texts might refer to Paris without using any of its unique locale. In Stendhal's *Le rouge et le noir*, characters walk or drive outdoors without the least reference to concrete places in Paris where their actions take place. Moreover, Paris in Stendhal's novel includes only private places: salons, attics, gardens, private rooms, dining-rooms; these are the places that constitute the city of Paris in this particular world. In the fictional world of Stendhal's novel, and from the point of view of its hero Julien Sorel, arriving in Paris from a provincial town signals his ascent on the social ladder and this is the only relevant property of Paris that applies to this fictional world. There is therefore no relevance to the concrete city life or public events in Paris, and the place serves only to connote a social dynamics. The lack of concreteness in referring to Paris can be illustrated from the following scene: when Julien and his sponsor (l'abbé Pirard) drive by cart to the home of Le conte de La Mole, neither their departure from l'abbé Pirard's house nor their taken route is described. Conversing at length on the way is not marked by any reference to the surrounding Parisian locale. Only upon their arrival at their destination does it become apparent that they have been *en route*. The overall confinement of Julien's adventures in Paris to the domestic area, the fact that the public domain in Paris is left out of the construction of the fictional world, produces a Paris very different from the one named and described in Flaubert's novel. Can we say that both fictional worlds are anchored in the same real place, Paris? Does the Paris of Stendhal imply all the concrete Parisian places that are nonetheless never mentioned? This illustration demonstrates that a novel can construct a place like Paris without reverting to a shared, well-defined set of features or to specific knowledge one has of the city. In such a case, the existence of a counterpart in reality proves to be of almost no consequence. In other words, properties associated with a name, including what intuitively seem to be its essential properties, are not necessarily ascribed to it in every possible situation. This is apart from the obvious fact that some of the properties attached in fiction to concrete reality counterparts, relate to fictional entities residing in or next to them. Napoleon in *War and Peace* and London in Conan Doyle's novels characteristically have fictional entities interact with them or reside in them. Since an empirical scanning of London will not reveal Sherlock Holmes, London cannot be the place where Holmes actually lived (see Routley, 1979: 15). Ascribing Holmes to London as one of its inhabitants is a true property of London in the context of fiction, but is false in reality.

Moreover, the decision as to which entities constitute the immigrants and which the natives of a fictional world is nothing but obvious. Fictional worlds can be anchored to real entities without these being explicitly named by the author. In Paul Auster's *In the Country of Last Things* the place where the futuristic fictional events take place seems to be a transformed New York city, an actuality variant of a place that carries no name in this novel; moreover, the things that take place in this variant of New York would be inconceivable in the real (empirical) New York of the present; they are not inconceivable of some *future* real New York. In this sense, whether a real entity is named or not by a fictional text has no correlation with the degree of reliance on our knowledge about the "real" world exhibited in that world construction. A real entity can be named within a fictional context and none of the knowledge associated with it outside fiction will be activated, whereas a place can remain unnamed and still activate a whole frame of knowledge associated with the place in extrafictional contexts.

"Truths 'copied' by the author and invented characters belong in an often indistinguishable fashion to the world of the literary text" (Pavel, 1983: 50). In David Lodge's novel *Changing Places*, Rummidge and Euphoria are introduced as places on an imaginary map. Yet, although figments of the imagination, Rummidge is presented as a typically unattractive industrial city in the English Midlands, while Euphoria conforms to the essential characteristics of an affluent state "situated between Northern and Southern California" (13).[8] The fictional name combined with a "true-to-life" characterization exemplifies the difficulty of distinguishing fictional from nonfictional entities in the literary world, of differentiating between types of knowledge activated in the construction of fictional entities.

The categorical distinction between fictional entities with and without a correlate in reality is therefore seriously called into question. This distinction is also questionable from another angle. It is assumed that the existence of a counterpart in reality for an entity constructed in fiction imposes specific constraints on the literary text which are not imposed when entities are native to the fictional world.[9] Yet constraints imposed by our common world knowledge are not related exclusively to entities with a counterpart in reality; various types of world-knowledge constraints can be equally violated in some possible world, fictional or other. The variety of ways of anchoring fictional

---

8 It is noteworthy that these imaginary places "return" in Lodge's subsequent novels *Small World* and *Nice Work*, thereby acquiring a certain transworld essentiality.

9 When I informally addressed a group of literary scholars asking why it was, according to their intuitive view, that literature tends to anchor itself much more in real times and places than to real (historical) persons, the results were instructive in this regard. Literature, it was claimed, can tolerate the constraints of reality less well in the domain of characters so central to the fictional world and so essential to the development of a narrative structure. Times and places are however less essential in this regard. Modes of anchoring fiction to real beings were therefore correlated with demands of the free play of imagination in the construction of a fictional world: the less a text relies on empirical reality, the more the realm of the imaginative can be explored.

states of affairs to real entities and the impossibility of distinguishing a fictional from a nonfictional domain within the literary world show that fictional worlds do not mix the fictional with representations of the real in any straightforward way. Paris-in-fiction (inhabited by fictional agents) and the fictional Rummidge (characterized by reality-like properties) have a similar status in the ontological sphere of their respective fictional worlds; although they differ in the way they activate world knowledge, their reliance on world knowledge is not correlated with whether the names they carry are fictional or real. Literary texts differ in the degrees and modes of their reliance on knowledge frames. These may range from frames of reference which recount concrete sets of attributes of objects in reality, through a general familiarity with laws and conventions according to which the world operates, to an acquaintance with symbolic or archetypal meanings associated with entities. For instance, "Paris" carries information about concrete locations and geographical features but also about a complex cultural-historical system associated with a capital and a metropolis of this kind. As demonstrated above, none of these frames is necessarily operated in all fictional worlds anchored to Paris. The ontological distinction between non-actual entities and "quasi-actual" ones (such as Paris, or Rummidge) is consequently converted into a problem of rhetoric.

This is indeed another literary maneuver destined to circumvent the logical incompleteness of fictional entities by showing that incompleteness, as a distinctive feature of fiction, is not a straight-forward logical criterion. Rhetorical strategies often render incompleteness unmarked in the fictional text; rhetorical manipulations might also either thematize or repress the difference between entities native to the fictional world and entities that have immigrated to it from the less or more familar country of real things and actual states of affairs. Rhetorically speaking, incompleteness can then predicate entities that have counterparts in empirical reality.

Theories of naming and the completeness of entities

In order to develop further the idea that from a literary perspective incompleteness is irrelevant to our understanding of fiction (Anna Karenina is logically an incomplete being, but she is not grasped as such in the process of reconstructing the fictional world) I will now return to theories of naming developed in the philosophy of language.

These theories, the gradual relaxation of criteria they have undergone in recent years (as discussed in chapter 1), and the kind of use they have been put to in the literary context, provide a basis for my claim about the mode of individuation of fictional entities, a mode which does not regard incompleteness nor matters of existence as relevant properties.

To understand how theories of naming can contribute to a model for all entities in fiction, it is necessary to delineate in brief for present purposes the passage from earlier to later theories about the relations between proper names and descriptions. As mentioned earlier in this study, the question of the meaning of names and of the logico-semantic relations between proper names and descriptions have been the subject of ongoing discussions among philosophers of language. Disagreements regarding the relations between proper names and descriptions, which are two kinds of "singular referring expressions" (Lyons, 1977: 640), touch on some of the substantial problems raised by fictional entities. Theories of naming center around two basic approaches, one identifying names with sets of definite descriptions and another which rejects such an identification. The basic question facing any attempt to explain the procedure of naming is whether names establish the link between words and world (names have referents but no meaning), whether names are kinds of descriptive expressions, whereby to each name a set of descriptions is attached which defines its meaning, or whether names are freely employed discursive means of reference, attached neither to descriptions nor to fixed referents.

Donnellan (1971) claims that proper names are always used referentially, while definite descriptions can also be used attributively (stating something about a thing and not just identifying the right referent). When used referentially, descriptions can be replaced by names and vice versa. For example, "Mr. Edwards" and "the man standing behind that chair" are referentially interchangeable in a particular context. Searle (1969: 85ff.) takes the extreme position, claiming that a proper name contains identifying descriptions that constitute the sense of a proper name. The name signifies a set of descriptions whose disjunction is analytically tied to the proper name by referring to an object that satisfies these descriptions. In other words, proper names are logically connected with descriptive characteristics of the referent and an identifying description can not only determine the right referent but can also replace a name.

However, the looseness of the sense of a name distinguishes its referring function from its describing function. Although the expression "the man standing behind that chair" or "the man with the white beard" can replace "Mr. Edwards" in determining a referent, the former are no more than contingent features of Mr. Edwards and therefore can serve as its descriptive substitutes only in specific contexts. In another counterfactual situation (when Mr. Edwards is not present or if he has dyed his beard) these will not constitute the meaning of "Mr. Edwards." The idea is that most names have no fixed sense attached to them and descriptions cannot be true of an object in any absolute manner. If the sense of a name was identified with a set of descriptions, that sense would change each time the said set of descriptions changed even remotely. In other words, whereas names seem to maintain a stable referent across different contexts, the descriptions attached to them in each context are likely to change. Since names resist an attempt to associate them with sets of descriptions, the question arises as to whether names carry any descriptive content whatsoever.

In short, those who believe that names have sense face the problem of the looseness of information related to a name and the unclear line dividing information necessary for the definition of a name from unnecessary information (that is, essential from contingent properties of the named object). The problem of the relations between names and descriptions is revealed particularly in counterfactual contexts, where the question of the necessary links between a given name and its identifying descriptions is central. Counterfactuals, as well as modalized propositions (propositions that appear with a qualifying modal operator, "it is believed that p," "it is possible that p"), touch on the question of whether descriptive substitutes can indeed indicate the essential sense of a name; they also touch on the problem of identity (what would Plato have been like had he not composed the *Republic*?). If descriptive substitutes are specific to a given context, in each possible world a different set of descriptions being attached to a name, does this mean that the named object changes its identity in each modal context, or is identity separate from meaning? In other words, does the identity of an entity remain stable across worlds despite the fact that in each world a different set of properties (designated by the appropriate set of descriptions) is ascribed to that entity? The second problem pertaining to names is whether the referring function of a name is stipulated by the existence of a referent.

If names had neither stable sense nor referent, there would be nothing that could generate descriptive expressions about them. If both referent and sense were not obligatory in exercising an act of naming, how would the continuity in referring to an entity with a name be guaranteed? Searle claims that in using names there is an intimate relation between our ability to use the name and our knowledge of the properties of the entity concerned. Therefore, when formulating the distinctive features of Aristotle, we know that not each and every one of the identifying properties is equally essential. It is only the sum total of identifying descriptions and the hierarchical structure they constitute that establish the identity of an object and enable us to refer to that object in a proper way. In some way, therefore, a name is logically attached to descriptions despite the fact that none is in itself analytically tied to the name.

Yet, our everyday referential intentions and practices are variable: names are sometimes used as defining abbreviations (when we say "water" we mean to talk about liquids that conform to the chemical definition of H_2O), sometimes to talk about alternative possible or counterfactual worlds (when we talk about what would have happened to Nixon had he not been elected president) and sometimes naming is warranted despite a worrying lack of information about the named object. This variety of practices have caused philosophers like Kripke and Putnam to relax the referential functions and the epistemological commitments attached to naming and to flex the idea of "essence" as the set of properties essential to an object and recurring in all possible worlds in which this object occurs. In view of the difficulty of associating names with descriptions Kripke (1972) has questioned the identification of names with sets of descriptions by distinguishing between names that are rigid designators (designating the same object in all possible worlds) and descriptions that express the properties of objects: "the properties an object has in every counter-factual world have nothing to do with properties used to identify this object in the actual world" (50). The sense of names is hence indeterminate and names enable us to refer without an absolute certainty regarding specific, rigidly assigned properties of the object concerned. Worlds other than the actual world can be imagined only because diverse descriptive conditions are associated with the same object in different possible worlds. The indefiniteness of the sense of referring expressions can hence be reduced when these expressions contextually fix the name. Singular reference is achieved not because we "have" the object, or because its properties are given to us as a stable set, but because we use a rigid designator (name or definite description) in a well-defined context. Following Kripke, it can be argued that a name designates an object even in worlds where the object is not self-evidently associated with the set of properties related to it in the actual world. One can hypothesize, for instance, another possible world in which Nixon was not the president of the United States. In such a world, "Nixon" refers to a well-individuated object although this same object carries a different set of attributes in each of the worlds concerned. In another possible world a rigid designator could identify an object although most of the important properties associated with the designated object do not hold in reality.[10] The perceiver of another possible world is not automatically sent to verify a set of descriptive statements he carries and associates with the name based on his established actual-world knowledge. Rather, another world might introduce a name and attach to it an idiosyncratic set of descriptions which, in that particular world, are identifying marks of the denoted object. Even when the name used to introduce an entity in another possible world already exists in the perceiver's stored knowledge of the world, the sense of the name in the context of that possible world may differ considerably from its sense in actuality, provided that world supplies the information necessary in order to form descriptive substitutes for the proper name, and descriptions that may replace the name only in the context of that specific world. Theories of naming, along the lines suggested by Kripke, Donnellan, Putnam and others, have emerged in order to separate reference from epistemology: to ensure the referential function of names regardless of epistemological conditions of knowing the referent, to explain rigid designation when the sense of a name is variable, and to account for stable identity across worlds.

As explained in chapter 1, both traditional theories of naming of the Russell–Frege type (linking names with a corresponding sense and

10 According to Kripke and others, there are minimal individuating requirements for a name to remain a rigid designator. A sufficient individuating feature can be the structure of the fertilized egg which later became Aristotle, for instance. The minimal requirements have to do with the causal chain at the beginning of which the object was baptized and a name was attached to it in a concrete moment. Other philosophers deny such minimal individuating requirements of the type specified by Kripke because they do not think that natural laws tell us what objectively could or could not be the case; Aristotle could therefore have been Chinese and still be Aristotle. See the discussion in Putnam, 1983: 55–58; 63–66.

with a referent), and new theories of naming of the Kripke–Donnellan line, both suggest a segregationist approach to fictional entities. Whereas traditional philosophies of naming were more explicit on the necessary presence of an existent, new theorists of reference expressed this dependence indirectly. What ensures the referential success of a referring act is a moment of "baptizing" when a name, as a rigid designator, was first attached to an object. This initial dependence of a name on a referent of the existent type, produces a sequence of felicitous uses of the name on subsequent occasions. Donnellan describes a historical chain going back to the moment of constituting a referential link between name and object while Kripke refers to a causal chain that establishes this link. When no moment of baptizing is reconstructible, the referring chain is claimed to end in a block and the use of the name has failed. Donnellan and Kripke both separate identifying conditions from existence. Our ability to refer with verbal expressions is disconnected from the speaker's intentions or from the scope of his knowledge about the referent.[11]

Philosophies of naming hence exclude fictional entities and nonexistents from the category of objects which can be rigidly and successfully designated with names. It is also clear that the exclusion of fictional entities as candidates of rigid designation is not an outcome of semantic considerations but of logical ones. Names can function as rigid designators in non-actual contexts because they satisfy the existence-condition, which guarantees the fixity of identity of the object concerned despite movements across world boundaries and into counter-factual states of affairs. Cross-referentiality is secured only when there is an existent that satisfies the name, a criterion relative to which fictional objects are obviously disqualified.

As shown in chapter 1, in a paper published in 1979 Pavel proposed a way of detaching the existential pre-requisite from Kripke's theory of naming and of adopting only that part of the theory that refers to our referential practices activated regardless of ontological considerations. Pavel's interpretation of Kripke hence enables, along the Kripkean line of argumentation, variable, context-bound modes of naming. Pavel's move was presented in that previous context to show

---

11 Rorty claims that the price for establishing principles of referring that guarantee a link between language and world, is that a proposition of the kind "Sherlock Holmes is a detective" are bound not to refer. Rorty therefore sees the Donnellan–Kripke line of argument as left-overs from a realism that still links semantics to metaphysics.

the conceptual gap between philosophers and literary theorists in their approach to the problem of fictional reference. Granted that we are aware of the conceptual leap necessary in order to apply new philosophical theories of reference to the problem of fiction, we are now in the position to grasp, following Pavel, the positive implications that literary theorists can draw from theories of naming for a model of fictional entities:

(1) If names never posit a stable association with a fixed set of descriptions, it might be claimed that, semantically speaking, names are always associated with incomplete sets of properties. In such a case, access to a correlate in reality does not matter when a name is made to signify within a given possible world. The only sense that can possibly be ascribed to a name stems from descriptions that gradually "fill" the name with meaning within a particular world. Maximality of the set of properties attached to an object is relative to a world and variability in this set is built in to every object regardless of the object's ontological status (in reality, in an alternative possible world or in a world of fiction).

(2) If a name does have descriptive content attached to it, this content includes only what is perceived in a specific context to be its essential properties; the essentiality of properties attached to a name is open to interpretation. The descriptive content associated with a name surely does not include every possible property that this entity might or might not have, essentially or inessentially, in any other world.

(3) If names ensure cross-world identity, they can rigidly designate entities whether these are real or imaginary, fictional or nonfictional. In other words, when names are claimed to withhold their referential power across actual and possible states of affairs, this entails a name maintaining its rigid capacity to designate regardless of the modality of the state of affairs which that object inhabits. Why, then, not extend the rigid use of names to imaginary worlds?

Definitization of entities and the completeness of fictional objects

Fictional contexts involve referential practices, practices that can be accounted for when we relax our criteria of warranted naming. Naming is warranted in fictional contexts as long as referential criteria are adjusted to the nature of fictional discourse. According to Inwagen

(1977), since fictional entities have no network of causal relations behind them based on a history at the beginning of which a link was established between objects and their names, *names* should be seen as secondary referential practices in fiction whereas definite descriptions are the primary means of referring. By changing the balance between names and descriptions Inwagen shows how referential practices can be implemented in a fictional context. Yet, reversing the preference for modes of naming reveals only one aspect of the referential practices unique to fiction. Another aspect is revealed when one reconsiders the question of whether the history of naming a fictional entity must indeed come to a dead-end. The history of naming a fictional entity can go back to the point where *the fictional entity is first named and introduced into the fictional universe*. In other words, the historical aspect of naming can be maintained in fiction and warranted naming be shown to be respected in line with the standard causal-relation mechanism linking name with object. Fictional texts transform standard mechanisms in a way which is unique to fictional contexts. The "baptizing" of the fictional entity has nothing to do with the moment when an object was actually attached to a name. A link between a name and a fictional object is established the moment a fictional entity is first designated as an individual in the universe under consideration. As I have shown, some philosophers would claim that variations of this first-instance of naming establishing referential relations is true in extrafictional naming practices as well: an object is designated as well-individuated, complete and distinct when a name or a rigid description first appear in a discourse. In fiction the link between a name and an object is established by the act of narration and fiction-making. Proper names and definite descriptions are the referring means apt for introducing singular entities into a world. I will claim in this section that *textual procedures of definitization* work to guarantee singularity of those fictional entities that are granted the status of fictional-world individuals, whereas other entities, whose individuation procedure is blocked, are granted a different status in the fictional universe.

Definitization is that stage or process in which it is textually indicated that a name or a description denotes a single, concrete, well-individuated, and distinct object. Names and descriptions are used in literary texts in a way that implies a history of causal relations between a name/description and a fictional entity. Fictional names and descriptions hence work as textual strategies for definitizing fictional entities. When a set of entities is characterized as a fictional set, a history of causal relations is reconstructed between the set of entities and a set of names and descriptions, the outcome of which is the domain of objects in that fictional world. Fictional entities are constructed because the literary text indicates a definite denotatum through the use of definite forms of expression. When a textual indication in the form of a name or a description is given, one may say that a fictional entity has been added to the domain of objects as one of its definite well-individuated constituents.

There are two basic strategies for definitizing entities. Especially because of the fictionality of the world, new elements are often introduced as if they are already known: the text conveys information about its fictional world as if that world is already there. Thus, many literary texts tend to present new entities from the very start by using expressions which are, lexically speaking, definite descriptions, although at the stage at which the expressions appear in the text the entity denoted by the description has not yet been sufficiently definitized. In such cases the definite form assumes a familiarity with a fictional referent whose essential properties are often not yet known. The other strategy is that of definitizing an object by specifying, in a series of descriptions, those properties which individuate the object in a particular fictional universe. Here, in other words, definitization relies on the accumulation of descriptive information.

"My dear, dear anxious friend," – said she, in mental soliloquy, while walking down stairs from her own room, ... The clock struck twelve as she passed through the hall ... She opened the parlour door and saw two gentlemen sitting with her father ... (*Emma*: 127–128)

Under certain circumstances there are few hours in life more agreeable than the hour dedicated to the ceremony known as afternoon tea ... The implements of the little feast had been disposed upon the lawn of an old English country house ... The house that rose beyond the lawn was ... the most characteristic object in the peculiarly English picture I have attempted to sketch. (*The Portrait of a Lady*: 5–6)

In the example from *Emma*, parts of the house are mentioned as if they are already known: definite descriptions inserted in subordinate clauses ("while walking ...," "as she passed ...") are textual indications of the definiteness of the entities introduced here for the first time into the fictional world (the house of Emma has not been described at any earlier stage). In the example from James, however, there is an opposite strategy of gradual definitization. The cluster of predicates suggests an attempt to definitize the place introduced: the text implies that despite the typicality of the scene, as long as there is more than one house satisfying the description, the lexical category remains that of an indefinite description. When later the name "Gardencourt" appears in the text as the house's name, the house has finally been definitized. Proper names and descriptions indicate at what stage in the process of constructing a fictional set of entities there appears to be only one object in the fictional world satisfying a specific description or identifiable by a name. In every text there is a particular moment when a definite description ("the house" or "him") refers to a well-individuated entity, a singular entity in that particular world.

Fictional definitization is a process in which literary texts work against a vagueness of instantiation. As long as one does not know whether there is only one entity satisfying a description, or what the identifying descriptions are that "fill" a name with contextual meaning, the fictional entity remains vague. Literary texts use a variety of means for definitizing the entities forming the relevant domain of objects. For instance, fictional worlds that do not rely on familiar frames and scripts have to introduce their basic categories before introducing concrete entities uniquely instantiating those categories:

For nothing is really itself anymore. There are pieces of this and pieces of that, but none of it fits together. And yet, very strangely, at the limit of all this chaos, everything begins to fuse again ... At a certain point, things disintegrate into muck, or dust, or scraps, and what you have is something new, some particle or agglomeration of matter that cannot be identified. (*In the Country of Last Things*: 35)

In Paul Auster's novel, where a world disintegrates, categories of matter and the self-identity of objects must be redefined. Literary texts of a fantastic, postmodernist or science-fictional type, therefore recruit definitizing means in order to construct a world, from its very basic categories to its concrete instances. Considerable explanatory effort is hence devoted in such cases to introducing the object-repertoire constituting the world concerned.

A vagueness of instantiation cannot be discarded unless the definite identity of fictional entities has been secured. Although in nonfictional contexts, vagueness disappears when the vague term is matched with a concrete object, a vague term can also be matched with any kind of construct, and getting rid of vagueness does not presuppose relating words to world. In fiction the matching of object to term is impossible and entities are definitized as part of the rhetoric of the text (which guarantees the construction of a world). The English country house has been definitized despite the fact that no complete set of attributes has been or could be ascribed to it (the house being fictional). When definitization is blocked, this demonstrates an alternative rhetorical strategy on the part of the author:

He travelled.
He came to know the melancholy of the steamboat, the cold awakening in the tent, the tedium of landscapes and ruins, the bitterness of interrupted friendships. (*Sentimental Education*: 411)

In such a case, the textual devices are used to denote *collective entities*, and the concrete places constituting this collectivity remain undefined. A nonspecificity here corresponds to the lack of attempt to overcome a vagueness of instantiation.

Note that the various modes of definitization fail to correlate with whether an entity has or lacks a "real" counterpart:

The little town of Verrières is one of the prettiest in Franche-Comté. Its white houses, with their red-tiled, pointed roofs, stretch out along the side of a hill. (*Le rouge et le noir*: 33)

Verrières, a point on the actual map of France, is introduced here formally; that is, there is no assumption of familiarity manifested in the mode of incorporating the place into the fictional world. Modes of definitization do not correspond, in any systematic way, to the *original* ontological status of the object introduced into a fictional universe.

In the textual process of definitization through rhetorical devices (definite and indefinite descriptions, names and categories), entities constituting the fictional object-domain are gradually or immediately introduced into the fictional world. Fictional ontology in general, the self-identity and the distinctness of fictional entities in particular, are hence dictated by the literary school to which a text belongs, its style and rhetorical purposes. Postmodernist fiction, for instance, "works to problematize the entire activity of reference" (Hutcheon, 1988: 152). But whatever the rhetoric of a literary text, unless explicitly stated otherwise, a completeness of the universe is always assumed.[12] A complete world is nevertheless not assumed in cases where a world is characterized by *radical incompleteness* (both p and ~p are attributed to

12 In this I differ from Pavel who contends that overcoming or minimizing incompleteness is a practice that corresponds only to a stable world view (1986: 108).

the same situation) or when the fictional world thematizes the collapsing of its domains, but these are the exceptions.[13]

Completeness of information is not a condition for definitizing fictional entities because fictional world-construction does not assume incompleteness on a logical level to be one of the world constructing conventions operating in fiction. For that reason detailed descriptions, or textual attempts to give as much information as possible about an entity, do not imply a stable ontology. Detailed descriptions are equally likely to appear in the most "realistic" novels, aspiring to present "une tranche de vie" (Zola, Flaubert, Balzac) and in fantastic or science-fictional fictions. "On the evening of the third day there, curiosity overcame his plans for seeing everything before visiting at Father Pirard" (*Le rouge et le noir*: 248), and the expression "at Father's Pirard's" remains the only textual manifestation of the place; the text does not even indicate what kind of place is involved (a hotel, a mansion, or a house). Yet the meagerness of information entails neither maximization nor minimalization of incompleteness. One might consider an opposite example where the text conveys as many details as possible about the domain of entities it constructs:

Two parallel arcades in the Moorish style extended right and left. The wall of a house took up the whole of the far end, opposite, and the fourth side, where the restaurant lay, was designed to look like a Gothic cloister with stained-glass windows. A sort of Chinese roof sheltered the platform on which the musicians played; the ground all round it was covered with asphalt; and there were some Venetian lanterns hung on poles which, seen from a distance, formed a crown of multicoloured lights above the dancers. (*Sentimental Education*: 103)

Flaubert's descriptions can go on and on without necessarily attaining an effect of completeness in the sense that they are "thematically

---

13 McHale (1987) illustrates the "cloudy" character of the ontic sphere in postmodernist fiction with the example of a novel by Sorrentino where parts of the ontic sphere are left vague, disappearing into the haziness of incompletely existing in a fiction (32).

Since many of the literary models for fictional ontology have emerged in view of postmodernist fiction (a literary school whose dominant is ontological), and since the postmodernist case has triggered the most elaborate models for fictional ontology, one might be led to generalize from the postmodernist case that most fictional worlds are radically incomplete and emphatically indeterminate. Yet postmodernism is an exception and theorists of postmodernism in fact prefer to believe that what they find in postmodernist fiction is unique and unprecedented, and that postmodernist poetics is radically discontinuous with all preceding poetics.

empty." In other words, the number of properties employed in a particular text to definitize a fictional entity has nothing to do with minimizing or maximizing incompleteness. The fact that literary texts assume completeness when carrying out procedures of definitization can also be proved by stressing the fact that definitization is a *process*. After a prior definitization a fictional entity can be referred to in terms of one of its salient or essential properties (essential in that particular world) or by anaphoric modes of reference.

Textual definitization is hence an inner mode of organization of the fictional domain of entities the nature of which presupposes the completeness of the entities introduced into a world. The fact that textual definitization rhetorically overcomes logical incompleteness does not in any way entail that fictional entities are as complete as real ones, that fictional characters are fictional *persons* or that fictional locations are fictional *places*. On the contrary, being creatures of fiction and *constructs of language*, fictional entities suspend the logic of actuals. The logic of completeness is therefore not automatically applicable as an inherent property of fictional beings. The possibility of definitizing an entity on the basis of extensive descriptions, on the basis of one salient feature or on the basis of no attributes at all ("at Father Pirard's") shows that the rhetoric of fiction is destined to construct its domains parallel to other world systems but not necessarily by analogy or by automatic application of their logical and ontological presuppositions.

Fictional entities, their incompleteness and manner of existence, have been, for obvious reasons, an object of discussion for philosophers. Fictional entities, like fictional worlds in general, serve for philosophers the purpose of illuminating the properties of existents, of complete entities and actual worlds. The philosophical interest in fictional entities hence emerges in a context whereby fictionals function as a foil to nonfictional existence and to actual completeness. Although literary theorists adopt the philosophical terminology in addressing the mode of existence of fiction, the logic (or nonlogic) of incompleteness cannot account for the distinct nature of fictional entities. The way fictional texts posit, manipulate and explore the fictionality of the entities they introduce as world-components, illustrates how the logical status of fictional entities offers but a partial account of the intricacy involved in fictional existence. The way fictional entities are constructed, the fact that in the fictional domain native and immigrant entities cannot be distinguished, the way incompleteness is manipulated by rhetorical devices, the naming mechanisms unique to fiction – these manifest the autonomy of fictional worlds, worlds that ground themselves in a distinct type of logic and semantics. Automatic transference of logical notions such as nonexistence and incompleteness, from actual and possible contexts to fictional ones, therefore provides an unsatisfactory explanation for fictional entities and for their mode of being.

The domain of fictional entities includes characters and objects that participate in the construction of the fictional world. The domain of fictional entities therefore has to do with the basic particulars (Strawson, 1959) or first-order entities that constitute the world of fiction. Two aspects of the mode of organization of fictional entities manifest the *fictionality* of the domain. These aspects correspond to the constraints imposed by the understander of fictional entities: (1) Every fictional domain is structured as a parallel and not a ramifying domain relative to reality or to its versions. The fictional domain of entities illustrates this parallelism in the fact that the centrality and actuality of entities in the fictional world is uncorrelated to the ontological status of these entities (to their being imaginary or real-world counterparts). (2) Every fictional domain has its unique mode of organization. The fictional domain of entities is organized by rhetorical modes of definitization that affirm the autonomy and self-sufficiency of the world constructed. In the domain of entities, as in other fictional domains, modes of organization specific to fiction are activated in a context. Facing a text known to be fictional, the reader understands the world textually constructed as a world uncommitted to reality (and hence a world where the ontological status of entities relative to the "real" world is of no consequence to the composition of that world). The reader also understands the fictional world as a world constructing its own set of referents; understanding fiction hence requires the activation of definitization procedures.

5

❖❖❖

Fictional events and the intricacies of plot

❖❖❖

Events, stories and plots have been topics of central importance in literary studies. Theories of narrative, from Aristotle to the present times, attest to the focal place that events, actions, their composition and manipulation occupy in the literary discussion. In formulating a model for fictional events that would determine the place of events in a fictional world, the centrality of notions like *fabula and sujhet, plot, action structures,* and *event sequence* to narrative theory has to be taken into consideration. Yet unlike the case of fictional entities (characters and objects) examined in the previous chapter, in the context of which both philosophers and literary theorists have paid much attention to the question of the *fictionality* of entities, in the present context the problem of what distinguishes fictional events and actions from nonfictional ones and the effect of this difference on the nature of narrative structures have been almost totally ignored until recent years. Only recently, after a long period in which narrative concepts, neutral with respect to questions of ontology, immigrated to other domains (to nourish research in such diverse fields as historiography, scientific discourse, legal rhetoric), did literary theorists start to be concerned with the narrativity specific to fiction and to be aware of the misleading results of using narrative notions across disciplinary borders (Cohn, 1990; Genette, 1990; Rigney, 1991). In addressing the topic of fictional events and action one faces therefore a total neglect on the part of philosophers concerning how fictional contexts change the logical structure of action and an almost total overlooking of the distinctive feature of literary or fictional narrativity on the part of literary theorists. Yet, since this neglect has different motivation, meaning and results in each of the disciplines involved, the situation is even more intricate than that. First, philosophers have no reason to concern themselves separately with the fictionality of action. Events that appear in fictional contexts are accounted for by a model describing nonexistence in general. All fictional entities, whether of first or second orders, blatantly breach logical laws. Whether we have a fictional figure like "Raskolnikov" or a fictional event like "Raskolnikov murdering the old lady," these are nonexistent entities and fictional entities that do not exist pose the same problem for logical suppositions and laws. Second, philosophers, when referring to action and events refer to types of (second order)[1] entities, to discrete (cognitive) units of narrative perception, whereas theorists of narrative, when referring to action and events refer to *higher order organization*, to events organized in sequences, in plots and stories. True, philosophies of action do refer to the relations cause-effect, action-consequence, reason-action, relations whose logical structure can change in modal contexts. Yet, whereas philosophers of action address action units as observable and well-distinguished discrete entities, theorists of narrative address action units as units of plot differentiated, as will be shown below, on the basis of *global* considerations of narrativity. Theorists of narrative therefore take into account a wholly different set of questions. For this reason, I will not consider the philosophical discourse on action and events as directly pertaining to a theory of fictional action and narrativity. Philosophy does not concern itself with overall narrative structures, with global action organization. Since this chapter aims to propose a theory of fictional narrativity and to describe the particular mode of organization of fictional events and actions, it is mainly narrative theory that developed within literary studies and that has addressed the question of higher order narrativity that would be our concern here. Moreover, although on face value, most narrative literary theory has absolutely ignored the question of fiction, and as such it might seem useless to a theory of *fictional* narrativity, narrative theory has, in fact, indirectly dealt with fictional narrativity, mainly through the concept of *plot*. I would claim that narrative studies in general, and narratology in particular, do not show an interest in discrete action units and address global narrative organization, thus revealing a possible link between action-structures and schemata and literary or fictional narrativity. In face of meager theoretical effort dedicated to fictional narrativity, this

---

1 First-order entities are physical objects located at any point in a space-time. Second-order entities (like events, processes, states of affairs) are entities which have a temporal duration and are located in a space-time. They are, like first-order entities, observable but identifiable only as perceptual and conceptual constructs (criteria of re-identification of an event, for instance, are not clear cut). For further description see Lyons, 1977: 442–447.

chapter will have to build up its arguments on the basis of indirect evidence. The claims made in this chapter will therefore draw on interpretation of the current state-of-the-art of narrative theory and also on analysis of the history of narrative studies. It would be claimed that recent semantic theories of plot that address the problem of fictional narrative, form a natural continuation to previous stages in research on the nature of narrativity within the literary discipline. This continuity is significant insofar as it evinces the way narrativity has all along been tacitly relying on a surrounding fictional context. Thus, despite radical changes undergone by the theory of narrative, these changes provide the essential explanation to what constitutes a fictional narrative.

In the context of the present chapter it should be noted again that by claiming that fictional events are differently organized from events in nonfictional narrative, it is not implied that there is something inherent to the events themselves that creates this distinction. Rather, in facing a sequence of events known to be fictional, the reader employs a series of conventions that directs his understanding of those events. These are plot-reconstructing conventions that lead the understander of fiction to search for a specific type of coherence in the events before him, and this coherence exceeds the coherence-demands applied to other narrative types.

Being constructed as a separate modal system, each fictional domain evinces its autonomy. Each fictional domain also displays its unique mode of organization. In this chapter that deals with the fictional domain of events, it will be shown in what ways fictional events create a modal structure of their own: events of the fictional plot are constructed as a system of possibilities, some of which are actualized and some are not, according to the thematic and semantic rules that dominate a given fictional world. It will also be shown that events in fictional narrative disclose a unique principle of organization. Fictional events do not only obey the logic of action and causality, they also conform to a type of "thematic" logic that interacts with the logic of action. The narrativity of fictional worlds is hence the outcome of an action-structure that manifests this specific type of logic unique to the fictional organization of events. This type of organization assures that fictional narrative is understood in a different way from nonfictional narrative.

The short history of narratology (narrative theory inspired by classical structuralism) has proven to be long enough for the discipline to undergo some substantial paradigmatic changes. Furthermore, although on the surface narratology manifests a relatively coherent and almost monolithic theoretical project, it includes in fact diverse methods and orientations. The first purpose of this chapter is to give an overview of a paradigm change in narratological models of plot and to describe it in terms of shifts within the range of conceptualizations available in the formalist–structuralist tradition. More specifically, this paradigmatic change consists of a shift from structural descriptions of action-structures in classical structuralism to semantic descriptions of narrative modalities in recent developments in narratology. Yet, this shift should not be described as a punctual transition but as a dialectical development leading from the earlier ideology of classical structuralism to the gradual domination of semantics in narrative theory. The historical survey of narratology which constitutes one central aspect of this chapter will justify current interest in fictional as opposed to nonfictional (historical, scientific) narrative. The direction of the paradigmatic shift in narratology can illuminate the type of model sought for fictional events and will allow me to show what distinguishes the action domain of fictional worlds. To delineate this paradigm shift, a twofold argument will be put forward.

(1) In theory, the concept of plot appears in classical structuralism as part of the attempt to describe the action-scheme in narrative texts. In practice, however, structuralist plot-models address a more comprehensive object and much broader questions. The gap between "official" pronouncements in structuralist poetics, in manifesto-like pieces, (Barthes, 1966b; Genette, 1982 [1964]) and implications drawn from structuralist practice in developing narrative models, is instructive. It shows that semantic considerations that have to do with literary narrative have permeated structuralist models from an early stage and that these models aimed at attaining a different explanatory power than was officially claimed. Structuralism has thus expressed a range of problems and questions signaling that plots of narrative fiction exceed the confines of action logic and constraints.

(2) Plot-models constructed within the framework of a narrative semantics seem to reflect a shift of conception in narratology, yet they actually revolve around old problems which traditional plot-models addressed but failed to solve. When the constraints of classical structuralist ideology were lifted from narrative theory, the shift to semantic systems became an inevitable sequel. Semantic systems supply the key to understanding the structure of fictional events.

As a point of departure for defining the conceptual framework in which narratological models of plot can be considered, I will first refer to Genette's (1988) insights on the matter:

there is room for two narratologies, one thematic in the broad sense (analysis of the story or the narrative content), the other formal or, rather, modal (analysis of narrative as a mode of "representation" of stories, in contrast to the nonnarrative modes like the dramatic ...)

But it turns out that analyses of narrative contents, grammars, logics, and semiotics have hardly, so far, laid claim to the term *narratology*, which thus remains (provisionally?) the property solely of the analysts of narrative mode. (ibid. 16)[2]

Genette's distinction between a narratology that studies narrative contents, grammars, logics, and semiotics, and a narratology that studies the narrative *mode* (indications of the presence of a narrator), is linked in his conception to the attributes "thematic" and "formal-modal" respectively. Genette's words first reflect uncertainty about what "narratology" as a field-name within narrative theory is all about (one would intuitively assume that narratology has more to do with grammars and logic than with narrative modes). This uncertainty partly explains why drawing a conceptual link between structuralist study of narrative grammar and later semantic considerations that have entered narrative theory, touches upon the core of the difficulty of delineating the boundaries of narratology. Genette thereby points at the central problem of dealing with fictional events: they involve both a logic of action and a semantics of fictional narration. Second, Genette might have chosen to refer here to two possible narratologies only heuristically (to back his view that the term "narrative" should be saved for "mode" only); in any case this methodical partition does not really hold. A glance at theoretical works as diverse as Barthes' "Introduction" (1966a) and Pavel's *move grammar* (1985) clearly shows that narrative semantics, logics and grammars are preoccupied with modal categories and that narrative modes are necessarily being incorporated into formal story-grammars.[3] Narratology therefore has

2 The claim to the term "narratology" is more widespread than Genette here argues, as attested for instance by Todorov's *Grammaire du Decameron*.
3 Barthes' level of *actions*, for instance (which is basically similar to the concept of *narrative domains* further elaborated and developed in Pavel), is closely tied with questions of mode (although semi-consciously). Modal notions are thus being incorporated into the grammar of a narrative.

to be considered as a field covering both narrative contents and narrative modes, narrative grammar and narrative semantics: the possibility of mapping the various concerns and inner branchings of narratology is problematic enough, as evidenced by Genette's hesitant approach to this field of research.

The formal side of narratology has to do with the supposition that every narrative text (transmitted through a narration) represents a sequence of *events*. It is commonly agreed that only events tied together by *chronology* and *causality* can form the basis for a narrative text (chronology is probably enough for *narrative*, but not for creating a *story*). Some causally connected event-sequences create an *action structure* (they form a *functional whole*) while other event-sequences do not obey a functional principle. Among events that create an action-structure, some have *a point* and some do not.[4] It is evident at this point that the question of what constitutes a story already involves the formal aspect of representing events and the thematic aspect of representing events that have a point. I will claim in what follows that plot-models in theory describe how events constitute an action-structure (a functional pattern of events) while in practice these models incessantly express the need for investigating and explicating the *narrativity* of the action structure, or, in other words, what turns an action-structure into a *story* (that is, an action-structure with a point).

Three types of problems emerge from classical structuralism and from plot-models in general, problems for which the semantics of narrative texts has in recent years outlined possible solutions.

(1) The problem of defining *the object of investigation of narrative theory*: does narrative theory presume to supply the sufficient conditions for producing a story, or does it address only necessary conditions of narrativity (a necessary level of events-scheme). The isolation of the action stratum in the narrative text necessarily raises some doubts regarding the status of plot-models. The ambivalence prevailing in narrative theory regarding its object of investigation will be described below.

Genette is thinking of course of *mode* (there is a narrator) and not of *modalities* in the semantic sense, yet, narrative domains are surely one possible result of narrating a chain of events, and are hence pertinent to Genette's narratology of modes.

4 The *point of a narrative* is a notion similar to the *evaluative function* in Labov (1972); it refers to the way a story indicates its aim, purpose and meaning. See also Shen, 1985, and Prince, 1982.

(2) The problem of narrative segmentation and of defining *the narrative unit.* Within narrative semantics, the narrative segment is presented as an intersection or as a complex of syntactic and semantic rules. Regarding the narrative segment not as an autonomous syntactic category but a locus where all narrative levels intersect solves in some senses the problem of defining narrative units in a fictional world.

(3) The problem of describing *the principle dominating narrative organizations* and defining narrativity. This problem is demonstrated in the structuralist attempt to define a narrative logic based on a unique principle of organization connecting the facts and events of the narrative world. This conception is replaced in narrative semantics with one whereby narrative structure is presented as a structure of alternative courses of actualization. This theoretical re-orientation creates a more flexible and dynamic view of the structure of plot, and accounts for the way fictional courses of events are actualized in the practice of fiction-making.

The following two sections will therefore observe a dual point of view: on the one hand, it will be claimed, narrative semantics solves some of the problems raised in the heyday of structuralism by introducing a new paradigm into narrative theory; on the other hand, narrative semantics will be presented as a direct continuation of the conceptual line and of the type of questions expressed in the early structuralist phase.

Plot-models and their object of investigation

Plot has always been a central concept in narrative theory. This trivial observation actually reflects a complicated state of affairs in narratology. Narratology interprets the centrality of plot in two different ways:

(a) First, plot can be considered central to any description of narrative texts because it is assumed that the action-core of narrative texts can be isolated and analyzed.[5] Such an interpretation orients narrative theory toward isolating the narrative core or scheme from other, narrative or non-narrative components. In a typical phrasing, the minimal definition of a narrative is "the representation of at least

---

5 This interpretation is one that meets Genette's notion of narrative contents: story considered in itself regardless of medium of transmission. Yet, as shown below, narrative models are never concerned just with an event-scheme.

two real or fictive events or situations in a time sequence, neither of which presupposes or entails the other" (Prince, 1982: 4). This definition ties the concept of narrative to the presence of an event-sequence or to the representation of a process of change. In this respect action, or plot in the restricted sense, forms the minimal and necessary condition for producing a narrative text.

(b) The second interpretation of the centrality of plot manifests the dominance of an Aristotelian orientation in narrative theory. Here, plot, as the domain of action in narrative texts, is situated as a superordinate of character and of thought. When plot is tantamount to an overall event-structure, it points not only at the centrality of action to the definition of narrativity, but to the role of the action-domain in organizing the narrative text as a whole. Plot is perceived as an overall organizing principle, and it is assigned the dominant organizing function and the power of narrativizing other textual components.

These two interpretations of the centrality of plot in narrative theory produce a gap between minimal and maximal definitions of narrative: narrative is an abstraction and reconstruction of causally arranged events; it is also the structuring functions attributed to that narrative core whereby plot is defined as a principle of organization, "the intelligible whole that governs a succession of events in any story" (Ricoeur, 1981: 167). This discrepancy reflects the ambivalent place assigned to the concept of plot in narrative studies, and it is in turn reflected in the actual use to which the concept of plot is put in narrative theory.[6] This discrepancy is well demonstrated in Prince's recently published dictionary of narratology where the concept of plot is defined both as "the main incidents of narrative" and as "the global dynamic (goal-oriented and forward-moving) organization of narrative constituents which is responsible for the thematic interest (indeed, the very intelligibility) of a narrative and for its emotional effect" (Prince, 1987).

The apparent disjunction between these two interpretations of the concept of plot is however reconciled in the object of investigation of plot-models. Plot-models claim to describe the movement from event-sequences to action-structures; in practice they attempt to address the

---

6 It is clear that a theorist like Ricoeur does not identify himself with the narratological project; quite the opposite. Yet his writings also manifest the same symptomatic unclarity about whether narrative theory should account for necessary or sufficient conditions for narrativity.

question of how a sequence of events turns into a story. To put it differently, the question that structuralist plot-models have addressed is the question of the value added to a set of events which transforms this set into a narrative whole – a story.[7] In this respect the object of investigation of plot-models merges the two interpretations of the concept of plot.

Even when plot is identified with a formal scheme of events reconstructed from the narrative text, such a reconstruction already presupposes a pre-processing and an over-all view of the thematics of narrative. Plot, even in its minimal sense, is the outcome of narrative understanding. Thus, definitions of plot, ranging from the Aristotelian tradition which situates action above other story-components, through Formalist dealings with narrative organization to structuralist attempts to grasp the logic of narrative, all reflect a belief in the cohering power of plot. As it turns out, plot-models make a distinction between the minimal occurrence of an event-sequence in a narrative, and the sufficient conditions for narrativity. They attempt to accommodate, through the concept of plot, a much wider range of narrative phenomena: (a) the type of organization by virtue of which the narrative, in its totality, is given a form: narrative organization should account for the generation of events and for the dynamics of narrative progress from the beginning through the middle to an ending; (b) plot should account for the way in which the narrative text incorporates into its structure elements which are not connected or not subordinated to the event-sequence (descriptions, non-narrative propositions, non-actualized events).

Plot as the object of narratology is actually treated as a conceptual equivalent to narrative logic and to the outcome of narrative understanding. This has been noticed by Ricoeur who uses his observation to subvert structural narratology:

the term "plot" does not appear in the technical vocabulary of narrative semiotics. In truth, it could not find a place there, since it stems from the narrative understanding which semiotic rationality tries to provide an equivalent for or, better, a simulation of. (1985: 52)

The discrepancy between necessary and sufficient conditions for narrativity can consequently be motivated in terms of the dual

---

7 Note, again, that many (quasi) structuralists would however agree that the zero transformation of an event (of set of events) would also yield a story, necessary conditions for narrativity being satisfied.

intention behind plot-models. Note that despite almost a compulsive tendency to define and to set up elaborate terminologies in narrative theory, the concept of plot (and also of story and narrative) is often used in an obscure enough way to camouflage that discrepancy.[8] In any case, the notion of minimal story has to be distinguished from those features in terms of which the quality of stories as stories is judged (Rimmon-Kenan, 1983: 18). Prince, who in many ways represents the mainstream of narratology, claims that the narrativity of stories does not derive only from the existence of a minimal sequence of events. The latter is a necessary condition, but there are degrees of narrativity and, by itself, the fulfillment of the necessary condition does not yield a high degree of narrativity. Narratives of high narrativity "will not merely describe change and its results but fundamental changes and results. They will take us from the origin to the conclusion ... from the onset of heterogeneity and difference back to homogeneity and indifference" (p. 153). Beyond what narratives have in common (a minimal action-structure), and even beyond features which account for the specificity of any given narrative, there are, according to Prince, degrees of narrativity, there is the distinctiveness of narrative determined by nonformal criteria such as *wholeness*, the *point of the narrative* and *orientation*. Prince's full exploration of the concept of narrativity implies that what makes the narrativity of texts should be defined on a wider scale than what classical structuralism had indicated as its formal object of analysis. "Plot" is used to refer to more than just a representation of a process of change in narrative texts.

Indeed, if one considers the kind of theoretical problems that plot-models claim to solve, one finds that concepts like "plot," "*fabula*" and "narrative macrostructure" are ways in which narrative theory attempts to explain how plot structure is responsible for imposing order and for organizing meanings in narrative texts.[9] Moreover, plot

---

8 Typical examples to this effect are Culler (1975) and Toolan (1988) where plot-structure is undefined, and where the concept of "plot" seems to be used in referring to a narrative logic or rationale of an intuitive nature.

9 "Plot ... is the organizing line and intention of narrative, thus perhaps best conceived as an activity, a structuring operation elicited in the reader trying to make sense of those meanings that develop only through textual and temporal succession" (Brooks, 1984: 37).
Here, Brooks almost puts plot in the reader (though he also wants to keep it in the narrative).

is perceived as an organizing principle in terms of which the aesthetic organization of a narrative text is differentiated from reality. Plot turns an agglomeration of materials into a closed and significant narrative structure. This presupposition, reconstructed from plot-models, that plot is a pivotal concept to which all narrative components are subordinated is a curious one since it implies that it is not the nature of event-sequences with which plot-models are preoccupied; this presupposition is also incommensurable with explicit statements of purpose expressed in structuralist models. Thus Bremond concerns himself with and dedicates his model of narrative logic to "the logical constraint that any series of events, organized as narrative, must respect in order to be intelligible." Yet, the status of his central objective is put in doubt when he claims that:

All narrative consists of a discourse which *integrates a sequence of events of human interest into the unity of a single plot*. Without succession there is no narrative ... Neither does narrative exist without *integration into the unity of a plot*, but only chronology, an enunciation of a succession of uncoordinated facts. Finally, where *there is no implied human interest* (narrated events neither being produced by agents nor experienced by anthropomorphic beings), there can be no narrative, for it is *only in relation to a plan conceived by man that events gain meaning* and can be organized into a structured temporal sequence. (my emphases) (Bremond, 1980: 390)

This conception of plot as an order-imposing principle, a principle of coherence in the face of a variety of meanings and a patternless world, is a conception that recurs, in diverse phrasings, in all attempts to cope with narrative-structures in general and with plot-structure in particular. Malmgren (1988) claims that a fictional world is composed of two fictional systems: *world* and *story*. The relation between these two components is analogous, according to Malmgren, to the one holding between the lexicon and the syntax of a language system. In the same way that syntax, as a systematic set of rules governs the order and arrangement of lexical items in language, so story "connects and combines the various entities that make up the *world*" (ibid. 27). Malmgren attributes here to the notion of story the type of functions associated with plots. It is the systematic set of rules determining the links and the type of interactions among the constitutive parts of a world repertoire. The notion of "unified action" clearly goes back to Aristotle who defines plot as the source of unity and order for all other components of the narrative: "so the plot, being an imitation of an action, must imitate one action and that a whole, the structural union of the parts being such that, if any one of them is displaced or removed, the whole will be disjointed and disturbed. For the thing whose presence or absence makes no visible difference is not an organic part of the whole" (*Poetics*, ch. 8).

Such claims indicate that narrative theory in general and narratology in particular create a gap between the practice of orienting narrative models toward a core of action and the ultimate conclusions drawn by narrative theorists which refer to the overall cohering function attributed to the narrative. Furthermore, it seems that narratologists do not content themselves with that abstracted scheme of action that is narratology's official object of observation. Story, *fabula* and *histoire*, are not just the reconstructed events that form the nucleus of narrative texts but yet the all-embracing patterns which, through the principles of organization they reflect, provide the necessary coherence to the narrative text in its totality. It is therefore no accident that plot, which often appears as the term covering the totality of narrative, is so central to the definitions of narrative texts, and that it has precedence over other components of the *mythos*. Without it, sequences of events, which are also part of our actual world, could not have been transformed into the hermetic and unified structure of a narrative, the world mass could not have been turned into a narrative world: "Plot is the principle of interconnectedness and intention which we cannot do without in moving through the discrete elements – incidents, episodes, actions – of a narrative" (Brooks, 1984: 5).

This view of plot as an aesthetic structure that turns a random sequence of events into a significant structure, explains the fore-grounded place of plot in narrative theories and it serves as a convenient point of departure for understanding the rationale of plot-models.[10] Literary narrative has at its core more than a simple sequence of events, and the myth of plot-unity turns out to be an effective and far-reaching presupposition. The broad definition of plot, the range of narrative phenomena that narratology attempts to account for in

10 "...narrative is not limited to making use of our familiarity with the conceptual network of action. It adds to it discursive features that distinguish it from a simple sequence of action sentences" (Ricoeur, 1984: 56).
    And also "[plot] is a mediation between the individual events of incidents and a story taken as a whole. In this respect, we may say equivalently that it draws a meaningful story from a diversity of events or incidents ... or that it transforms the events or incidents into a story" (ibid.: 65).

terms of plot characteristics, constitute the background for understanding fictional narrativity and higher-order narrative organization.

Plot-models and structuralist ideology

Narrative models identify plot with the comprehensive unity of a
narrative structure, a theoretical conviction which orients narrative
theory towards dealing with two problems: one central problem
concerns principles of organization unique to narrative, the other has
to do with a definition of narrative units. These problems enfold the
wide range of questions pertinent to the study of narrative, and they
constitute the main criteria for testing the explanatory power of
narrative models. Structuralist descriptions of narrative units and
structuralist investment in the attempt to isolate a principle which
dominates narrative organization both reflect a concern with
"narrativity" (the definition of plot as a principle of overall unity) and
hence an interest in the concept of plot which transcends the official
object of description of narrative grammars and semiotics.

Plot-models can be classified according to the way in which they
delimit the *narrative unit* and to the level at which narrative units are
defined. A narrative unit is expressed through language: "Raskolnikov
lifted the axe." Such sentences can be grouped around a generalizing
proposition describing an event forming the surface narrative unit:
"Raskolnikov murders the old lady." The move from a linguistic unit
to a surface narrative unit should be describable through various
procedures of semantic integration. Such an integration could explain
how a linguistic sequence is turned into a narrative one. Barthes
(1966), for instance, describes a procedure of *naming a sequence*. In a
further process of abstraction, surface narrative structures are replaced
by a narrative unit like "crime" or "murder" abstracted from the
semantic content of the narrative text under consideration. This and
the next level of description require not just abstraction but also a
consideration of distributional relations between an event and its
results at a later stage of the narrative sequence. The definition of the
narrative unit is grounded on functional considerations which delimit
a narrative unit in terms of a deep narrative structure. At this stage, we
are already dealing with categories of a universal narrative grammar.
Raskolnikov's crime is represented on this level of abstraction not
according to its place in a chronological sequence of events but
according to the function it fulfills in a schematic narrative structure.

Categories composing a narrative grammar were variously termed and articulated. In a simplified manner one can say that the narrative sequence dealing with the murder of the old lady fulfills the function of "complication" or "problem." The difference between the two levels of abstraction is roughly the difference between Propp's paradigmatic functions and story grammars like Pavel's, Bremond's and others.[11] Propp defines the unit of *function* as "the act of a character, defined from the point of view of its significance for the course of the action" which assumes both the semantic content of the unit and its functional relations with other plot-constituents. Pavel, on the other hand, employs the categorial vocabulary of Move, Problem, Solution, Auxiliary, Tribulation, which may be understood as deep-level abstract categories, covering a great number of concrete situations.

The notion of narrative grammar − that narrative units are delimited and described according to their function in a deep narrative scheme − implies that events of the narrative are defined as syntactic units forwarding the narrative process. The content of a narrative unit is nothing but a contingent filling of a functional category. The kidnapping of the princess by the dragon can constitute a *problem* in one story and a *solution* (for the persecuted grooms) in another. The nonreferential approach has indeed dominated narratological grammars both of the type descending from Propp or Bremond, and of the type descending from the abstract semantic categories narrativized by Greimas. The moratorium on referential questions is apparent in definitions of narrative units, as it is in attempts to describe narrative-specific principles of organization. Both concepts manifest a similar interest in constructing a logical narrative mechanism free from semantic and referential considerations.

Note that "semantic" carries two distinct meanings in this chapter: it refers to considerations of content that figure in "bottom−top" models that arrive at categories of narrative grammar through the

---

11 A narrative unit can also be represented in an abstract semantic deep structure and not necessarily in a narrative deep structure. According to this structuralist view, initiated in the works of Levi-Strauss and continuing in Greimas' structural semantics, a story is constructed on the basis of an abstract semantic scheme, composed of abstract semantic categories of the form /x/ /non-x/, representing relations of opposition and negation. Such a semantic pattern constitutes a deep structure generating narrative structures.

See Jefferson (1977) for an exploration of Greimas' case-study of a Maupassant's narrative "Deux amis."

contents of specific units of text (which is the case in Barthes' sequence-naming operation, for instance). "Semantic" also refers to the abstract categories of semantic grammars that build their categories (à la Fillmore) on the basis of a semantic functionalism (as is the case in Greimas' structural semantics, but also in Pavel's move-grammar, and in Doležel's narrative semantics). Early structuralism claimed to be neutralized of semantic considerations in the first sense:

Literature had long enough been regarded as a message without a code for it to become necessary to regard it for a time as a code without a message. (Genette, 1982 [1964])

To locate the structuralist orientation in plot-models, it might be productive to note that definitions of narrative units may be aligned with one of two possible perspectives on narrative structures. Doležel (1978) proposes to distinguish between narrative models of a *thematic* type, an orientation best represented by Tomashevsky's concept of the *motif, and narrative models with a syntactic* orientation, represented by Propp's concept of a *function*. Doležel grounds this theoretical and methodological distinction on the difference between grounding narrative structures on thematic segmentations in a given text (through the story motifs), and viewing narrative structure through the prism of a deep level of abstraction in relation to which the function of a story unit is decided. Whereas the motif is delimited according to its position within a concrete narrative sequence (in *Crime and Punishment* the hero's penitence is a bound motif), the function is a syntactic category relatively autonomous in relation to the semantic content of a specific unit. What characterizes the syntactic approach is both the mapping of concrete semantic units (murder) by abstract semantic categories (complication) and the fact that the syntactic value of a semantic unit is determined on the basis of its overall functional relations with same-level units of action (its effect on the total structure of events).

Both orientations face a similar problem regarding the way one moves from narrative surface structures to narrative deep structures, yet, it is clear that a syntactic type of model has to account for a substantially different abstraction procedure from a theme-oriented motif description. One of the most problematic aspects of structuralist studies of narrative is the lack of an account of the formal procedures describing the passage from surface linguistic units to deep-structure units of the narrative *langue* (see Pavel, 1988).

Doležel points here to one of the substantial differences between the formalist concepts of *fabula* and *sujhet* and the narratological concept of a narrative grammar. Whereas the formalist orientation is mainly thematic (in the above sense), within the narratological framework, characterized by a strong anti-referentiality and a functionalist approach, the narrative text is viewed as a sign-system whose signified is a narrative abstract grammar. The signified of a narrative text is not described in semantic terms, or in terms of the world constructed by textual signs, but in terms of a deep narrative structure which maps every new act of narrative production. Thus, whereas Tomashevsky's thematics operates as a model for describing compositional and combinational procedures in concrete stories, the structuralist trend, at least in its explicit pronouncements of purpose, operates toward a definition of the syntactic rules which constitute a narrative grammar, and toward a description of narrative paradigms regardless of specific semantic contents.[12] In the work of Propp, for instance, specific units in the folk-tales under examination are perceived as *variables* of constant functions that is, as contingent contents of an abstract sequence of functions that form the narrative backbone of the entire corpus.

The problem of recovery procedures for arriving at syntactic narrative units is coupled with the problem of attempting to divorce the syntactic function of a unit from its semantic content, both leading to the need for a different type of narrative segmentation.

Plot-models differ in the type of principle isolated in order to define plot-structure. Since, as claimed above, plot should assign order to the totality of narrative, the question of the means through which plot can organize its discrete elements, thereby differentiating the external world from the world in its narrative–aesthetic guise, becomes of central concern. The question thus formulated does not necessarily appear in structuralist plot-models; yet, as I will suggest, attempts to isolate a formal principle of functional organization (defined in terms of causality, chronology or equivalence) are reflections of the need to answer this problem. In other words, attempts to isolate a singular

---

12 "... Its object [of the science of literature] could not be to impose a meaning on the work ... It cannot be a science of the content of works ... but a science of the *conditions* of content, that is to say of forms: it will concern itself with the variations of the meanings engendered and, so to speak, *engenderable* by works ... its object will no longer be the full meanings of the work but on the contrary the empty meaning which underpins them all" (Barthes, 1987: 73–74).

organizing principle prevalent in the narrative, is actually a way for explaining how plot turns event-sequences into a structured closed and complete whole. Furthermore, I would claim that the attempt to isolate organizing principles specific to narrative reflects the anti-referential inclination of structuralist poetics; the totality of a story can be reduced to one narrative principle of organization since the semantics of a given narrative and its specific world-structure are disregarded. The incompatibility between the attempt to describe the total order of plot and the attempt to reduce this totality to one dominant principle of organization, is typical of structuralist descriptions of plot-structure, and it reflects the gap between action-oriented definitions and story (narrativity)-oriented definitions of plot, a gap deeply rooted in structuralist poetics from its very beginning.

One of the characteristics of structuralist narrative models is the attempt to isolate and define the logic of narrative. The question is: what type of relations hold among elements of the narrative and determine the narrative overall structure? Plot-organization is described, both within semantic (Greimassian) models and within syntactic models, according to various principles: causality, chronology and equivalence. These are apparently three qualitatively different principles: whereas chronology is a mimetic organizing principle, causality is a logical principle and equivalence can be described as a semantic type of organization. *Chronology* means that a temporal relation exists among events reconstructed from the text since the ordering of events follows a life-like (and hence extratextual) pattern of temporal order. *Causality*, on the other hand, means that plot structure reveals a pattern of solidarity among its parts and that plot forms a closed system of interconnectedness between events. Functionality and the distributional relations which tie together plot components and create a plot dynamics seem to me to lead in narratology to a type of determinism where beginning, middle and end phases of the narrative are perceived as equally present and as given.[13]

I will concentrate on the concept of causality, since in narratological

13 To prove this point, it is enough to examine the way Popper describes the intuitive idea of determinism:
"... the future co-exists with the past; and the future is fixed, in exactly the same sense as the past. Though the spectator [in motion-picture film] may not know the future, every future event, without exception, might in principle be known with certainty, exactly like the past, since it exists in the same sense in which the past exists" (1982: 5).

studies time and chronology are often perceived as part of a surface structure and not as immanent to deep narrative schemata.[14] Brooks and Ricoeur both draw our attention to the fact that narratological studies miss the dynamics of temporality in plot as part of their ideology. As Ricoeur expresses it, narratological rationality "requires for its models of the deep grammar of narrative an achronological status as a matter of principle, in relation to which the diachrony of transformations, displayed on the surface of a narrative, appears derived and inessential" (1985: 159).

Unlike diachrony, the principle of causality in its theoretical formulation is presumed to be a part of the deep structure of narrative grammar. Following Aristotle who compares history to dramatic plot and attributes a precedence to the logic of action over chronology, Barthes argues that temporality is not a logical principle and therefore cannot form the ground for a narrative grammar. He claims that the temporal connection between events is no more than a referential illusion. The only temporality that exists in a narrative text is not the reality-like temporality but a semiotic time of the narrative system requiring the introduction of elements one after the other. Consequently, Barthes' view requires that chronology be replaced by logic.[15]

Pavel (1985), whose plot-model was proposed twenty years later, provides the formal explanation for rejecting chronology as a principle of plot-organization. Pavel shows that in deep narrative structures there is a level of abstraction in which the order of presenting plot-components (events) in the narrative tree, differs from the temporal order of their occurrence (33ff.). Pavel concludes that chronology is not part of the deep level of plot but of the surface structure of the narrative. That is to say, chronological links exist only on a surface narrative level, whereas the deep narrative structure is autonomous in relation to the chronological order of events. Such claims motivate the focal position of causal-functional relations in structuralist models. Although in practice it is rather difficult to disconnect causality from chronology, causality is conceived as the immanent principle of narrative structuration.[16]

---

14 In classical structuralism this is true mainly of Greimas, less so of Bremond and Todorov.

15 Note that time, as an essential principle of narrative, can be considered part of the deep structure because at the very least a narrative includes one event, one change of state from anterior to posterior.

16 Not only does causality imply chronological relations, both principles are in fact present in narratological plot-models. Barthes, for instance, after expressing the

Narratological studies of plot make a direct connection between plot-structure and causality. The more hermetic the causal connection between events, the more apparent the way in which plot imposes order on narrative elements. From Forster to Prince, precedence is given to causality as the central principle of narrative structuring. Forster (1927) distinguishes plot from story by differentiating temporal connections from causal ones. Prince, who relates causality to degrees of narrativity, likewise underscores its centrality to plot-structure. The principle of causality is of special interest since it reflects the attempt of structuralists to isolate a logical principle unique to narrative. First, if events of the plot obey a logical causality, it will be possible to understand in what sense a narrative manifests a unified, complete structure whereas reality is just an accidental aggregate of materials. Second, the connection between problem and solution in the action-structure is a logical connection between cause and effect, and this causal pattern can be actualized in endless possibilities and contents. As shown above, the logical connection between cause and effect does not require a chronological contiguity, and it is therefore appropriate for defining a narrative-scheme which can be semantically and sequentially actualized in endless ways. Causality is welcomed by narratological models since it is possible to deal in terms of causality with organizations immanent to narrative while disregarding their meaning. The attractiveness of causality also derives from its being, in principle, an objective kind of relation which does not depend on interpretation or on the subjective reconstructions of one reader or another. Such a logical principle can also explain various aspects of plot-structure: it can explain turning points in the plot, it can explain the centrality of events to narrative structures, and it can explain why a plot has a beginning, middle and end. In other words, the functionalist orientation in structuralist poetics substantially depends on the prevalence of causal links between events of the story.

Is causality indeed a consistent, unique and objective principle of organizing events in a narrative text? Causality implies a link between the glass falling off the table and its being broken. The two events are causally linked (although the latter is not a necessary effect of the cause: the glass can fall without being broken). Yet it is sufficient to examine any plot to see that causality, as a principle for organizing the

---

theoretical ground for distinguishing between the two, proceeds to describe a plot-model which makes use of mimetic chronology.

narrative, includes causal relations of various kinds: causal relations proper to which are added functional relations among aims, problems and results decided retrospectively on the grounds of a narrative understanding. Causality in the strict sense rarely explains the move from one event of the plot to the next.

The eclectic type of arrangement implied in the principle of causality can be illustrated in the case of "Oedipus Rex." The following events are all part of the Oedipus story (not all, though, are in the drama):

1 Predictions about Oedipus' fate.
2 Oedipus is expelled and then is adopted by the king of Corinth.
3 Upon discovering the prophecies, Oedipus runs away from the palace of his adoptive parents.
4 Oedipus kills a nobleman on the road.
5 Oedipus solves the Sphinx's riddle.
6 Oedipus is crowned and marries Jocasta.
7 The plague.
8 Revelation of the truth about Oedipus' identity.
9 Revelation of the truth about the identity of Laius' murderer.

Structuralist attempts to account for the structure of plot, to isolate a syntactic narrative principle of organization, raise many problems. In the plot of *Oedipus Rex* there are various types of links which are causal in different senses. Some events stand in relations of psychological motivation (hearing the Sphinx's prophecy motivates Oedipus' escape from Corinth); some are based on direct causality (6 causes 7); some just (remotely) enable other events (5 enables 6; 4 enables 6),[17] and some causal links depend on conventional assumptions. Moreover, since we deal here with a case where the entire sequence unfolds within a deterministic teleology (the gods will all events and so are the final cause of all effects), a specific event, like the marriage of Oedipus to Jocasta, causes the plague only according to the thematic rationalization characteristic of the drama, where such a sin brings about the gods' rage. The remote dependence of the plague on the marriage between mother and son can be demonstrated by the fact that these are events brought about by two different agents. The plague, which is the gods' doing, is an outcome of Oedipus' sin only in a world where it is normatively assumed that divine and human deeds are correlated. Yet, likewise, events linked by direct causality in

17 See Shen (1990) for an analysis of types of causality and the logical relations each type entails.

non-deterministic worlds, always assume a conventionally (or contextually) based causality (cancer is an effect of tobacco use only in a world where smokers assume a causal relation between the two; with no such assumption, cancer cannot be said to be caused by tobacco use). In accounting for the relations among events, and for the interaction between action domains of different agents, a strict logical principle of causality is evidently insufficient.

Causality turns out to provide a problematic explanation for the plot-structure of this narrative. While the structuralist "syntactic" methodology strives to isolate and abstract the narrative *langue* and the logic of the narrative system, the structure of events does not seem to follow a strict causal principle; events are subjected to an action-structure in which the constituent parts are functionally linked, which means that causal links originate from a prior integration or from a narrative understanding. The attempt of narratology to elucidate the concept of plot in terms of a logical principle of organization (causality) should be seen, partly, as a reflection of a presupposition characteristic of all plot-models: the presupposition that plot is a central and dominant structuring principle of narrative texts. By tracing the way structuralist plot-models transgress the theoretical principles they set for themselves, it is possible both to follow the move from traditional narratology to what is commonly termed *narrative semantics*, and to explain from whence the fallacies of the narratological conceptions of plot emerge.

Plot-models attempt to isolate the principles ordering narrative texts (causal chronology or psychological causality linking events, spatial relations between descriptive components, oppositional relations between characters) when, as it turns out, plot structure is no more than an eclectic set of ordering rules, which only together, and from a functional perspective, can explain the dynamics of plot, and the relations between components of the narrative.

In the foregoing discussion, various difficulties emerging from the suppositions and practice of classical narratology, have been enumerated:

(a) that segmentation into narrative units cannot but combine thematic (bottom-top) and syntactic (top-bottom) procedures;

(b) that narrative organization cannot be based solely on logical relations of functional causality. Narrative structure derives from an aggregate of possible semantic relations (equivalence, chronology, causality, motivation).

Structuralist models have been concerned with constructing a *narrative logic* within a *syntactic model* and in view of an *antireferential ideology*, which led to an impasse (since causality and functionality presuppose a prior semantic integration). It is in response to structuralism that more recent narrative theories propose to replace the above with a comprehensive model of *narrative semantics*.

Narrative semantics – from syntactic to semantic plot-models

In view of various difficulties involved in structuralist plot-models, attempts were made to situate narrative logic elsewhere, to relate the logic of narrative to a more general grammar of texts where semantic notions (like coherence, semantic axioms and maxims active in fiction, modalities) are conceived of as "the base, formative component" (Doležel, 1976: 129). Indeed, one of the main claims against structuralist poetics was that the descriptions it provided of narrative language could not account for the semiological specificity of narrative texts. Definitions of narrative units provided by structuralist poetics were arbitrary, the principles of narrative organization definable only in view of the meaning structure of a specific text, and the connection between narrative events almost never a priori causal. Structuralist studies of narrative structures, being basically teleological and functional, cannot isolate an autonomous logic of narrative which is describable outside a specific plot. As Peter Brooks claims in justifying the association he makes between the Freudian psychoanalytic concept of desire for death and the narrative notion of an ending "the narrative must tend toward its end, seek illumination in its own death. Yet this must be the right death, the correct end" (103). An ending is not autonomously correct outside the meaning structure of a specific life, of a specific narrative.

The anti-referential ideology that explains the persevering attempt to talk about a syntactic logic of narrative dominated structuralist thought for some time, until it started to give way to what Pavel describes as a reconsideration of "the moratorium on referential issues" (1986: 10). The structuralist program, from its initial formulations (in the works of Levi-Strauss, Barthes, Greimas and Todorov) to its later manifestations in the narratology of Prince, Bal, Rimmon-Kenan and others, situates in the center of its project, paradigmatic structures of a narrative syntax or of a narrative *langue*. Ideologically, the preoccupation with narrative paradigms excludes any dealings with the level of meaning and with specific semantic organizations. No wonder one of the main arguments against structuralism pointed at the fact that in view of the notion of empty forms, structuralist poetics was not really capable of addressing the semiology of narrative texts and that therefore its concentration on the abstract level of common narrative structures was doomed to failure.

The shift from the structuralist belief in a narrative logic to narrative semantics is a natural outcome of the difficulties and dead-ends encountered by classical narratology. As mentioned above, conceptual and procedural problems emerging from classical structuralism created the need for alternative, or rather rectified models that would incorporate what was learnt from the earlier phase of structuralism. New narrative models showed a growing awareness that a text semantics should be the base for any text grammar and that, in the case of narrative, abstract narrative structures should be tied to semantic constructions. This theoretical orientation is illuminating in the account it provided of the semantics inherent to narrative grammars, in this way carrying the structuralist project to more fruitful directions.

It is already evident in Barthes' early work (1966a) that the contents of story-units are taken into account in constructing models of narrative structures. The procedures for moving from units of text to narrative categories and functions are implemented through processes of semantic integration as reflected in the titles or headings given to narrative sequences. The need to relate narrative grammar to a semantic domain is already apparent in early structuralist plot-models, and it has become more pronounced in later developments in narrative theory where a semantics of narrative is assigned various places of prominence. Culler (1980), for instance, expresses some profound doubts about the possibility of reconstructing a logic of narrative and he can hence serve as a handy example in tracking down these developments. Culler investigates the concepts of *fabula* and *sujhet* with a skepticism which undermines any attempt to divorce narrative syntax from semantics. Culler argues that *fabula* and *sujhet* do not represent a certain logic of plot-organization (organization by the chronology of narrated events in the *fabula* as opposed to chrono-logical deviations in the *sujhet*); rather, they represent an order of a thematic nature applied to a given text. The *fabula* is not a pattern of story-materials abstracted of modes of narration, but a structure which derives from narrative modes of signification. Hence, the relations between *fabula* and *sujhet* in "Oedipus Rex" are not the outcome of chronological deformation (Laius' murder by his son is recounted at the end of the narrative chain but belongs to the initial moves of the *fabula*); Culler suggests considering the place of the event in the *sujhet* as indicative of its function; it is the outcome of the narrative meaning-structure, an outcome necessitated by everything which precedes it. Laius' death is not caused by circumstances or fatal prophecies, but by the demands of plot-structure making Laius' murder by Oedipus retroactively unavoidable. In Culler's view every narrative is articulated in terms of a dual logic: the logic of chronology and causality, and the logic of signification (the order of events in the *fabula* of *Oedipus Rex* corresponds to a thematic structure of truth revelation and exposure to one's true identity).

Although Culler's proposal here constitutes more of a provocation than a proposal for alternative formal procedures for activating a narrative semantics, he does raise an important doubt regarding the ability of narratology to explain the dynamics of plot in terms of a narrative grammar. Note also that Culler points here at the need to make room for text semantics within the narratological paradigm itself.[18]

Plot as a constellation of possible worlds

The orientation of narrative is a substantial problem which many plot-models succeed in evading. Most plot-models describe the structure of the narrative as a given. This is possible because the functional principle immanent to structuralism dictates that plot and plot-dynamics are always viewed retrospectively; from a functionalist point of view all parts of the plot are equally present. Both syntactic and thematic-semantic models express the view that only the narrative ending can determine plot structure:

By simply *retelling* the story we immediately discover what may be omitted without destroying the coherence of the narrative and what may not be

18 Culler, to be more specific, shows that the plot-structure obeys both a syntactic type of logic and a semantic structuration. Beginning, middle and end are therefore not just units in a causal chain but also functions in a structure of signification. The identity of Laius' murderer not only constitutes the last unit in a causal chain but it also opens up the complication around which the plot is structured. Events recorded as deviant in terms of natural chronology, can be regarded as thematically essential and naturally positioned.

omitted without disturbing the connection among events. (Tomashevsky, 1965: 68)

Such plot-models often acknowledge the functional dependence of the narrative structure on its ending: "many narratives can be viewed as teleologically determined ... Narrative often displays itself in terms of an end which functions as its (partial) condition, its magnetizing force, its organizing principle" (Prince, 1982: 157). For the very reason that plot is viewed from a functional–retrospective point, such plot-models will tend to describe narrative structure on the basis of factually presented events. The hallmark of narrative is assurance, claims Prince,[19] and unactualized possibilities are divorced from plot-structures.

One of the claims against such views has to do with their inability to account for plot-orientation and direction. It was this very problem which Bremond addressed in his writings, describing plot-structure as a mechanism of choices among alternative narrative sequences. Every point in a narrative chain opens up alternative options for actualization. In similar terms Barthes (1966) refers to *cardinal functions* in plot as being "the risky moments of a narrative" (95). Note that modal categories have also entered classical structuralism yet clearly remained at the fringes of narrative models. One can refer in this context to Todorov's grammar (1977) where *mood (the relation which a character sustains with a narrative proposition) is among the secondary categories* of the grammar. The same is true of Greimas' grammar (1977) where modal utterances form one class in the typology of narrative utterances, a class determined by the specific semantic restrictions imposed by modal classemes (like "savoir"). The presence of modal categories even in early structuralist models points, however, at the link between these early models and models of narrative semantics that officially place the play among alternative modes of actualization at their center.

Within narrative semantics Eco (1979) describes plot-structure as a process of activating some semantic possibilities, while narcotizing others. The *fabula* is eventually structured as a process of choosing among alternative courses or possibilities of actualization and the

19 "If narrativity is a function of the discreteness and specificity of the (sequences of) events presented, it is also a function of the extent to which their occurrence is given as a fact (in a certain world) rather than a possibility or probability. The hallmark of narrative is assurance" (Prince, 1982: 149).

narrative structure is the outcome of this process. The options opened by the text, the fact that the narrative is a structure of diverging alternatives, are reflected in the reader's active participation which includes inferences, forward anticipations and gap filling.

Plot-models describing plot-structure as a process of selection among alternative courses of events and states show how the narrative creates its structure through linear dynamics, yet they too cannot explain the orientation of a narrative because of their forward-oriented perspective, and because they lack modal concepts which could account for alternative logics of narrative change. In a Bremondian approach the narrativity of narrative is dependent on the particular course selected to be actualized, whereas in more or less teleological approaches, the narrativity of narratives depends on a satisfying ending.

Plot-dynamics can be approached retrospectively or linearly. The articulation of modally oriented plot-models in recent years derives from some of the narratological conceptions on narrative structure. In what follows I will briefly present the solutions proposed by models of plot within the framework of a possible world semantics, in a natural continuation to structuralist models of plot. It is a system which answers some of the substantial objections to structuralist studies of plot.

We have seen in earlier chapters that the theory of possible worlds was developed in modal logic as an attempt to assign concrete ontological content to modal concepts. Possible worlds have produced several metaphors which have proven to be useful working hypotheses for the study of narrative. The metaphor of *possibility* adopted by narrative semiotics refers to procedures of actualization and inference which concern individuals and properties belonging to different possible worlds imagined by the reader as possible outcomes of the *fabula* (see Eco, 1979: 217ff.). The other metaphor related to possible worlds, and which bears on developments in modes of theorizing about plots, emerges from the idea of *a plurality of worlds*. The idea here is that possible worlds enable us to describe the universe not as a single, determinate and determined set of facts but as a constellation of possible and impossible situations. Along the same line, it is proposed to describe narrative texts (and narrative worlds) as composed of a constellation of states of affairs that are modally different. The plurality of worlds enables us to describe the inner semantic structure of a fictional narrative in terms of a modal system:

The narrative text is represented as an ordered ensemble of CP worlds [textualized worlds that establish the relation between logical world-systems and the narrative text]. (Vaina, 1977: 4, my translation)

The idea that a narrative text composes a constellation of possible worlds, that each narrative situation is modally indexed, and that a selective actualization of narrative possibilities produces an action-structure has opened a new direction in narrative theory.

One of the forerunners in the study of plot within the conceptual system of possible worlds is Vaina (1977) who describes the possible worlds of the narrative text from the strict perspective of a logic semantician and in this respect stays very close to concepts of modal logic and semantics. Once the text has been segmented into its worlds (each world or sub-world consists of a set of truth-valued propositions that form a state of affairs), one can continue identifying the entities that compose the textual world. The properties of these entities are then specified (that is, an inventory of individuals and properties is elaborated), and the relations between individuals' properties are established. At the next stage changes of state are described, and the concept of *event* is introduced into the model through the notion of a change of state. The history of the textual world is composed of transitions from one total state of the world to another. The logic of change and action is therefore a derivative of the logic of state as a set of propositions. We can easily see how action vocabulary is directly connected and even derived from the vocabulary of semantic logic.

The last part of the model aims to describe not just the structure of change but the structure of the *fabula*. For that purpose modal concepts are employed:

It seems reasonable to us to pose the problem of the attitude of individuals vis-à-vis a sequence of events in which they participate, or even vis-à-vis certain "states of affairs" determining the choice of a future action. One operates on this level with a (modal) logic of propositional attitudes. (7)

Propositional attitudes (like recall, dream, perceive, hope, desire, believe, know, ignore) divide the possible worlds of the text into those compatible with the particular attitude of an individual and those incompatible with it.

This basic model proposed by Vaina was later succeeded by modified versions which created a more articulated integration of narratological concepts with the semantic concepts emerging from the possible worlds framework. Paradigmatic examples are Pavel (1980) and Ryan (1985). Ryan appropriates Pavel's main supposition that "a plot is split into *more than one* narrative domain, and is accordingly divided into several distinct sets of propositions. The nature of these propositions is heterogeneous. A domain contains ontological, epistemological, axiological and action propositions ... " (106). Ryan indeed starts with the supposition that narrative worlds are modally stratified, thus adding a dimension to the basic semantic model of narrative logic proposed by Vaina. According to her claim "the worlds of the modal system of narration fall into two main categories: (1) those with an absolute or autonomous existence; and (2) those whose existence is relative to somebody, that is, which exist through a mental act of a character" (720). In other words, the analogy between the inner structure of a narrative world and the inner structure of the universe is grounded on the fundamental distinction between factual propositions and modalized propositions. The narrative universe has an actual world of its own, free of specific propositional attitudes: the domain regarded as actual and real by the characters of the narrative universe. Other domains of the narrative universe are subjected to propositional attitudes and are therefore relative to the world-representing acts of individuals, their beliefs and wishes, predictions and inventions.

Modal differentiations added to narrative logic produce a hierarchical dimension which privileges one domain of events and states as the *factual domain* of the narrative universe; the other domains are viewed as *relative worlds* of the narrative universe (epistemic or knowledge worlds, hypothetical worlds, intention worlds, wish worlds, worlds of moral values, obligation worlds and alternate universes). Ryan adds a dynamic dimension to the modal conception of world-structure by integrating it with narrative concepts of plot construction. The relations built up between worlds can result in *productive conflicts* when the individual experiencing the conflict "is in a position, and is willing to take steps toward its resolution" (733). Note that the metaphor of "possible worlds" not only allows for an account of semantic principles that modally structure the narrative universe, but also serves as a conceptual instrument for describing the structure of plot and its movement.[20] The description of a fictional world as a constellation of possible worlds (including a factual domain)

20 Note that in all these models from Vaina to Pavel, one can detect a slide from narrative to fiction. The narrativity of worlds is tackled through modal concepts of actuality and possibility, concepts which were primarily adopted by literary theory to account for the fictionality of worlds.

is combined with a narrative logic.[21] The advantages of such a model for describing the narrative structure of plot over more traditional narrative semantics, are significant:

(1) The semantic procedures for describing narrative worlds and their interrelations are at the same time paradigmatic rules describing the components and logic of the narrative system and operational rules for describing plot movement. In this respect, the description of plot as a modal structure overcomes the theoretical discrepancy, so typical of structuralist poetics, between paradigmatic rules and syntagmatic operations.

(2) The emergence of a narrative semantics from modal conceptualizations produces plot-models which elude one of the most serious problems in structuralist studies of plot. Within the conceptual framework of modal semantics the narrative unit is perceived as a relational situation holding between a set of possible worlds. Such a semantics of narrative generates a segmentation which has the following advantages:

(a) the narrative unit takes into account, at the same time, the overall narrative structure and its linear build up; that is, a given narrative situation necessarily reflects its position in the total plot-structure, and it incorporates situations which constitute alternative options for plot-development;

(b) the dynamics of plot and the concept of change are inherent to the delineation of any narrative situation;

(c) a narrative state of affairs contains syntactic and semantic information which derives from a general logic of narrative, but it also demonstrates the particular laws established by a given narrative world; thus, in a psychological novel the relations among events mostly depend on mental causality and motivation (types of causation are only classifiable within a general semantics of narrative); the specific type of mental motivation dominating the narrative has to do with the concrete semantic rules operative in a given text. In addition to those axioms that every narrative postulates, there are ramifying variants that are world-specific.

(3) The relations implied in concepts such as states of affairs, productive conflicts, and constellations of possible worlds are such that they enable narrative semantics to exit the boundaries of the

---

21 "... le récit ne comporte pas qu'un seul état d'affaires mais plutôt une succession de mondes inscrite dans une temporalité representée par la structure narrative elle-même" (Chateau, 1976: 214).

actual. Eco (1979) has shown the need for describing all the shared factors and knowledge frames involved in the semiotic process of narrative understanding. He insisted that narrative structure cannot be accounted for unless the totality of knowledge a narrative text activates is taken into consideration. It is apparent that within such a conceptual framework it is possible to describe the way in which the narrative text incorporates elements which are not connected or not subordinated to the event-sequence (descriptions, non-narrative propositions, non-actualized events). Plot-structure includes both factual domains and non-actual domains of a narrative or non-narrative nature.

(4) The concept of *productive conflict* is both a comprehensive concept (a conflict can be activated by any principle of narrative organization) and a concept that takes into account the specific semantic and syntactic laws operative in a given narrative world. For this very reason, describing the dynamics of plot in terms of productive conflicts certainly provides a more fruitful mode for describing the logic of plot advancement.

This chapter has traced stages in the history of narratological studies, from classical structuralism to current semantics of possible worlds, as stages located along one continuous line of theorizing about plot-structures. These stages have indicated that, first indirectly and then explicitly, semantic and thematic considerations have permeated the outright syntactic functionalism that had characterized earlier phases in narrative theory. This overall gradual change can be detected in the current centrality of narrative semantics over syntax; in the replacement of attempts to describe a logic of narrative around a single principle with a more dynamic and eclectic view of narrative organization; and in the movement from an anti-referential conception of narrative to a renewed interest in the referent and in the structure of the narrative universe. These very levels of change are indirect reflections on the distinctive conventions activated in the context of fictional narrative and they indicate the tacit supposition that fictional narratives are thematically unified and structured. Hence the need detectable in the history of narrative theory to supplant syntactic functionalism with narrative semantics reflects the belief that in fictional action-structures syntactic and thematic-semantic components interact. The need to replace a single principle of organization with a variety of organizing possibilities further reflects the nature of fictional events organized in a plot; plot being a comprehensive structure in which actualized events form only part of the overall narrative (the belief in unity constituted through heterogeneity). The urge to suppress an anti-referential conception of narrative likewise emerged from the need to make room for questions about ontology and reference, questions so central to defining the unique status of fictional narrative that constructs and refers to its own universe. Thus, although fictional narratives are not necessarily different "objectively" from nonfictional narratives,[22] the understander of fiction approaches the question of narrative emplotment with specific expectations for high integrativity, for an overall thematic structure and for a representational relationship with the real world.

22 Questions of narrativity and "storiness" also occupy a central place in current theories of narrative in general; see in this context Vilensky, 1982.

❖❖

6

Focalization and fictional perspective

❖❖

Is focalization specific to fiction?

Worlds, both actual and fictional, are discoursive constructs. Worlds are therefore dependent on instances of discourse responsible for the selection and arrangement of world components. Since information about worlds always has a source, a world can be viewed as being mediated by a variety of speakers and positions; these mediating positions operate on world-components determining their nature and their status in a given world. It is the perspective-dependency of worlds that detain us from opposing fiction to reality; all worlds, including the actual one, are perspective-dependent and hence only versions of reality. Yet the dependence of a world on a perspective is varied: each type of world establishes its own dependency relation with the perspective presenting or representing it.

Where are these perspectives located relative to the world on which they operate? The fictional world, as other world-types, contains among its sets of objects, a set of perspectives interacting with all other sets of objects contained in that world. Yet, if worlds are, if not constituted by discourse (as in Goodman, 1978), at least mediated by discourse, the problem is whether in the case of a fictional world a unique type of interaction between mediating positions and world-elements is assumed. That is, can we distinguish a fictional domain of points of view from nonfictional types of interaction between worlds and perspectives? Does the fact that in the fictional world both world-components and perspectives are fictional affect the type of re-lationship assumed between these two sets of elements? The dependence of worlds in general and of world-versions on discourses that construct or mediate them can be demonstrated in the notion of authority underlying a world construction. The cultural effects of more or less authoritative versions of the fictional world (presented by an omniscient narrator, by an unreliable narrator and so forth) are analogous to gradations of authority revealed when we compare the reality-version of a scientist or a logician to that of a sham or a politician. The fact that all worlds obey grades of authority is presumedly what enabled literary theory of point of view to describe the conventions of literary authentification and authority control in acts of narration without even addressing the question of fictionality of the facts constructed through those very points of view.

A perspectival arrangement of elements generates a *modally structured universe*. Yet in fiction, as has been noticed by several scholars (Ryan, 1985, Martinez-Bonati, 1983, Doležel, 1980) the authority of fictional speakers and narrators determines the factual or nonfactual nature of propositions about the fictional universe; that is, as readers of fiction we follow the authoritative say-so of a speaker in establishing the facts of fiction. In literary contexts, then, authority is conceived as a convention attributing more power of construction to an external speaker, and less power to an internal and restricted speaker. Once a speaker has been situated outside the fictional world with omniscience and omnipotence on his side, the events and situations narrated are likely to be viewed by the reader as facts of the fictional world. In short, a higher degree of authority with which the speaker is equipped determines the degree of authenticity or factuality of propositions originating from that speaker. Variations of authority produce a fictional world whose structure is fundamentally modal, containing sets of fictional facts alongside sets of relativized elements attributed to characters' knowledge, beliefs, thoughts, predictions. The interaction of speakers with propositions produces a world hierarchically organized where facts, quasi-facts and nonfacts constitute the totality of the world. In view of these aspects of fictional mediation and the world-structure thereby produced, fictional worlds become self-sufficient: no unexpected discovery of facts about a real-historical Hamlet can change the fictional facts established regarding that character's self with the help of an authoritative textual source.

The hierarchy of world components according to degrees of factuality does not only derive from the authority behind speaking subjects; prior to the fictional world's being transmitted by a voice, components of the world interact with perceiving subjects, with focalizers that act as the primary determinants of degrees of factuality. Focalization precedes narration in this respect and like narration, I would claim, where object of narration cannot be abstracted from mode of narration, focalization is inseparable from the focalized object.

Focalization and fictional perspective

The concept of *focalization*, introduced by Genette in 1972, was destined to cover one central aspect of mediation in texts. Focalization will also serve as a central metaphor in this chapter illustrating the operation of perspectives in fictional worlds; it will be shown that when *narrative motifs*[1] are considered on the level of focalization (and not on the level of narration),[2] the identity of the focalizer and the type of focalization carried out pre-determine the degree of authenticity or the degree of (fictional) factuality eventually assigned to the narrative speech-act. Consequently, types of focalization are significant in accounting for the degree of authenticity assigned to narrative motifs: each type of focalization ascribes a different degree of authenticity to fictional entities. The fact that the authenticity of world components is dependent on modes of perception and narration is a distinctive feature of fictional world-construction.

The modal structure of the fictional universe is hence produced by the interaction between entities and focalizers that are two sets of world components. This interaction produces a world structured according to varying degrees of authenticity of the narrative motifs involved. This structure reflects another facet of the autonomy of fictional worlds: a fictional world provides its own criteria for discerning fact from nonfact, and for distinguishing authenticated from nonauthenticated domains. Intraworld criteria of authenticity are generated by the system of focalization and narration. Both fictional and actual world-models are modally structured. The differences are nevertheless significant, and they have to do with the global conventions instigated when understanding fiction. These conventions are specifically reflected in the way perspectives and points of view are interpreted in fiction.

(1) The main difference between fictional worlds and worlds which constitute versions of reality is that the latter assume that beyond all versions there is *the world as it is*. As a result, in nonfictional contexts one can assume that, ontologically speaking, the perspectival arrangement of a world remains hypothetically independent of the very elements this arrangement makes accessible. In fictional contexts it is not only that world-components are filtered through perspectival

---

1 A narrative motif is a set of fictional entities that form a narrative unit (a unit is defined relative to the narrativity-constraints pertaining to a given world).

2 The distinction between *focalization* and *narration* clearly optimizes, in theory, what are, in practice, two inseparable facets of mediating information. Note also that focalization has heretofore mainly been explored in narrative texts.

positions, the interaction between the two sets is all-encompassing. Perspectives affect our ability to reconstruct a world and they motivate the way a world is characterized and structured because, ontologically speaking, in fiction we do not assume that world-components exist prior to or independently of the perspectives arranging them.[3]

(2) In reality-versions, facts of the world do not maintain an a priori correlation with types of focalization: the factual core of the world is independent of perspectival arrangements.[4] If one hesitantly expresses the formula water $= H_2O$ as a belief, this attitude of the speaker could not change the chemical factuality of the formula. The validity of propositions about the world is not affected by the attitude or authority of speakers. In actual contexts nonfactual domains are regarded as hypothetical non-actual domains; that is, whatever passes as having a doubtful factual status cannot be considered part of actuality. In fiction, however, nonfactual domains are not necessarily non-actual they are just relativized with respect to a given narrating or focalizing source. In fiction we face a strict correspondence between types of focalization and degrees of factuality.

(3) In the fictional world model the source of authority generating a modal structure is itself fictional, which means that there are no a priori criteria of validation for fictional facts. The norm for determining authenticity is internal to the fictional world. There is nothing immanent to fictional world-components that determines their degree of factuality in the fictional world: a factual narrative motif might

3 There can be no analysis of meaning or of the information about specific referents and frames without considering the dimension of speech and position. The same is true in reverse. In order to grasp the position of a speaking (or perceiving) character we must understand his place in the fictional world (Hrushovski, 1979: 374).

4 By relating here to the factual core of the universe I do no more than quote the accepted version of philosophical realism about the actual world; a convenient version since it acts as a foil to the way fictional worlds are perceived. Yet, my point still holds even if an opposite view is taken into account, one that views this "realist" version as illusory (as do philosophers such as Goodman and Rorty), and sees the factual core of the world as no more than an accepted belief, version or interpretation of the world. Even if facts are regarded as no more than institutional interpretations, a chemical fact, for instance, will be regarded as valid in scientific discourse even if the majority of world population is ignorant of this fact or has no access to it. Therefore, whether the world beyond all versions of it is not believed to exist or whether it is just viewed as inaccessible to us *as it is*, is of no consequence to the present topic. Questions of metaphysics and ontology do not have to be settled to proceed in theorizing about the mode of being of fiction.

represent a supernatural element or events that contradict each other. If the authoritative say-so of a speaker establishes the fictional existence of a square circle, this impossibility becomes a fictional fact. Authenticity in fiction is hence not restricted to specific types of facts. Since, in fiction, motifs are not inherently devoid of the ability to become (fictional) world-facts, the convention according to which world components are distributed into factual and nonfactual domains is world-specific.

The main concern of this chapter emerges from these general observations regarding the place of focalization in the fictional world model. This chapter will present various modes of interaction between focalizing instances and fictional entities and ways in which focalization operates on fictional worlds. I will attempt to show that since in a fictional world focalizers are inseparable from other world-components (every fictional object is presented from a point of view), the ontological implications invested in focal-differentiations are crucial to any description of fictional worlds. Prior, however, to analyzing the interaction between focalizers and world-components in fiction, one should investigate further in what sense this interaction can be regarded as unique to fiction, or, in other words, in what sense fictional focalizers are immanently inseparable from world-components. It would be claimed that reading of the fictional world as focalized is a central convention employed by the understander of fiction, and points of view are always understood as being essential components of such worlds.

Focalization on the fictional world

In coining the term *focalization*, Genette aimed at distinguishing, in the act of narrative mediation, between the mediating act of perception and the mediating act of narration. A term widely used by narratologists, focalization has the clear advantages of allowing us to regard perspectival positions in isolation from modes of narration: "focalization is not an independent linguistic activity but an aspect of its contents" (Bal, 1981: 206). Focalization is a principle according to which elements of the fictional world are arranged from a certain perspective or from a specific position. Narration concerns the mode of verbalizing the perceiving process and the objects of perception; it is the principle according to which elements are textualized in particular manners of expression carried out from a narrating stance.

Focalization is one aspect determining what gets narrated, the factor filtering world-components; only at a second stage considerations of narratability are imposed on the results of focalization (which clarifies why this chapter concentrates on focalization, rather than on acts of narration, as what reflects perspectival determination of fictional worlds). By superimposing focalization on narration, by claiming that focalization pre-determines narratability, one can examine the composition of a fictional world model prior to narration. A world consists of objects (objects of a first, second and third order) and of acts of focalizations. That is, focalization is itself constructed as a fictional domain alongside other domains of this (fictional) world-type. The basic structure of a fictional universe can be described as a structure in which entities interact with modes of focalization. Furthermore, because acts of focalization stipulate the selection and combination of fictional world-components, the modalized structure of a fictional universe can basically be treated as the outcome of acts of focalization and of narration. Who sees determines the status of a fictional element no less than the authority of the narrating source conveying information about that element. This brings us to the more general claim (which will be tested in the present chapter) that in fictional worlds, focalizers and other world-components are ontologically commensurable: they are of the same ontological order. To put it differently, the domains of entities and of focalizers are inseparable: focalizers are not independent of entities. Properties of focalizers are reconstructed through entities selected to constitute the fictional world and through the mode of arranging these entities. Entities are not abstractable from focalizers: they are constituted by acts of focalization.

The interaction between fictional entities and focalizers does not only determine the degree of factuality of world-components; this interaction motivates the very selection of elements forming domains of the fictional world. Whatever a fictional world contains is conditioned and dictated by what the mutual determination of objects and focalizers allows for the production of. This principle of selection is prior and fundamental to the organization of the fictional universe.

To further pursue this line of analysis, I will concentrate on one fictional domain composed of a set of perceptible objects: the set of *spatial entities*, or of *places*. By isolating one specific domain it will be possible to examine the particular working of perspectival arrangements in determining the nature of that domain. The perceptible nature of places makes them a case of particular interest since they can test my initial claim that in fiction world-components do not exist prior to or independent of focalization. Being perceptible entities, places are, on the one hand, more susceptible to perspectival distortions and manipulations. Yet this particular nature of places enables them to sustain appropriation by a subjective perspective without losing their properties. To put it differently, the perspectival arrangement of places, perceived as an operator over the fictional domain of space, should be complemented by the apparent fact that places seem to have a fictional existence apart from, though filtered through, the perspective conveying information about them. Yet, as will be shown below, fictional elements do *interact* with perspectives on the fictional world, and a perspective can hence determine which places are presented, in what textual manifestations, in what degree of factuality, in what position in relation to other places and with what significance. The fictional place can nevertheless be abstracted, identified and even objectified from the perceiving perspective. In a fictional description of Paris, for instance, the construct of the place as emerging from the text is perceived as the intersection between perspectival manipulations and (fictionally) objectified traits. Concentrating on a set of perceptible elements is therefore a strategy for examining the effects of interaction-procedures which sets of fictional objects undergo. The effects of focalization on the nature of first and second-order entities and on the structure of their domains can demonstrate why in the fictional world focalization is a central principle of organization. It will also clarify how variations of perspective affect the mode of arranging places and the way places are selected to serve as locations for other fictional entities (events, situations and characters). This direction of analysis should not only contribute to our understanding of the way fictional worlds are structured. It also contributes to the ongoing theorizing on perspectives and points of view. The following analysis can prove of particular interest since changes in perspective are typically tracked down, in theories of focalization, through changes in types of information (shifts from external events to inner situations or vice versa). Here, changes of perspective will prove to be detectable without changes in the nature of the information conveyed.[5]

---

5 Note also that theories of point of view, or of focalization for that matter, aim at recovering positions of focalizers or of narrators whereas in the present study the

Information about fictional places implies information about mediating perspectives and it motivates what gets selected in the fictional universe. Note that selection in a fictional world has a specific meaning: it is associated with the order of appearance of fictional elements, the position from which elements are selected and so on.[6] Since the literary text is the only source of information about the world it constructs, selection of elements in one context is describable only against the background of the totality of elements mentioned throughout the text, and shifts in perspective on the fictional world can only be detected in these relative organizations of fictional elements:

First and foremost, what I mean by this concept [focalization] is *the result of the selection from among all possible materials of narrative content.* Then, it consists of the "view," vision also in the abstract sense of 'considering some things from a certain perspective.' And finally, presentation [my translation. (Bal, 1977: 37)]

An act of focalization is therefore an act in which the totality of fictional elements is restricted in a specific context according to one principle or other. Vitoux (1982) claims that in a non-delegated focalization (focalization in which the narrator does not delegate the power of focalization to a character) "the focalizer does not seem to impose an a priori restriction on his field of vision, whether a qualitative or a quantitative one" [my translation (ibid.: 361)].[7] Yet, as demonstrated in focalization models (and also in the present study), an omniscient narrator in a zero act of focalization (with no apparent restriction on his field of focalization) necessarily manifests a restriction on selection. Any construction hence reflects a restricted point of view and once such a restriction is identified it is either attributed to the narrator–focalizer or is imposed on a character to whom the power of focalization has been delegated.[8]

opposite direction of analysis is aimed at: different perspectives recognized in a text are considered only insofar as they motivate the organization and relative arrangement of fictional world-components in general, and of places in particular.

6 Selection is commonly defined as a choice of a subset of elements from a complete set. Selection, in this sense, only pertains to worlds which are, naively speaking, independent of discursive practices, whereas constructed worlds involve the type of selection described here.

7 This reflects a traditional approach to point of view according to which *omniscient* narration is opposed to *selective* narration (Rossum-Guyon, 1970: 477).

8 Cordesse (1988) studied in detail the ways in which the author creates narrative situations by diminishing his control and by enacting a procedure of *split*

A perspective (or point of view) is the position from which an act of focalization is implemented. The position of a character or of a narrator is not necessarily identified as a perceptual perspective. Focalization can reflect various principles of organization at work. The effect of focalization on the structure of the entity-domain in the fictional world is not necessarily motivated by perception. Focalizers interact with entities in other modes too. Focalization is a general name for a whole range of perspectival determinations of entities. The same focalizing subject may therefore have different perspectives, visual, auditory, verbal or otherwise, on the same fictional object manifested in discrete acts of focalization. The type of perspective adopted determines the aspect of the fictional entity that is to be actualized. Note that it has been recognized in recent theories of point of view that focalization and its associated concepts are inherently *anthropomorphic*. As such they translate textual strategies into mimetic terms which are sometimes misleading. The term "focalizing subject" reflects an attempt to avoid a personification of focalizers. Likewise, Rimmon-Kenan (1983) proposes seeing these subjects as *agents* (ibid.: 138).[9] Indeed, one of the purposes of the present discussion is positively to define the working of a focalizing agent when it carries no perceptual or individuating properties and to investigate the implications of "impersonal" focalization for the structure of the fictional universe.

A perspective or a focalizing position allows diverse principles of organization or different modes of focalization to be implemented. A perspective can be described in terms of *perceptual restrictions* on a character, in terms of the *ideological attitudes* of an external focalizer or in terms of a *logic of action*. Such principles are needed to motivate the appearance of specific elements as objects of focalization and hence as

(débrayage). The author holds five functions (the acting function, the perceiving function, the narrating function, the writing function and the fictionalizing function), each or all of which can be delegated, thus creating a distance between the author and the subject fulfilling the function. Cordesse's study is reminiscent, in many respects (despite a difference in terminology and methodology), of Uspensky's seminal work on point of view (1973).

9 Avoiding anthropomorphic terms is particularly crucial when an anonymous, external focalizer displays objectivized narrative motifs. Ryan (1981) claims that the concept of narrator is logically necessary in all fictions. Impersonal narration, however, is an abstract construct of fiction since in this case the subject holding the ability to narrate the story is attributed a zero degree of individuation and no psychological foundation. A similar claim can be made regarding external focalizers.

world-components. The diversity of these principles also justifies the neutralization of anthropomorphic overtones in the concept of focalization.

All principles of organization operative in fiction are, by necessity *textually manifested* (Uspensky, 1973).[10] Some perspectival positions are explicitly marked, while others function as underlying principles recovered in order to naturalize the unfolding of fiction (Culler, 1975: 200). Identifying perspectives thus also imposes coherence on the materials composing a fictional world.[11]

Types of organization that focalization imposes on fictional domains

Genette (1972) distinguishes between zero, internal and external focalizations based on a diminishing degree of access to the psychology of characters. In internal focalization, for instance, the character is limited in his authority to provide information about psychological perceptions and mental activities of other characters.[12] Bal, on the other hand, distinguishes internal from external focalizations based on the intra- or extradiegetic locus of the focalizer, regardless of psychological penetration. Since I concentrate here on focalization in interaction with places, it is only the latter terminological use of internal and external focalizations which is applicable to the present analysis. An internal act of focalization is the one carried out by a character and is opposed to external acts of focalization in which the focalizing subject cannot be identified with a character. Thus, it is possible to define the spatial coordinates of the character-focalizer's perceiving position inside the fictional universe, whereas the position of an external focalizer cannot be defined in terms of perceptual limitations of a spatial-temporal nature. Since there are no recognizable perceptual restrictions on the position of external

---

10 Uspensky discusses the deep and surface compositional structures which manifest the various semantic spheres in which point of view may be considered.

11 Sternberg (1981) provides a thorough discussion of principles of organization postulated and imposed on descriptions. Since descriptive sequences denote co-existing elements, point of view is considered one of the principles which order the unordered. This, like other studies of description within narrative theory, aims at identifying modes of organization which can motivate the arrangement of non-narrative series.

12 For a critical review of focalization and the first-person narrator, see Edmiston, 1989.

focalizers, the principles organizing fictional elements in external acts of focalization obey alternative types of restriction (that would be explored below).

The following description aims to contribute to a definition of the type of positioning relevant to external focalization and of its effects on the nature of world components. First, let us perform a comparative examination of two examples. In the first, the arrangement of places following the attributes of "near" and "distant" is relative to a perceptually restricted focalizer; changes in the position of the focalizer motivate changes in the arrangement of fictional places. The relative arrangement of the places described as near or distant is relative to the position of a perceptually restricted focalizer.

The shore, which rising and falling, became steadily more distant and more peaceful. (*To the Lighthouse*: 169)

They were close to the Lighthouse now ... the Lighthouse one had seen across the bay all these years ... The island had grown so small ... (187)

When the focalizer's position cannot be described in these terms, places are nevertheless considered as near or distant as an outcome not of their distance from a perceiving subject, but relative to their *distance from the action or situation* narrated; from the here-and-now of the fictional world where characters are engaged in action or in a situation. In the example given below from *The Portrait of a Lady*, the immediate surrounding is identified according to the spatio-temporal location (the here-and-now) of the situation depicted; other places are accordingly arranged:

It is not, however, with the outside of the place that we are concerned; on this bright morning of ripened spring its tenants had reason to prefer the shady side of the wall ... In an apartment ... one of the several distinct apartments into which the villa was divided ... a gentleman was seated in company with a young girl ... The room was, however, less sombre ... for it had a wide high door, which now stood open into the tangled garden behind. (ibid.: 226–227)

Once the human situation being narrated is located in one of the apartments, other places (the other apartments in the house and the garden) become secondary to it, that is, distant to varying extents from the here-and-now of the situation in focus. The arrangement of places and their relative positioning thus follow a perspectival principle which is, in the present case, tantamount to the logic of the situation. Selecting a location or changing a location is then caused by the situation depicted or by a change in the situation depicted. Focalization can also be identified with the logic of action and then put constraints on the sequential ordering of places. When under external focalization, the appearance of places in a specific order follows a logic of action: change of location is then dictated by the demands of causal relations in a sequence of events.

The companions drove out of the Roman Gate ... they reached the small superurban piazza ... Isabel went with her friend through a wide, high court ... Mr. Osmond met her in the cold ante-chamber ... and ushered her, with her conductress, into the apartment ... (ibid.: 253)

Constraints on the arrangement of places implemented in external acts of focalization where perspective is equivalent to a narrative focus, hence identify the here-and-now of the fictional world. Hamburger (1975) defines the "here and now" of fiction as the zero point of the system of reality. The here-and-now designates the originary point of experience: "even if a 'present time' ... is not indicated at all ... we experience the action of the novel as being 'here and now,' as the experience of fictive persons, or, as Aristotle said, of men in action" (ibid.: 97). A *narrative focus*, like a perceptual position, functions as a type of focalization motivating modes of arranging places (or other fictional entities). An external focalization, originating from a narrative stance outside the fictional world, is therefore neither a synonym for unrestricted selection nor equivalent to a random arrangement of places; it rather defines the here-and-now of action, and reveals that focalizers and entities can interact on nonperceptual grounds.

Although external focalizations also reflect perspectival constraints, though self-imposed, in a context where the arrangement of places cannot be accounted for in terms of the scope of perception of a particular character (to whom one tends to attribute focalization in that particular context), an external focalizer is posited to motivate the selection. In such cases the informativeness of a textual segment with respect to the place described seems to circumvent the perspectival restrictions on the character to whom the power of construction has formally been delegated:

Then there was a silence. They could hear nothing but the crunch of the sand under their feet and the murmur of the weir; for the Seine is divided into two above Nogent. The stream which turned the water-mills disgorged its overflow at this point, to meet the main current of the river father down; and coming from the bridges, one could see a grassy mound on the right, on the other bank, dominated by a white house ... (*Sentimental Education*: 249)

From "for the Seine" what is conveyed transcends the particular mental restrictions and awarenesses of the character's perspective. At the point where details of the landscape cannot be attributed to the perceptual faculties of the character, an act of external focalization emerges from the description. The selection of places and their characterization are no longer restricted by the perceptual position of the character. Sometimes an external focalizer is inferred because there is no human agent around to serve as a candidate for perception. Such is the case in the second part of Woolf's *To the Lighthouse* where no human agent is present in the house to motivate the particular selection. Particularly in view of the variety of internal focalizers who govern the other parts of the novel, the absence of a human agent who may function as a focalizing subject requires that an external focalizer fulfill the function of selecting and arranging places and their features.

So with the house empty and the doors locked and the mattresses rolled round, those stray airs, advance guards of great armies, blustered in, brushed bare boards, nibbled and fanned, met nothing in bedroom or drawing-room that wholly resisted them ... Only the shadows of the trees, flourishing in the wind, made obeisance on the wall, and for a moment darkened the pool in which light reflected itself. (ibid.: 120)

Fictional entities cannot be selected and introduced apart from a focalizing subject. Although the external focalizing subject does not have the perceptual restrictions which constrain internal focalizers (the perceiving subject is at the same time inside and outside the house), the focalizer is self-restricted by the natural situation to which its perspective clings. Following the movement of the "stray airs," the focalizer, although potentially unrestricted, actually restricts the scope of its perspective to the house and its immediate surroundings.

The sequential ordering of entities in internal focalization follows other constraints. An internal focalizer's position is always related to a point in space (whether this position is static or dynamic). Since internal focalization is primarily qualified by perceptual constraints, whenever a narrator delegates the power of focalization to a character, there is an immediate restriction on the perceptual field:

His face was turned towards the house, but his eyes were bent musingly on the lawn; so that he had been an object of observation to a person who had just made her appearance in the ample doorway. (*The Portrait of a Lady*: 15)

Here the house, the lawn and the doorway are places selected in discrete acts of focalization (one internal, one external) and their arrangement is determined by the specific perspectival order to which they are subjected.

The perspective of internal focalizers restricts the scope of selectable places to those which, being a part of the focalizer's perceptual field, are related *in a space-continuum*:

Pansy was not in the first room ... He took his course to the adjoining room and met Mrs. Osmond coming out of the deep doorway ... There was another room beyond the one in which they stood – a small room that had been thrown open and lighted. (*The Portrait of a Lady*: 366ff.)

Mr. Rosier, making his social round, is looking for a moment of intimacy with Pansy. His moving perspective directed by his interest explores the relative positions of the reception-rooms and integrates them in one topographical frame. This topographical arrangement is not neutral; it emerges from the interaction between the internal focalizer and the space before him. Topographical relations between places can be however confused and the fictional space fragmented when an internal focalizer incorporates into his field of vision both entities directly perceived and entities invoked by memory, aspirations and so on.[13]

Since the major constraint on internal focalization is removed from external focalization, and since external focalizers are not confined to a human perceptual field, this focalization type can allow, in principle, looser spatial relations between places. An external focalizer, unbounded by a topographical continuum that defines its perceptual scope, usually imposes alternative constraints on the construction of series. This is relevant mainly in descriptive segments where the logic of what is described replaces the logic of visual or mental perception and dictates the order and arrangement of the entities selected. In the case of places, these are often selected according to a topographical logic which dictates the arrangement:

The little town of Verrières is one of the prettiest in Franche-Comte. Its white houses, with their red-tiled, pointed roofs, stretch out along the side of a hill where clumps of chestnut-trees thrust sturdily upwards at each little bend. Down in the valley the river Doubs flows by, some hundreds of feet below fortifications which were built centuries ago ... .High above the town, and protecting it on its northern side, rise the jagged peaks of Verra, a branch of the Jura mountains. (*Le rouge et le noir*: 23)

13 Eco (1979) describes such elements as forming the *subworlds* of characters: these are imaginary courses of events characters set up in the course of the plot and are distinguished from actual states of the fabula.

This opening passage of the novel is a panoramic description of the village, panoramic being itself a type of constraint imposed by the topological order of the place itself. Following this order, parts of the landscape are arranged according to principles which disregard perceptual limitations; alternative principles which allow the construction of places unlimited in scope.[14]

One may conclude that in internal focalization the continuum of space is subordinated to perceptual provisions. In external focalization the ordering of a set of places is constrained by the topological logic of the focalized places. It can even be claimed that the absence of perceptual restrictions in external focalization tends to result in a more obvious spatial relation among places (relations of adjacency, containment, proximity or distance) whereas internal focalization can produce incoherent or fragmented sets of places which can only be "naturalized" by a compound act of focalization (incorporating places viewed, dreamt about, recalled or imagined).

She was under the apple tree and Darl and I go across the moon and the cat jumps down and runs and we can hear her inside the wood. (*As I Lay Dying*: 204)

In this example, the heterogeneous set of places is naturalized through reconstructing a sequence combining immediate perception of the focalizer with the associations raised during the perception through memory and fantasy. The position of the focalizer (inside or outside the fictional universe), and constraints on focalization, are hence detectable in the mode of presenting objects. This is of particular interest since, as mentioned above, internal focalization was commonly distinguished from external focalization on the ground of the distinction between perceptible and imperceptible objects. An external focalizer has often been recognized by its capacity to operate the literary convention of penetrating and reporting mental activities. Yet, as shown here, fictional perspectives do not interact with (perceptible or imperceptible) entities which are pre-given. We do not gain access to fictional entities through their perspectival filtering: the very fictional existence, nature and structure of fictional entities is stipulated and is the outcome of focalization. The "fingerprints" left by a focalizer of any type on the objects of the fictional world, are therefore recognizable regardless of the class of objects considered. A prior delimitation of one type of information (in our case, information about

14 The notion of *the size of fictional worlds* is discussed in Pavel (1986: 94ff.)

perceptible elements of space) reveals sufficient indications as to the type of focalization through which that information has been conveyed. Focalization has a significant role in determining and in organizing fictional domains and it thus works not only as a mode of categorizing types of information but also as a convention for motivating and distinguishing between different kinds of arrangements in the fictional universe.

Another constraint on focalization which is reflected in fictional domains has to do with the scope of entities which compose a fictional domain and in the present test-case the scope of places that compose a fictional space. A character can visually grasp an expansive place (such as a city) only in specific contexts. Although "expansive" and "compact" are obviously relative terms they can tentatively be defined according to the boundaries of human visual perception. This is the case, for instance, when a place is approached from the outside:

He was little impressed by his first view of Paris seen from a distance. (*Le rouge et le noir*: 246–247)

The specific circumstances under which internal focalizers select expansive places indicate that internal focalizers are restricted in the scope of the place they can indicate to be their immediate surrounding.

When a set of places attributed to an internal focalizer includes an expansive place, one either sees the perspective of an external focalizer behind this selection, or the internal focalizer is assigned an exceptional position which allows him to expand temporarily his field of perception (such as a view from a tower). Transitions from expansive to compact places are usually understood as reflecting a shift from external to internal focalization, and the correlation between the scope of places and types of focalization is thus maintained:

The visitor had not been announced; the girl heard her last walking about the adjoining room. It was an old house at Albany, a large, square, double house, with a notice of sale in the windows of the lower apartments. (*The Portrait of a Lady*: 23)

The shift from internal to external position of focalization is indicated in the broadening of the perspective on the places described. Likewise, the panoramic description opening *Le rouge et le noir*, quoted above, gives way to descriptions of smaller places inside the village of Verrières, and this change is correlated with a shift from the external focalizer to the perspective of an internal focalizer: a hypothetical traveler visiting Verrières.

Following O'Toole (1980) it is possible to describe each domain of entities as organized in levels, as stratified according to its inherent logic. Places, as one domain of entities in a fictional world, are organized in a hierarchy of *containment* (a country contains a hill which contains a church-yard which contains a church which contains a well which contains a magic egg). Similar hierarchies can be easily constructed for other fictional domains. In the domain of characters, shifts in levels of information from exterior to interior, from conscious to subconscious data about the character would manifest shifts in types of focalization. Transitions between levels of a fictional domain indicate transitions in levels of focalization. Transitions from one level to another in the system of topological relations among places indicate changing restrictions imposed on internal focalizers or a shift from internal to external focalization. In the following example, the character's distancing perspective is manifested in the movement from places lower in the system to locations which belong to a higher set:

He gazed through the mist at spires and buildings whose names he did not know, and took a last look at the Ile Saint-Louis, the Cité, and Notre-Dame; and soon, as Paris was lost to view, he heaved a deep sigh. (*Sentimental Education*: 15)

Changes of scope in the type of entities described are understood as corresponding to changes in type of focalization.

Types of organization that narrative modalities impose on fictional domains

The case of internal focalization has been defined in the previous section as a selection principle identified with a set of perceptual constraints. Internal focalizers can however incorporate into their perceptual field objects invoked through memory, imagination and wishes and not only through perceptual faculties. The question is whether a character–focalizer's mental acts can be subsumed under the general category of internal focalization, or whether a character's mental activity obeys constraints which diverge from perceptual constraints in internal focalization. This is a significant question which illuminates the way focalization is interpreted by the understander of fiction. Where focal-differentiations are discerned by the understander of fiction, they affect the status of fictional world-components (that is, different types of focalization carry different ontological implications for the way a fictional universe is reconstructed). Since the authority of a focalizer does not correlate with the type of information conveyed (an element is relative to a character's mental world whether that element is imagined, known, or seen by that character), the question stands whether visual perception is assumed to differ from other modes of internal focalization. Thus, if in the process of reconstructing the fictional world, the mental activities of an internal focalizer are assumed to produce an additional and separate type of focalization, the understander will assign a different, possibly lower, degree of authority to the relevant narrative motifs. Is it possible, in other words, to claim that perceptible objects are assigned a decreased degree of authenticity as the character distances himself from his immediate surroundings, plunging into his inner world of memories and fantasies?

The choice of an entity as an object of focalization, within or without an internal focalizer's immediate surroundings, is always a significant choice: world components are not presented as if they come more or less easily or directly as objects of focalization according to their distance from the focalizer. Moreover, the immediate surroundings of a focalizer are, in themselves, a composite construct; they consist of entities in different degrees of proximity. Distance from or proximity to the focalizer cannot be in themselves sufficient conditions for distinguishing between types of internal focalization, and hence between sets of entities mediated through these different acts. Besides, an internal focalizer can select a distant place which becomes accessible despite the distance, through other sensuous impressions:

Sometimes they heard the roll of drums far away in the distance. It was the call to arms being beaten in the villages for the defence of Paris. (*Sentimental Education*: 325)

Places in proximity to the focalizer do not necessarily enter more readily into his field of perception than distant places (or other distant entities). When the internal focalizer's focus of interest lies beyond his immediate field of perception, the distinction between types of internal focalization in terms of immediacy are greatly problematized:

And then, she reflected, there was that scene on the beach. One must remember that. It was a windy morning. They had all gone to the beach. Mrs. Ramsay sat and wrote letters by a rock. (*To the Lighthouse*: 149)

Focalizing on entities through visual perceptions or through memories cannot differentiate sets of entities in terms of their degree of authenticity, in terms of an intensity of interest, nor in terms of the significance implied in their choice. What is then the justification for imposing different conventions of world-reconstruction for modes of internal focalization? Does the understander of fiction isolate visual perception from other mental acts through which internal focalization is being carried out? Note, again, that this problem is related to the general question concerning the role of narrative modalities in determining the structure of a fictional universe, a question of direct relevance to the present attempt to describe the implications of the interaction between focalizers and fictional domains. Without solving these queries here, suffice it to acknowledge at this point the complex relationships holding between narrative modalities and the relative arrangements of fictional world-components.[15] Focalization is a general name for a complex of narrative modalities that can correspond to a variety of world-reconstructing conventions.

Mental acts (such as recalling and dreaming) as alternatives to perception in spatial proximity, add fields of perception to a focalizer. An internal focalizer can select entities belonging to various contexts (from his immediate surroundings or from remembered or imagined contexts). Although all entities selected by an internal focalizer, in whatever type of focalization, are immanently of restricted factuality (being subordinated to a focalizer's limited authority), their arrangement in fragmentary or incongruous sets can be motivated by the variety of mental acts through which a character operates his focalization-capacity. That is, in understanding a fragmentary domain, the reader assumes a range of mental acts to naturalize this fragmentation.

The Polish girl ... made him long to hold her to his heart while the two of them travelled in a sleigh across a snow-covered plain ... The Swiss girl ... opened up vistas of tranquil pleasure in a lake-side chalet ... the Bacchante ... made him dream of greedy kisses in oleanser groves, in stormy weather ... (*Sentimental Education*: 126–127).

In this case, the set of places, taken from diverse contexts, is motivated by the character-focalizer's elaborated dreams. In defining types of focalization according to vision and other mental acts through which entities are selected and arranged, it is possible to differentiate domains of entities and at the same time define their interrelations and relative authenticity. Focalization through a memory is regarded as complementary to the act of focalizing on an immediately perceived

15 See Ryan, 1984.

entity located close by. In particular, by pointing at the relations between various entities the focalizer selects, types of focalization not only motivate the selection of entities from distant contexts, but also motivate the particular choice of entities and the significance attributed to them.

So now, Mrs. Ramsay thought, she could return to that dream land, that unreal but fascinating place, the Mannings' drawing-room at Marlow twenty years ago; where one moved about without haste or anxiety, for there was no future to worry about ... she knew the end of the story, since it had happened twenty years ago, and life which shot down even from this dining-room table in cascades, heaven knows where, was sealed up there, and lay, like a lake, placidly between its banks. (*To the Lighthouse*: 87)

In Mrs. Ramsay's mind the uncertainty of the current flux of life is replaced by the sealed experiences of the past; the immediate, anxiety-ridden surroundings are replaced by the dream land of a peaceful past. The shift to a place from the distant past satisfies the focalizer's need which cannot be equally gratified by her immediate surroundings. Places in memory thus become more attractive than her surroundings, fully absorbing her attention.

The differentiation between types of internal focalization is nevertheless justified since it corresponds to the modal structure of the fictional universe. There is indeed a detectable correlation between types of focalization (external, internal-perceptual, internal-nonperceptual) and the degree of actualization of entities (which entities are *present* in the here-and-now of the fictional reality). For instance, in the domain of places one can differentiate the places actualized as the here-and-now, the immediate surroundings of events, actions, states and characters, from other places. The boundaries of the here-and-now are directly linked to the system of focalization. Places which lie outside the immediate perceptual field of an internal focalizer are not likely to be included in that part of the fictional domain actualized as the here-and-now of the story. Differentiations between types of internal focalization hence correspond to modal differentiations in the structure of the fictional world. For example, in *La chute*, although all places constructed are subjected to the utterance acts of a limited focalizer, Amsterdam, forming the context of these acts is the actualized part of space, whereas Paris, invoked through memory, clearly has a different status (function) in the overall structure of the fictional world. Yet the motivation for excluding sets of places from the here-and-now of a story by subjecting them to indirect modes of focalization, and the reason for assigning places with varying degrees of actualization in the fictional domain, is often problematic. In *To the Lighthouse* the place "at the window" where Mrs. Ramsay sits with her son before Lily Briscoe's eyes, and the place "on the beach" invoked through Lily's memory of the past, where Mrs. Ramsay was writing letters, belong to different types of focalization with which they interact. The motivation for introducing similar places through diverse acts of focalization involves the particular thematics of that fictional world. In this type of world (a stream of consciousness novel) mental acts of all types play an equivalent role. It is thus clear that the interaction of a set of places with the system of focalizations in general, and the specific interaction between focalizers and places that form the story's here-and-now, are also related to the set of conventions operating in the construction of specific worlds. That is, some world-reconstructing conventions are culture- or period-specific.

It has been demonstrated in this chapter that focalizers and entities are two separate fictional domains in constant interaction. As a result, the selection and arrangement of entities are motivated by the superposing of focalization on world-components. The definition of types of focalization and of possible positions of focalizers account for constraints imposed in the construction of fictional domains, whether a domain of places or of other world-components. Constraints on focalization also motivate the possibilities open before internal focalizers for selecting distant or imagined entities outside the field of their immediate perception.

In more general terms, it has been shown in this chapter that both modes of selecting and combining fictional elements and the modalized structure of the fictional universe can be accounted for in terms of the interaction between focalizers and other world-components. This line of analysis reflects one aspect of the unique nature of fictional universes: that information about them is always perspectivally determined. Unlike other worlds where perceiving and narrating subjects filter or mediate information, in the case of fictional worlds, domains of entities are constituted through perceiving and narrating acts. It can further be claimed that the way focalization interacts with fictional-world components suggests another area of research where ontological considerations intersect with narrative principles and concepts, such as point of view, responsible for the organization of narrative texts. One can therefore conclude that when commonly used narrative concepts, such as *focalization*, are regarded within a modal framework for the fictional universe, they can account for modal differentiations within the fictional world. That is, within such a modal framework, the meaning of a concept like *focalization* is modified, thus contributing both to our understanding of the explanatory scope of the concept itself, and to our understanding of the way fictional worlds are constructed by discourse.

7

Fictional time

States of affairs take place in time and space, as do stories that are composed of narrativized states of affairs. Since it is the overall claim of this study that fictional worlds form parallel worlds they should, as such, be autonomous in relation to nonfictional versions of the world. The domains of space and time should likely be constructed according to the logic of parallelism, a parallelism entailing the autonomy of fictional time and space in relation to the temporality and spatiality of the actual world – assuming such an autonomy still does not circumvent possible affinities between the two world systems. Fictional events are too markedly anchored in the history and geography of the world to be appropriately accounted for by a model suggesting a breach between fiction and reality.[1] Yet, one might ask, is the logic of parallelism not undermined by the fact that fictional space and time so markedly rely on times and places of reality? Fictional worlds are very often anchored in real times and places. In fact, fictional worlds are much more massively anchored to times and places of the real world than they are to historical figures. Whereas a historical figure rarely makes a central character in a fictional story, narratives of realistic, fantastic and even science fictional kinds, usually relate their spatio-temporal structure to the times and places of reality drawing on the chronology of world-history and on the geography of world-topography. If fictional worlds are so massively anchored in real times and places, is it valid to maintain that the fictional world posits a spatio-temporal system separate from the spatio-temporal system of the actual world?

---

1 A collection of essays published in 1987 (Mallory and Simpson-Housley) centers on the question of how novelists and poets use geographical places and how this can contribute to regional studies thus creating a common ground for the two disciplines. If one disregards the radical mimeticism presupposed by such a study, this collection can be seen as evidence to the massive reliance of fictional space-construction on the geography of the real world.

I would claim that the autonomy of fictional spatio-temporality has to do with the *logic* of constructing fictional domains, and not with the content of this construction. Fictional autonomy is therefore perfectly compatible with the extensive modeling of fictional events on real ones, and of fictional dates on historical ones. The possibilities for fictionally locating events in space-time are varied: fiction can actualize in fictional time events and situations that never were actualized in history; it can locate imaginary events in a familiar historical moment; it can actualize in a real geographical place fictional events and inhabit this place with imaginary individuals, and it can locate historical events in an imaginary place. Yet, since fiction constitutes an independent parallel ontology, when events that belong to the French Revolution occur in fiction they are neither treated as possible non-actualized events located in historical time and in real places nor as actual events imported into fictional time and space. As claimed in chapter 3, once worlds are projected as fictional, their fictional status implies that we attribute autonomy to the fictional domain as a whole and to each of its sub-domains (including the spatio-temporal domain). As readers of fiction we know that the Franco-Russian war in which a prince Andreij participated is not the same war recorded in history books; we hence know for certain that as much historical accuracy as *War and Peace* contains, no person identified as that same prince could appear on the list of injured heroes of the Napoleonic war outside fiction.

Thus, despite being heavily anchored to "world knowledge," and regardless of the degree to which fiction relies on real entities, the time and space of fiction form a domain in an autonomous world (autonomous in relation to nonfictional versions of reality and in relation to possible worlds alternative to actuality). In this sense the present chapter continues the argument forwarded in chapter 4 showing how on the level of organizing fictional individuals in spatio-temporal relations, the ontological origins of a given entity (be they in reality or in fiction) are of no consequence. It is the business of this chapter to explore the nature and implications of this autonomy of fiction, particularly in the domain of time. What is, in other words, the type of temporal organization imposed on states of affairs in the context of fiction?

The analogy between time of fiction and time of actuality

Speaking about the autonomy of fictional time relies on the assumption that fictional worlds posit parallel spatiotemporal systems. To explicate this assumption, it should be noted that every world links its components in spatiotemporal relations. Since a *world* is a constellation of spatiotemporally linked elements, temporal relations can serve as a primary criterion for drawing the dividing line between worlds: when elements cease to be spatiotemporally related, they must be attributed to separate worlds. It was shown in earlier parts of this study that unlike possible worlds that ramify from the actual state of affairs, fictional worlds unfold parallel to actuality. This difference in position relative to the actual world between possible and fictional worlds also applies to the spatio-temporal organization of a world. The actual world, its versions and possible divergences are all interrelated in one spatiotemporal system: the most fantastic possibility ramifying from the actual state of affairs remains spatiotemporally linked to the world's actualized center. Each fictional world however assumes a spatiotemporal system of its own, distinct from the spatiotemporal system to which the actual world, its parts, versions and ramifying possibilities are tied.

The system of fictional spatio-temporality is analogous to the spatio-temporal system of "reality" (or its versions) in the sense that in both ontologies world-components are bound together. It will be the concern of this chapter to show that the understander of fiction constructs a separate temporal system for the fictional world and that fictional temporality obeys differently constructed temporal inter-relations. Yet, if we succeed in showing that fictional time is a concept belonging to another spatiotemporal system, how do we ensure that in a separate world time does not cease to be a relevant concept? It could be possible that we ascribe the term "fictional time" to a principle of organization that does not resemble anything we refer to with the term "real time" in the context of actuality-versions. Note that with regard to the concept of "real time" I refer to the intuitive way people understand the rudiments of the operation of time in the world: that things occur in time, that time is irreversible and so on. The question, then, will be whether notions about the working of real time also hold in the context of a fictional world or whether fiction entails a different time conception, and whether temporal organization is interpreted in a similar manner within fiction and without.

The analogy between actual and fictional temporality is however based on the notion that the relevance of temporal organization to fictional narrative worlds is one of the strongest conventions assumed by readers of fiction and a prevalent supposition in narrative studies.[2] Yet, granted that the status of fictional worlds differs from the status of courses of events alternative to the actual world (that fictional worlds and possible worlds assume different logical relations with the actual world), this analogy should be qualified: the understander of fiction interprets the temporality of fiction in a specific manner. Although notions of present, past, future, chronology etc., are used in relation to fiction, these are not treated as constructing possible past, present, or future states of the actual world. Fiction has its independent notions of past, present, and future, as will be shown in this chapter. In fact, it will be shown that time concepts are interpreted differently in a fictional world, that different temporal relations are reconstructed and a different type of temporal organization referred to in fictional contexts. Time notions carry a different (not necessarily temporal) meaning in fictional contexts because such contexts tell the reader to activate the relevant convention in order to reconstruct the domain of fictional time. It is the purpose of this chapter to recover these relevant conventions by showing the particular ways in which readers interpret fictional time and fictional temporal organization.

To embark on the thesis I intend to advance in the present chapter, I will claim that fictional time imposes a system of relations that is only marginally analogous to the system of relations interrelating components of the real world. "When a system of relations is analogous to the spatiotemporal relations, strictly so called, let me call them *analogically* spatiotemporal" claims Lewis (1986: 76). In what sense is the nature of fictional time analogous to actual time and what are the specific features unique to its operation? Lewis provides the conditions that make two systems analogical. He explicates the concept of *analogy between spatiotemporal systems* by describing the relations holding between two alternative physical world versions: a Newtonian theory and a relativistic world. A spatiotemporal system built for Newtonian mechanics posits the concepts of absolute

---

2 There is also a solid enough tradition that attributes to spatiality a prominent place in narrative organization (see Frank, 1945; Mitchell, 1980; McNeil, 1980; Smitten, 1978).

simultaneity (a zero distance in time) and absolute rest (a zero distance in space). Conversely, in our relativistic world any two points in space-time have only one distance between them. A relativistic system therefore does away with the concept of absolute rest. The differences between a Newtonian world and a relativistic world show that two analogical space-time systems can be mutually exclusive by posing spatiotemporal relations of different kinds. Despite this extensive difference in the spatiotemporal interrelations among elements posited by Newtonian and relativistic ontologies, this difference can still provide the basis for talking about analogous systems: although each paradigm interprets the notion of space-time differently, and each system assumes a different kind of spatio-temporal relations, any selected point in space-time can be described according to one or the other system of relations. That is, although the physical versions are mutually exclusive, they share a world of referents to which both allude, and they share the supposition that these referents are spatiotemporally linked. Fictional time is analogous to actual time in a similar but somewhat modified sense. On the face of things concepts of time in fiction are modeled on concepts of time in actual world versions. Yet in fiction spatiotemporal concepts will prove to refer to a fiction-specific mode of organization. Fictional concepts of time and "real time" concepts, rather than acting as diverse models for addressing a shared phenomenon, seem to be similar terms that refer to separate ontologies. Thus, in the present context I refer to analogous modeling not in the sense that two versions refer to a shared world, but in the sense that one terminological system of time-notions is applied to worlds of different ontological orders. That is, in fiction, as in extrafictional contexts we can say "event B occurred after event A" (Natasha married Pierre after Napoleon invaded Russia), but these temporal relations carry diverse meanings in fictional as opposed to nonfictional contexts.

Fictional time diverges from real time in particular modes. The modeling of fictional time on actual time is constrained by two general principles:

(1) The time of fiction cannot be treated in the same way as real time because in fiction we do not assume that (even ideally) there is a world beyond its fictional projection. Fictional world-projection is subjected to points of view and to discursive practices: that is, there is no objective measurement of temporal durations and relations beyond point of view determinants (perspectives, speakers, positions)

and textual devices (tense, temporal connectives, aspects) to which time is subordinated in fiction. Therefore, as claimed above, we do not assume an objective time dimension apart from the mode of the discursive construction of the fictional universe. In fiction the perception of time movement is triggered by the perspectival arrangement of materials and by the linguistic formulation of sentences.

(2) Fictional worlds allow, in principle at least, radical deviations from the regularities of time in the actual world. That is, fictional worlds do not necessarily obey rules of the physical operation of time in "the world as it is." Thus, fictional worlds can include time paradoxes where time is presented as reversible or bilateral. Although such cases often occur where time serves as a theme, in texts that thematize the concept of time, these cases indicate that fictional time differs from "real time." The possibility of projecting a fictional world where temporal interrelations among world components are deviant relative to temporal interrelations among our world-mates indicates that fictional time forms part of a separate, although analogous world system. Likewise, the possibility of actualizing an impossible situation in fiction is symptomatic of fictional worlds belonging to a separate ontological domain from that of possible worlds.

Given the above general constraints on the fictional construction of time, in line with similar constraints at work in other fictional domains, the following section is dedicated to a description of the distinct nature of fictional time and to an exploration of the specific meaning of temporal concepts in the context of fiction.

The reliance of temporality of fiction on the modal operation of temporal concepts

The history of cultures and sciences provides numerous versions about the nature of time. These versions describe various aspects of time on the grounds of a commonly held understanding that things in the actual world are temporally related, that temporal coordinates define the position of world components, and so on. In general, ways of talking about the working of time in the organization of the world can contradict each other. There is most strikingly an acknowledged discrepancy between definitions of time as a physical concept and definitions of time based on our limited access to it. This discrepancy can be detected in the work of St. Augustine and later writers in the way phenomenologies of time, developed in various branches of philosophy, attempt to bridge the gap between the intuitively perceived temporality of the world, on the one hand, and the evanescence of time on the other. Thus, in Roman Ingarden's phrasing, we should distinguish between the "objective" time of the real world and the "subjective" time of an absolute conscious subject, or between a "homogeneous, 'empty' physicomathematically determined world time [and] concrete intuitively apprehendable intersubjective time in which we all live collectively ..." (1973: 234).

This discrepancy gains a particular emphasis when the concept of a "present" is being addressed. In physical terms the present defines the objective temporal coordinates identifying the constantly changing zero reference point: everything that precedes a given point is past, while everything that succeeds it is future. In phenomenological terms there is nothing but the present time. The present is indivisible and ceaselessly vanishing. According to Augustine, for instance, the three dimensions of time – past, present, and future reduce themselves to one, the present, in which the past survives as a memory, and the future pre-exists in the form of anticipation. Each period and culture inherits and nourishes another vision of the universe and hence elaborates a different conceptual system for time (see Patrides, 1976). Yet, whatever the approach to the problem of time, the difference between past, present, and future seems to be a difference in modality. That is, perceiving the existence of things in time raises the question of how the present is understood in relation to past and future times, the access to which is less direct.

Time versions which make up our notion of the temporal existence of things in the world often attempt to grasp the reality of time through its mental appearances in order to answer the disconcerting question posed by Augustine: "What, then, is time? I know well enough what it is, provided that nobody asks me; but if I am asked what it is and try to explain, I am baffled" (St. Augustine, 1961: 264). In various models that describe real time, it is assumed that time has an objective existence (which physics, for instance, strives to account for), and there are versions or models of time that attempt to describe the ways in which time is experienced through the limitations of a human mentality.

The time constructed by fictional texts is to be distinguished both from the objective dimension of physical time and from the subjective dimension of experienced time. The question that should be addressed is therefore what distinguishes the time represented by fictional texts from other time dimensions. Although studies of time in narrative fiction have been numerous, I believe none of them has actually addressed the property of fictionality as a determinant in distinguishing fictional time from extrafictional time dimensions.[3]

In exploring the nature of the analogy between fictional and extra-fictional time, it can be claimed that, unlike objective physical time, fictional time only exists through points of view relating information about the world of fiction. Thus, although the relativization of time and of temporal order to a point of view is also characteristic of subjective experiences of time, this relativization is all encompassing in fiction. As will be shown later, narrative theory extensively attests to the fact that the understander of fiction does not assume the same kind of discrepancy between fictional time in its (fictionally) objective existence and the phenomenology of fictional time; objective and subjective times are interpreted differently in the context of fiction. Attempts to discuss fictional time by referring to the temporality experienced by fictional characters as similar to the temporality experienced in reality (see for instance, Paul Ricoeur, 1985), are basically misleading in this regard, because the "objective" time of fiction is also perspectivally determined. But the fact that there is no "objective" time in fiction supplies only part of the picture. Fiction operates unique differentiations between temporal modalities; "objective" and "subjective" are hence inadequate in accounting for the modal varieties of fictional time. Fictional modalities of time distinguish between temporal locations on the actual time line of a story and temporal locations that are off that time line. Yet what is included in the story time line is not necessarily correlated with what factually occurs in the story. The event of Anna Karenina's death, which presents a fictional fact, is included in the story time line because of the way it is narrated and not because of its place in the narrative. Had this same event been recounted by a character who had allegedly witnessed the heroine's suicide, the event would still be on the story's time line, despite its being subjected to a subjective point of view. Had it however been recounted as succeeding the story's ending, the event would not appear on the story time line, it would not be part of the narrative present. Being on or off the time line is uncorrelated with

---

3 An exception is Paul Ricoeur's study of time in narrative (1984, 1985) which dedicates separate volumes to time in historical narrative and to time in fictional narrative.

questions of "objective" or "subjective" time-conceptions. The particulars of the ways in which readers of fiction reconstruct fictional time will be discussed below. At this point it should be noted that since all temporal segments, including the authenticated actual time of the fictional universe, are conveyed from a certain perspective, one cannot distinguish between the way things are in time and the way things are recounted or textually presented. Fictional time is tied to the nature of fiction which assumes no world beyond the discursive mode of this world construction. In the case of a work of literature, the language of the text establishes its world and refers to it at the same time. The words on the page are sufficient to create the illusion of time flowing steadily forward "just as time does in the real world" (Dry, 1983: 19); yet in the case of fiction a separation between the mode of textual disposition of event-sequences and the present, past, and future times thereby constructed cannot be assumed. In fiction, physical time and the subjective observation and recovery of time – through words and points of view – are one and the same.

The major questions regarding *how* an experience of time emerges from the temporality of fiction, or, in other words, how the semiotics of fiction elicits an experience of time and what the unique nature of time in fiction is, have yet to be answered. One step toward answering these questions lies in the perspectival determinants of fictional time following which durations, orders, and temporal segmentations are subjected to points of view. This supposition is complemented by the second claim that in fiction, temporal concepts (a time line; order ; past, present, and future; exposition ; and so on) function as modal indicators and are invested with ontological content. That is, *in fiction temporal indicators and temporal concepts are understood as signifying modal differentiations and not only temporal relations or temporal dispositions*. It is not my intention to deal in this chapter with the physical and philosophical differences between real time and fictional time but to show that the constraints imposed on fictional world-construction are unique.

In order to show how the organization of fictional time reflects the ontological autonomy of fiction, a critical reading of familiar notions of time in narrative fiction will be pursued. The fact that narrative theory refers to fictional time with similar concepts to those used in referring to "real" time, raises the question of whether and how this notional similarity is motivated in narrative theory. In other words, here as in previous chapters, data is provided by theoretical formulations which narrative theorists tend to use. These would divulge the relevant constraints and conventions activated by theorists–readers in understanding and accounting for the working of fictional time. The idea is to show how notions of time deliberated and employed by narrative theorists are interpreted both in temporal terms and as indicating specific constraints on the fictional construction of time. In other words, time notions employed by theorists of narrative temporality (such as present, past, and future, order, chronology) can be shown to refer differently within fiction.

Time notions employed in current narrative studies can be classified according to three types of theories proposed, each privileging a different level of analysis for locating the temporality of literary texts.

1 Narrative theories that identify the temporality of fiction with the narrativity of fictional texts.

2 Narrative theories that primarily attribute the temporality of fiction to the temporality of events and states of affairs projected or constructed by the fictional text.

3 Narrative theories that primarily attribute the temporality of fiction to the temporality of the textual medium and to verbal means of presentation.

I would claim that each of these temporal modulations in each type of theory grounds itself in a metaphorical extension of a familiar time concept. That is, in order to locate the temporality of fiction on one of these levels of organization, theoretical models of narrative time extend or manipulate the meaning of a temporal concept. This is done in order to allow for a description of fictional temporality in terms similar to those with which, allegedly, the operation of the temporal system in actual world versions can be described. Locating the temporality of fiction in narrative structures is best revealed in the metaphorical use of the concept of *a narrative present*; locating fictional temporality in the order of events projected by the literary text depends on the metaphorical use of the temporal concept of *chronology*; identifying fictional time with the temporality of textual disposition depends on a metaphorical understanding of the concept of *tense* and of *order* as implying relations of temporal ordering.

Fictional time and the narrative present

Some narrative models identify temporality with the narrativity of texts. Although theoretical models addressing the problem of narrative temporality do not restrict themselves to narrative fiction, this non-differentiation between fictional and nonfictional narrative is itself instructive in hinting at the problems raised by the notion of fictional time. I will first trace the kind of argumentation developed when the notion of temporality is identified with narrativity.

Temporality acquires a particular pertinence in relation to narrative texts in which time is considered a major organizing principle: "narrative texts are the clearest temporally based systems" (Reinhart, 1984: 805). It is claimed, or tacitly assumed, in narrative studies that temporality should be explored in narrative texts where it functions as a dominant principle of organization. Since a narrative structure is teleological (or in less extreme formulations, it reflects functional relations), it has a beginning and an end, and therefore must include temporal materials organized along a time line. The time stream along which events are located is a dimension of primary importance in the narrative world. Present, past, and future are hence the various stages in the forward movement of narrative time (certain events occupy the narrative present and, once being recounted these events become narrative past). Present, past, and future times of narrative can also be claimed to refer to the modalities of fiction: what is narrated but has not been actualized as narrative present is either interpeted as narrative past, preceding the beginning of a story, or as a future possibility of the narrative succeeding its ending. In both senses the present, past, and future of narrative, and the temporality of narrative in general, are identified with the forward-movement which is at the very core of narrativity. Hence, in various theories of narrative time, the mere representation of temporal material does not produce in itself narrative temporality: events do not merely exist in time and are not simply chronologically organized; their order reflects a narrative functionality. Without narrative time, the story could not move forward.

This notion of narrative time in the context of which temporality is identified with the essence of the narrative configurational act, explains why narrative theory is often concerned with the question of whether narrative deep-structures are indifferent to temporality. This is of major concern to narrative theory because if the time movement is the condition for narrativity, narrative deep-structure should also be temporalized. Narrative theory hence addresses the problem of the temporality which is at the very bottom of narrative. It is in this context that the narrative differentiation between *fabula* and *sujhet* comes up, reflecting the consensus among researchers that the chronology of *sujhet* is not immanent to narrative structure (there is an underlying reconstructible order from which the *sujhet* can deviate in many ways). Narrative theory undertakes, as one of its main projects, to explicate the temporality inherent to narrative structures, to show why the chronology presented by the *sujhet* is secondary to the prior chronology of the *fabula*. This is the background behind specific attempts within narrative theory to formulate the difference between "deep level" temporality and "surface level" temporality.

All proposed varieties of narrative structures ... have at least an abstract narrative level, in which the order of the ultimate constituents (events) can be different from the chronological order ...

Chronological order is thus a property of *individual events* rather than of entire *Moves*. As a consequence, it cannot be located at a very abstract level of plot-structure ...

If so, then a preferable way of dealing with the temporal order is to consider it a property of individual narrative leaves (events). (Pavel 33ff., italics in the original)

Linking narrativity to temporality is based on the functional organization of events along a time line with a beginning and an end. Identifying temporality with narrativity is presupposed in definitions of the narrative present. Narrative structure is such that only some of the events or moves included therein are placed at the center of that structure. The intimate link between temporality and narrativity is not only responsible for the dynamic forward movement of the narrative, it is also responsible for the hierarchy of centrality or salience that exists among events of the story. The narrative time line is not one monolithic sequence: the time line is segmented into a *foreground* and *background*, or into a *narrative present* and a nonpresent, and the question is whether this division into foreground and background of the sequence of events is just a general narrative mechanism or a division related to the temporality specific to fiction. "Foreground" and "narrative present" indeed reflect this dual functionality. The narrative determination of a universe motivates the segmentation of the time line into foreground and background (the former is treated as the present). The concept of narrative present is, indeed, developed as a central metaphor of time that indicates narrativity, and it is the nature of this metaphoricity which will reveal how theorists grasp the nature of temporality in the context of narrative fiction.

Definitions of the narrative present as a central concept of narrative temporality are of very different kinds, and they express diverse theoretical convictions. From a *linguistic* point of view the narrative present is defined as those sections of the narrative that propel the story time line (Dry, 1981: 234ff.) or as the foregrounded narrative sequence (the sequence of temporally ordered event clauses) that moves the reference time forward (Reinhart, 1984: 785). From the point of view of literary narrative theory the beginning of the fictive present is described by Meir Sternberg (1979) as the point marking the end of the exposition in the *fabula*, a point considered important enough to be worthy of a scenic treatment in the *sujhet* (21). From a different stance, Hamburger shows that the here-and-now of fiction is an undifferentiated timelessness, the entry into which marks the entry into fiction (in her model there is therefore no room for segmenting fictional time into present and nonpresent).

Without going into the details of each model, it can be shown that *linguistic* and *literary* definitions will each produce a different narrative present. A telling example in this regard can be found in Dry (1983), who refers to Sternberg's distinction between scene and summary. The former reflects the narrative normal ratio (1: 1) of reading time to represented time. Dry refers to Sternberg in order to exclude summary from the narrative time line and to thereby mark the boundaries of the narrative present. Yet her reasons for excluding summary from the narrative time line are very different from Sternberg's reasons for excluding summary from the fictive present. Sternberg refers to the rhetorical effects of shifting from summary to scene as a means of marking selection preferences of a narrator and hence the beginning of the fictive present; it is not however that Sternberg excludes summary from the narrative present as a matter of principle (summary is a relative notion determined by the overall textual norm). Dry however does exclude summary as a matter of principle since summary refers to time-spans and not to punctual occurrence in time. Some other examples of the difference between linguistic and literary definitions of the narrative present may be found in linguistic approaches which do not allow statives to be included in the narrative present (since the states reported are perceived as continuing to exist while the temporal events reported in the foreground take place), while literary approaches do not exclude states from the fictive present. Another example relates to the function of dialogues in regard to the narrative present. One may presume that when a dialogue or embedded speech appears, the content of that speech will be deemed present or nonpresent in a literary analysis, whereas in a linguistic analysis the speech acts themselves, or the dialogue's replications, will count as forwarding the narrative time line. Despite these differences between the two approaches, their common denominator lies in their attempt to provide formal indicators (of linguistic, compositional or ontological order) which demarcate the boundaries of the narrative present in any given text. Moreover, these theories share a similar procedure: although the boundaries of this present vary from model to model, the narrative present is defined as a demarcated segment in the narrative time line. In both linguistic and literary models the present is demarcated from nonpresent segments of the story, and the present is defined as a temporal concept, although the decision about how to demarcate this segment of time has very little to do with temporal considerations. The narrative present is treated as a concept correlated with literary composition or with linguistic considerations. Both linguistic and literary approaches identify temporality with narrativity, and the present thus has to do with the mode of narrative existence and organization. The criteria for separating segments of the foreground or of the narrative present from other segments range from linguistic criteria to compositional ones, none of which grounds itself in purely temporal considerations.

In view of the complex relations between narrative present and basic notions of time, my counter-proposal to this first notion of temporality in fiction is grounded in the nature of the narrative present. My claim is that definitions of the narrative present reflect the temporality associated with fiction. The present, which is literally a temporal concept, works as a metaphorical substitute for a modal concept:[4] "situations on a time line ... are presented as actually occurring in the narrative world, as opposed to being merely talked of, expected, or hypothesized" (Dry, 1983: 21). This criterion of presentness is internal to the narrative: it treats worlds of narrative, and their division into foreground and background as unrelated to

4 This metaphoricity is implied in Reinhart (1984) where the narrative present, as the reference time line, is defined by the foreground sequence of the text. The demarcation of the temporal foregrounded segments is oriented, according to Reinhart, by perceptual principles. The author even concludes that a "narrative organization system is obtained by a metaphorical extension of the spatial perceptual system" (805): that is, temporality is viewed as a metaphorical extension of spatial relations.

extranarrative temporality. Thus among the propositions referring to the story time line, not all trigger a perception of temporal movement. Moreover, sequenced points can trigger perception of time movement although no change of state is thereby implied. In other words, temporal considerations are not the ultimate criterion for determining the story time line or for conditioning the perception of time movement in a story. Language can move time even if the temporality of what is narrated is radically blurred. Linguistic models of narrative foreground thus establish the grounds for inner-worlds criteria for temporal segmentation, criteria which are necessary to understanding the notion of narrative present in the fictional world. The present of fiction (or the foreground of the narrative) stands as a descriptive metaphor for the notion of *presence, immediacy* or *actuality*. The actualization (or presentness) of parts of the narrative world, rather than the inherent temporality of narrated events, is the primary condition for delimiting the present of narrative. The prevalent intuition which equates the term "fictive present" with the notion of "presentness" is indeed shared by such theorists of fictional and/or narrative time as Sternberg, Mendilow, Dry and Ingarden. Yet what is lacking is an explanation as to why such an actuality of part of the narrative is associated with temporality and why the fictive present, as a descriptive metaphor, is correlated with specific textual or linguistic markers of temporality.

My claim is that the fictive present is a specific narrative level with no a priori formal features or factors that can delineate its boundaries: events of the narrative present are not necessarily continuously arranged along a time line; temporally arranged event clauses might be included in what is defined, from a functional point of view, as nonpresent; scenic presentation is not necessarily an indicator of entering the narrative present; and so on. In short, the delimitation of the fictive present follows the specific modal structure of a given fictional universe; each narrative text selects different (and not necessarily temporal) materials to be actualized as its present.

The idea of narrative levels was introduced by Genette in order to systematize the notion of embedding, of subjecting one level of narrative to another. The primary narrative is the diegetic level of an extradiegetic narrating stance. Genette, in other words, attempts to provide a criterion for distinguishing between narrative levels by relating them to the formal source of narration. The primary level of the narrative is assigned to the narrating act of a first-level narrator, whether this narrating function is fulfilled by someone situated *in* the fictional world (extradiegetic homodiegetic) or by a narrator situated outside the story he narrates (extradiegetic heterodiegetic). Definitions of levels therefore have nothing to do with thematic importance revealed through an interpretation (Genette, 1983: 55ff.) This is in line with Ricoeur who demonstrates that the temporality of fiction cannot be separated from the concept of narrative configuration or emplotment: concepts of fictional temporality are tied up with divisions and structures of the narrative.

To narrate a story is already to "reflect upon" the event narrated. For this reason, narrative "grasping together" carries with it the capacity for distancing itself from its own production and in this way dividing itself in two ... [Fictive features of narrative time] are in a sense set free by the interplay between the various temporal levels stemming from the reflexivity of the configurating act itself. (Ricoeur, 1985: 61)

While also acknowledging that the concept of narrative levels and of temporality in fiction cannot be separated, Genette differs from Ricoeur in explicating narrative layering in formal terms of acts and levels of narration, rather than in the more abstract terms of principles of narrative configuration and emplotment. Genette's model can explain why the temporal coordinates of events, positioning them inside or outside the narrative present, involve questions of fictional layering and embedding. What Genette achieves in his model is an explication of the concept of "primary narrative" as the level of narrative most directly and immediately conveyed on the extra-diegetic level of communication. In a way Genette's notion of primary narrative and its formal definition explains why the time line of a narrative is constituted by what actually occurs in the story.

Genette's terms for designating primary and embedded narrative levels reveal why narrative levels correlate with the modalized structure of the fictional universe. Each level of the narrative implies shifting to another world, to another modality relative to the actual "presentness" of the primary level of narrative. As McHale (1987) has aptly put it, "each change of narrative level in a recursive structure also involves a change of ontological level, a change of world. These embedded or nested worlds may be more or less continuous with the world of the primary diegesis" (113). Shifts in narrative levels imply ontological shifts and temporal segmentation carries ontological implications. Since the time line of a narrative (the fictive present) is included in the primary narrative level, inclusion or exclusion from the time line bears on a story segment's degree of actuality or immediacy. To illustrate this point, let us refer to Nabokov's *The Real Life of Sebastian Knight* (1964) where the story is structured around two narrative axis: the narrator's (Sebastian's brother, V) hunt for evidence concerning Sebastian's life, and Sebastian's life as reconstructed through indirect evidence. Both levels are grammatically presented as narrative past relative to V's act of narration:

Again, whatever the weather, hats and umbrellas were tabooed, and Sebastian piously got wet and caught colds ... Fifteen years later, when I visited Cambridge and was told by Sebastian's best college friend ... of all these things ... (37)

In those last and saddest years of his life Sebastian wrote *The Doubtful Asphodel* ... Where and how did he write it? In the reading room of the British Museum ... At a humble table deep in the corner of a Parisian "bistro" ... In a deck-chair under an orange parasol ... In many other places which I can but vaguely conjecture. (146)

The narrative present yet consists of those past events subordinated to the narration of V and relating the details of his journey of seeking the past. On a less immediate level, Sebastian's own life is being reconstructed from various sources. Each narrative level is attributed a different ontological status and *has its own time dimension.* Since narrative levels are arranged according to levels of actuality or immediacy, in considering the temporality of events the narrative level to which an event belongs should also be taken into consideration. The time of a story is segmented into ontologically divergent sections indicating the degree of actuality of the events included in each time section.

The narrative present is the outcome of the narrative configuration in which certain events and states are selected to form the primary ontological level, the level of immediately presented and actually occurring narrative events. The narrative present is organized in a time line whereas other narrative segments of a less immediate nature or of a lower degree of actuality are organized relative to the temporal domain of their own narrative level. For this reason there is no point in theoretically imposing an a priori restriction on the type of materials the narrative present might include (as reflected in the exclusion of statives, of nonscenic materials and such like constraints). Moreover, subjected to the narrating act of the narrator, the entry into the narrative present may be indicated in diverse ways (by syntactic or semantic indicators, by speech-act indicators and so on) according to the modal composition of a given fictional universe. From the point of view of the extra-diegetic narrator, who controls the primary diegetic level, narrative segments may either be considered actual or of diminishing degrees of actuality.

To sum, the division of narrative fiction into foreground and background is not just a temporal division (into what is located on the narrative time line and what is presented as off the time line); the narrative present reflects the fact that the time of narrative fiction exhibits its own modal structure in which some events are presented as actually occurring (and hence part of the primary narrative level) whereas other events and situations are presented as only expected, talked about, hypothesized etc., in a sequenced or unsequenced form.

Fictional time and chronology

The temporality of fiction is attributed by some models of narrative time to the temporality of events and states of affairs projected or constructed by the fictional text. It is a central supposition in narrative studies (from Aristotle through the Russian Formalists to modern narratology) that since fictional texts present temporal material, they are inherently temporal. Attempts to locate the temporality of fiction in the chronology or achronology of events rely on the theoretical assumption that events presented in fiction in a certain order have a prior chronological order which is reconstructible from the text and independent of its textual manifestation. Thus, in Tomashevsky's phrasing "plot is distinct from story. Both include the same events, but in the plot the events are arranged and connected according to the orderly sequence in which they were presented in the work (in brief, the story is 'the action itself,' the plot, 'how the reader learns of the action.')" (1965: 67). The belief in the existence of a zero degree, where a perfect temporal correspondence is maintained between narrative and story, is supported "by a conception of discourse as consisting of sets of discrete signs which, in some way, correspond to (depict, encode, denote, refer to, and so forth) sets of discrete and specific ideas, objects, or events" (Smith, 1980: 221). Barbara Hernstein Smith claims that the conception of a prior scheme of chronologically ordered events and their subsequent discursive presentation in a deformed or original order, and such like assumptions that dominate contemporary narrative theory, are reflections of Platonist propensities inherent to this field of study.

The implausibility of assuming a prior absolute order is more specifically explained by Smith through her claim that no narrative version can be independent of a particular teller and occasion of telling (215). The fallacy of assuming a prior perfect order, as implied in narrative studies, is a clue to explicating the *metaphoricity of chronology* when used in relation to fictional temporality. There is no particular determinate set of events in some particular determinate (untwisted) order or sequence prior to and independent of a narrative in question. Smith herself proposes an alternative grasp on discursive temporality that obliterates altogether this hiatus between the telling and the told.[5] Goodman (1984) has a more moderate proposal that both avoids the Platonism of assuming a prior objective chronology of events and is more satisfactorily compatible with one's intuitions regarding the twistings of orders. Granted that chronology is a relevant organization of events, we can opt, with Goodman, for the assumption that the twisting in the telling is always relative not to an absolute order of occurrence but to the order of the told:

I am not supposing that order of occurrence is an absolute order of events independent of all versions but am rather drawing the distinction between order of the telling and order of the told ... I am by no means conceding that there is some underlying story, some deep structure, that is not itself a version. (122–123)

The idea that the told events in their chronological order form one possible version of retelling and not a prior Platonic order of a privileged ontological status is not revolutionary in itself. It implies, however, a denial of any theoretical attempt to root the notion of fictional temporality in the "natural" chronology of prenarrated events. Chronology is no more than an order of telling tied to the semiotics of world construction.

In extrafictional contexts chronology is an essentialist concept accounting for the "natural" concatenation of events independent of any perspectival interference (whether such a chronology of events in

5 One of Smith's strongest claims against a division of discourse into two time axes is that it is virtually impossible for any narrator to sustain an absolute chronological order in an utterance of more than minimal length. Chronology is therefore of no necessary relevance to fictional narrative.

reality is accessible or not is a question of a different sort); in fictional contexts the chronology of reported events is the outcome of the order and mode of their presentation. There is no order prior to the perspectivally determined mode of telling. Although it is doubtful whether chronology in general is not an idealized concept which assists us in coming to terms with the mass of events around us, regardless of the way we answer this metaphysical question, it is clear that even if such a positivist definition of chronology is accepted regarding "the real world," it definitely bears no relevance to fiction. That is, the way the order of fictional events is described in narrative studies and the mode of applying the distinction between *fabula* and *sujhet* to the issue of fictional chronology, are based on terms that extend, metaphorically, an essentialist conception of chronology understood as an absolute order of temporal materials.

To demonstrate the impossibility of divorcing the order of events from modes of telling, one can refer to two types of data: a literary text which foregrounds the notion of chronology by undermining any attempt to reconstruct the chronology of events and a theoretical model grounding its concepts of textual composition in a correlation with a reconstructed chronology of events. First, it is easy to demonstrate how in literary texts the order of the told can be manipulated to such an extent through modes of telling that chronological order loses its hold on the organization of the fictional world. Such is the case, for instance, in Robbe-Grillet's *La Maison de rendez-vous* (1966) where the order of the told is radically manipulated by modes of telling:

various essential points remain to be settled, for example: did the patrol's arrival take place before or after the theatrical performance? Perhaps it was even in the middle of the performance ... Then comes the knocking at the main door ... The audience is obviously unaware of what is happening in the rest of the house ... (149)

Simultaneity of logically consecutive events, conflicting versions of the same occurrences, contradictory retellings – all these are modes of telling demonstrating that the told does not exist apart from the telling. This text does not deliver to its readers a sense of a camouflaged or dissimulated absolute order; rather chronology does not seem to condition narrative organization or to be relevant at all to the organization of this narrative world. The sense of order is not undermined by the modes of telling characteristic of this text by

Robbe-Grillet; it is only the notion of a chronological order of prenarrated events that loses its pertinence. The example of Robbe-Grillet does not therefore provide a means of rejecting the relevance of order to some texts or a means of showing that chronology is relevant only when it is in the interests of the narrator to enable the reader to make certain inferences regarding the order of events narrated. It is rather that chronology as a temporal order inherent in events and prior to their narration is not a concept that pertains to the organization of fictional events. It is language that triggers the illusion of movement in time and of a chronological order of events; these are but the outcome of narrative manipulations and cannot reflect the temporal relations among the represented events. Fictional discourse constructs temporal relations in the narrative world, it does not *reveal* these relations.

The difficulty of tying chronology, as a mimetic principle organizing events in a pre-established level of action, to what is actually involved in fictional temporality can also be demonstrated in a theoretical model that grounds the notion of exposition on the chronological ordering of events. According to Sternberg, exposition (and the fictive present) is a concept belonging to the reconstructed order of events existing prior to aesthetic composition:

The point marking the end of the exposition in the *fabula* thus coincides with that point in time which marks the beginning of the *fictive present* in the *sujhet* – the beginning of the first time-section that the work considers important enough to be worthy of such full treatment as will involve, according to the contextual scenic norm, a close approximation or correspondence between its representational time and the clock-marked time we employ in everyday life. (1978: 21)

Every literary work establishes an internal norm which sets a relative standard for distinguishing between the time ratios of scenic and nonscenic presentation. Exposition is therefore defined as the time section in the *fabula* that precedes the point where the first event is treated scenically in the *sujhet*. Without elaborating on the details of this model, one may notice that in defining exposition Sternberg distinguishes between the reconstructed order of events, included in the retrospectively defined structure of the *fabula*, and the textual indicators that belong to the modes of presenting this structure. That is, in this respect the order of chronology is treated as prior to and independent of modes of presentation. Yet, in the attempt to supply a formal criterion for defining the temporal boundaries of the exposition, Sternberg switches between references to the distinction between *fabula* and *sujhet* as based on the absolute terms of chronology and references to modes of textual presentation which belong to the order of the text. That is, textual modes supply the evidence for marking different segments on the prior level of the *fabula* in order to explain the segmentation of the chronology of the *fabula* into exposition and nonexposition. By assuming that a temporal segment in the *fabula* correlates with specific nonscenic proportions of presentation, this model presupposes that textual modes represent or convey temporal relations that exist prior to these very modes. There are however many cases in which the proportions of presentation (scene versus nonscene) do not correspond to the division of time into an expositional part and a fictive-present part. A case in point is, for instance, the opening chapter of Patrick White's *Fringe of Leaves*, where an expositional segment in terms of chronology (presenting the past background of the protagonists) is presented scenically as a conversation between marginal characters, who disappear from the narrative scene thereafter. Yet this type of leap between reconstructed and textual levels is characteristic of many narrative models that assume a priority of chronological order and reconstructible temporal relations. As long as the reconstruction of parts of the *fabula* is based on textual principles of composition, there will always be texts that will counteract such a correlation. The idea that a chronological order of events can be reconstructed is only a tentative convention employed in reading fiction: this convention is not always treated as valid and it definitely cannot be correlated with pregiven textual indicators. When the convention of reconstructing chronology is activated, whatever textual features are present can be in the service of this activated convention. Yet the reconstruction of chronology is not always activated, and there is very little a priori correlation between the temporal delimitation of segments in fiction (as exposition versus fictive present) and the reconstructed chronology of events making up these segments. Exposition (determined textually by its nonscenic presentation) might include preparatory elements (*The Brothers Karamazov* opens with an expanded exposition, the first element of which relates the future murder of the family's father), or it might include events which chronologically come after the first scene in the *sujhet* (in Flaubert's *Un coeur simple* the first expositional chapter recounts events that chronologically succeed the events scenically presented in the second chapter).

On top of the theoretical difficulty of making mimetic assumptions about the relations between a *fabula* and a chronology of reconstructed events, there is the practical difficulty of correlating textual exposition with a specific domain of the *fabula*. The latter is however a telling difficulty: as Sternberg claims, exposition is a segment with a unique status in the overall structure of narrative events (a "nonprivileged" segment according to the internal textual norm). The segmentation of fictional time into exposition and fictive present can therefore be claimed to exceed questions of order even if a mimetic principle of chronology is accepted. I will claim that the chronology of the exposition and the fictive present cannot be seen as sequenced (that is, exposition is not the segment chronologically preceding the beginning of the *fabula*) because the sets of events that belong to each segment are of diverse ontological orders; the order of events in fiction is not of one modality. Chronology in fiction is subjected to the modal structure of the fictional universe. A text marks an ontological level which we choose to call *exposition* (according to quantitative indicators − nonscenic presentation − or according to qualitative indicators)[6] since this level is presented as separate from the level composed of events actualized on the primary narrative level. I would suggest describing the shift from exposition to fictive present again as a shift in levels, and describing the chronology of sets of events relative to the pertinent narrative level. Exposition can present a temporal domain additional to the time of the fictive present not on chronological grounds but on ontological grounds: the exposition includes materials, temporal or nontemporal, that were not selected to be actualized on the primary narrative level. Genette himself would have probably rejected the distinction between exposition and primary level altogether because expositional material is often presented as belonging to a separate narrative level (that is, as embedded in the primary narrative). Thus, chronology pertains to fiction solely in the semiotic sense of the order of the told; moreover the chronology of told events is relevant only when the events described form part *of the same ontological-narrative level*. Exposition and fictive present are hence of two different ontological orders. Exposition, narrative present, and other segmentations in the order of the told (narrative past, narrative

---

6 See Sternberg's own reservations about the possibility of employing only quantitative criteria in all cases when delimitation of the expositional segment is required (especially 28–29).

future, ending, and so on) hence function as temporal concepts that carry ontological implications differentiating distinct modalities and levels of actualization in the structure of the fictional universe.

Fictional time and modalities of tense relations

Some models primarily attribute the temporality of fiction to the temporality of the textual medium and to the nature of verbal presentation. The classical division of the arts (Lessing opposes painting to poetry) is determined by the spatial as opposed to the temporal order: reading occurs in time and the signs which are read are uttered or inscribed in a temporal sequence.[7] The linearity of the textual medium imposes a temporal organization that cannot be eluded. Thus Gertrude Stein (1962) expresses the impossibility of escaping the time of composition:

If the time in the composition is very troublesome it is because there must even if there is no time at all in the composition there must be time in the composition which is in its quality of distribution and equilibration. (522)

The temporality inherent to linear disposition is related to discursive structures in general, and it therefore has limited bearing on the particular problem of time in narrative fiction. Temporality as the linearity of discourse is also too obviously a metaphor to be discussed any further here. There is, however, another aspect of verbal presentation which is considered to be a test case for time in fiction. This is the temporality of the grammatical system of tenses and the order relations implied in this system.

The relationship between the grammatical system of aspect and tense and temporality is not a priori obvious. The question that the semantics of tense and aspect poses in relation to the temporality of narrative worlds is if and how the grammatical distinction between past, present, and future forms of verbs indicate temporal relations between the events reported by these verbs. In other words, do linguistic categories carry temporal meaning in fictional discourse, and does the distinction between past, present, and future tenses indicate interrelations of past, present, and future between the events narrated?

---

7 This division has itself been disputed in recent years. The abolition of the space–time differential as the basis for the generic distinction between painting and poetry can also be demonstrated in Lessing himself, who was originally responsible for the distinction, as shown in Mitchell, 1986.

A related problem, mostly addressed by linguists, is whether categories of grammatical aspect have implications for the construction and segmentation of the fictional time line (through the distinction, for instance, between continuous and punctual action correlated with aspectual differentiations). Attempts to address both the aspectual system and the tense system move along two lines:

(1) Some theorists deny any temporal meaning to grammatical categories in the context of fiction. Such is Hamburger's classical approach to the logic of literature where she claims that "fictionalization, action presented as the Here and Now of the fictive persons, *nullifies the temporal meaning of the tense* in which a piece of narrative literature is narrated: the preterite meaning of the grammatical past tense, as well as the present meaning of the historical present" (1973: 98, italics in the original). Hamburger bases her argument on the distinction between assertive and fictional discourse: unlike the speaker in the assertive mode, the speaker of a fictional discourse is himself fictional, which implies different logical principles governing fictional discourse. Hamburger shows how temporal meaning signified by tense is neutralized in fictional discourse as manifested in unique verb forms (the epic preterite) and in ungrammatical collocations (past tense in combination with present adverbials, mental verbs in past tense registering the concurrent flow of thoughts, and so on). Being ungrammatical in extrafictional contexts, such forms serve in fiction only as indicators marking the entry into fiction and hence the atemporality of fiction. In fiction, grammatical tenses do not imply temporal meaning. Likewise, Ingarden claims that in fiction there is a certain leveling of all the represented time moments. This equalization of represented time moments is symptomatically reflected in the fact that "in the vast majority of literary works, events and objects are represented in terms of the past" (1973: 236). The common denominator of these claims is that the logic of fiction cuts the time of fiction off "real time" and imposes a reinterpretation of the linguistic means for representing time in a fictional world. The attempt to dispense with the temporality of tense is based on the idea that grammatical tenses in fiction are "free-floating," having no reference point in relation to which past tense can be differentiated from future or present tenses. As a result, in fiction all grammatical tenses refer to the same here-and-now of the fictional characters.

(2) According to an opposite approach, the temporal intention of the tenses is conserved, despite the break established when we enter

the realm of fiction. What the system of tenses does achieve, according to Ricoeur for one, is the suspension of the reader's involvement in his or her real environment. "It suspends even more fundamentally the belief in the past as having-been in order to transpose it to the level of fiction ... An indirect relation to lived time is thus preserved through the mediation of neutralization" (1985: 75ff.). Ricoeur aims in his book at grounding the experience of time in fiction by explicating the temporal meaning inherent in different principles organizing the fictional universe. With respect to the system of tenses, he claims that the temporal intention of tensed verbs is conserved because the reader understands the present or past tenses as relative to the narrative voice: the present of narration is understood by the reader as posterior to the narrated story; the told story is hence the past of the narrative voice. Along a similar vein Pinto (1989) claims that fictional time does not advance automatically and that elements in the narrative sequence are semiotically marked in different ways. Fictional narrative constructs two different orders: the order of the narrated, which is semantically marked by the past tense (past in relation to the narrating act of speech) and the order of commentary marked by the present tense reminding the reader of the act of speech of a narrator and hence of the fact that the text is fiction and is to be understood as such. For both Ricoeur and Pinto the system of tense continues to operate in the context of fiction but it signifies different things. When past tense is used, for instance, it does not refer to past time but to a specific textual level and to a concrete fictional modality. In this way tenses reflect the particular nature of the narrative act of fiction-making.

The attempt to maintain, yet modify, the temporal meaning of tenses in fictional contexts relies on the belief that tenses in fiction are not totally cut off from an Archimedean point that allows fiction to uphold the whole system of tenses and to maintain their temporal differentiation. The zero point of reference has to do, again, with the relations between the axis of presentation (the telling) and the axis of the represented (the told): the temporal location of events is relativized to the time of narrative.

Both types of approach posit a question regarding the temporal meaning of past, present, and future tenses when these tenses position textual segments relative to the present of narration, rather than relative to present time. Both approaches, although oppositional in their conclusions, imply that fictional time is a separate independent temporal system obeying its own logic and principles of organization.

The meaning of tenses is characteristic of the fictional mode of being in time. The concept of fictional time is subject to the reservation that grammatical tenses carry a temporal meaning which is relativized to a present point of reference, the fictional present of the narrative act. In view of the fictional act that dominates the temporal system, Hamburger denies tenses in fiction any temporal meaning while Ricoeur positively maintains that tenses preserve their meaning relative to an alternative (fictional) reference point.

Attempts either to attribute temporal meaning to the system of tense or to neutralize it from any temporal meaning seem somewhat dubious at the outset because they appear to rely on an extremely purist view of language. Both views portrayed above are extreme in their solutions because they describe fictional temporality as a deviation against the background of an essentialist view of tense use. They assume that in nonfictional discourse tenses carry a distinct, unquestionable, and "uncontaminated" temporal meaning. As noticed earlier in this study, it is not at all certain that the use of tenses is more constrained in extrafictional contexts and that ungrammatical constructions of the type Hamburger enumerates ("tomorrow was Christmas") cannot appear outside fiction. Various options for employing tense forms in discourse in general indicate that the semiotics of tense can elude the temporality of past, present, and future implied in the use of such grammatical categories even in nonfictional contexts.

Yet regardless of whether in nonfictional discourse grammatical tenses are temporally intended, the above approaches to the tense system in fictional discourse are problematic for another reason. Both presuppose the priority of a present and its centrality to maintaining a temporal system of any kind. A present point of reference is needed to maintain the temporal meaning of tenses because present time is associated in these models with the "real time" concept of present which has

a decided ontic advantage over the "real" past and – to a still greater degree – over each future. And indeed, each "now," as well as that which is really present in the "now-moment," delineates a pronounced *actuality*, which inheres in neither the past nor the present – This *in actu esse* in a strict sense inheres only in the present and in what really exists in the present. (Ingarden, 1973: 235)

According to Ingarden, the ontic priority of the present is only maintained in real time. In represented time, however, the actuality of the present is only simulated; the relations between past, present, and future only maintain the sense of order but carry no ontic implications. Ingarden's observation can thus motivate the type of discussions involved in investigating the working of grammatical tenses in fictional discourse. The temporal or atemporal meaning of tenses is seen as the product of whether the segments correlated with the prevalent grammatical form of tense in a given text are attributed a privileged ontic position. The actuality of the fictional narrating act provides, according to some of the theorists, the necessary ontic vantage point for maintaining the operation of the tense system. The function of tenses in fictional discourse is hence closely tied to the way the concept of present is perceived, as a privileged reference point in the domain of which things are actualized. Thus, when the fictive present is identified with the present of speech, the reference point of time movement moves with it ensuring the stable pastness of narrated events. When fictive present is identified with the here-and-now of narrated events, the movement of time is neutralized by being reduced to an ever dominant ever present here-and-now of fiction; movement is then confined to a meta-temporal domain where all times are equal. Thus it is clear that the function of grammatical tenses in fiction is closely tied to the concept of an actualized present, and to the way the notion of present is interpreted in each given model. The idea of linking the present of fiction with the meaning attributed to tenses in fictional discourse is implied in the various models examined above and it further fortifies my argument that in fiction the use of grammatical tense is not only relative to a point of narration but is mainly correlated with the segmentation of fictional time into present and nonpresent. The temporal meaning of tenses is determined relative to that narrative segment being actualized as the foreground of the story, as its fictive present. To determine the function of grammatical tenses in fictional discourse requires a consideration of the position of a tense-determined given event in relation to the fictive present. To clarify the function of the fictive present as a factor in determining the meaning of tenses in fiction, I will briefly refer to an example. In James's "The Beast in the Jungle," one can show how the working of grammatical tense distinctions can only be motivated in relation to the fictive present. The story commences with a renewal of acquaintance of the main characters of the story, a man and a woman, who previously met eight years earlier. Marcher, the character whose perspective dominates the narrative, vaguely remembers the first encounter. May's face "affected him as the sequel of something of which he had lost the beginning" (1458). Thus, at the beginning of the story, tense differentiation supports the distinction between narrative present and the past encounter: "the present would have been so much better if the other, in the far distance, in the foreign land, hadn't been so stupidly meagre" (1460). But shifts in tenses also serve to differentiate actualized from non-actualized happenings.

He would have liked to invent something, get her to make-believe with him that some passage of a romantic or critical kind had originally occurred. He was really almost reaching out in imagination – as against time – for something that would do ... (1460)

In the final sections of the story, Marcher, following May's death, discovers that, by being preoccupied with his egocentric secret, he has missed the opportunity of living a full life of love with May. The insight he has about missing his chances and misinterpreting his whole life is signaled by a resort to a past perfect tense which appears to express the delayed understanding of those parts of his life and hence of the impossibility of actualizing their potential in the narrative present:

The fate he had been marked for he had met with a vengeance – he had emptied the cup to the lees; he had been the man of his time, the man, to whom nothing on earth was to have happened ... So she had seen it while he didn't ... that all the while he had waited the wait was itself his portion ... (1491)

The shift to the past perfect tense clearly functions here not only to signal a past further from the "past" of Marcher's flow of thoughts, but also the recognition that comes too late to change anything. The use of tenses here underlines the modal function of tense use in general. Tenses do not only produce an order of past, present, and future – they also carry implications regarding the actualizability of a given situation. The modality of tense is hence a prerequisite for interpreting the meaning of tenses in fictional discourse. At Marcher's present state the past cannot be revived, and lost situations are lost for ever. Likewise, in the first scenes of the story tenses mark the play between memory and forgetfulness in Marcher's reconstruction and speculation as to what really happened in their initial encounter. In the closing scenes, the modal significance of tenses lies in the distinction they signal between what Marcher now understands and the pastness of events to which his understanding applies. Tense differentiation does not necessarily carry temporal meaning (shifts in grammatical tense are often not motivated by temporal shifts). The tenses rather mark degrees of actuality, of recognition and of knowledge at various stages of the story.

In a similar fashion, in Nabokov's novel *The Real Life of Sebastian Knight*, there is no tense differentiation between textual segments in which the narrator V relates events or occurrences in his own life and events related to Sebastian's life, which took place in a distant past relative to the point of time at which V reconstructs Sebastian's life. This lack of linguistic differentiation is one possible symptom for the conflation of levels characteristic of this novel.[8]

The "anomaly" of tense usage in fictional contexts noticed by theorists of diverse convictions, yet does not necessarily mark the total loss of temporal meaning the tense system undergoes in fiction. Shifts in the meaning of tenses rather indicate that the function of tenses is determined by the organization of fictional time into foreground and background (into fictive present and nonpresent). Again, the insistence on preserving or denying a temporal meaning of tenses amounts to an attempt to find a distinctive vantage point in relation to which the use of past, present, or future tenses can be motivated in fiction. In any case, in fiction, where the use of tenses and the construction of temporal relations among events is subjected to a point of view of a narrating self, which both fluctuates and is internal to the fictional system, past, present, and future necessarily become relativized concepts. In this sense, the temporality inherent in textual modes of presentation, in the linear disposition of segments, and in the meaning of grammatical categories, is a temporality which obeys the specific constraints of fictional world re-construction.

Tenses in general indicate modalities within a universe of discourse. In fiction the linguistic categories of tense imply relations of order (between past, present, and future events); this order reflects not just temporal relations but also the modal structure of the fictional world according to degrees of actuality. As a result, the actualized present is that segment marked by a dominant tense form (usually the past or the epic preterite), while other tense forms are attributed diminished degrees of actuality. Even if we agree that grammatical tenses are measured against the temporal point of narration (which explains why

---

8 For a full analysis of the novel's Chinese-box structure and the interdependence among narrative levels, see Rimmon, 1976.

the prevalent tense form in fiction is the past form), tense differentiation is not employed to mark varying distances between the time of narration and the time of the narrated but to indicate the degree of actualization of the told events. In the fictional world, the shift in grammatical tenses and hence the shift from fictive past to fictive present or future, are shifts which imply a change in modality.

The very core of fiction lies in the projection of a world through textual modes of presentation, which produces a modally stratified world structure. The system of fictive time and temporality that interrelates elements in fictional worlds is hence also a reflection of this modal structure and it manifests the two distinctive properties of time in fiction. The first property of fictional time that emerges from its particular mode of being is connected to the fact that time in fiction constitutes a parallel and autonomous temporal system; the second property is related to the correlation between temporal relations and the degree of actuality of given fictional situations (whether a situation is an actual state of affairs in the story, or only a hypothetical or talked about state of affairs).

The fact that fictional time is sensed to be separate (yet analogous) from other temporal systems is expressed in narrative models that address the time of narrative fiction employing time-referring expressions yet attributing to these expressions specific meanings appropriate for a narrative fictional context. The interpretation given to notions like fictive present, order, chronology, time line and tense differentiations in narrative theories, expresses the logic of parallelism characteristic of the distinct nature of the temporal systems of fictional narrative. These terms indicating time, work only as metaphorical extensions of time-referring expressions used in nonfictional contexts. More specifically, narrative theories, in their dealings with fictive time, reveal a view on this temporal system as requiring a unique and distinct time conception different from those at work outside fiction. The tacit belief that in fiction time works differently can be illustrated in showing that, for instance, the fictive present constitutes a privileged ontic sphere, that the time line of a story is not just the organization of events in a specific order, but also the foreground of the story. The fact that time-parameters organize states of affairs of the fictional world according to degrees of actualization shows that the fictional world is understood to be modally and not only temporally structured. Extant theories of narrative temporality hence reflect what has been explicitly argued in this chapter: that the time of narrative fiction constitutes an autonomous temporal system, and that this autonomy is manifested in the modal structure of the time of fictional worlds: that is, in the fact that time in fiction follows modal considerations and not only questions of temporal location and organization.

Conclusion

This study of possible worlds and fictional worlds aims to provide a conceptual exposition of how the two terms relate. Since possible and fictional worlds interact both in the philosophical discipline and in the domain of literary theory, my conceptual exposition switches constantly between discourses of both. The overall task of the analysis presented in this study is twofold: for one, this study exhibits an attempt to uproot the mechanism behind interdisciplinary borrowings. The case of possible worlds supplies an intricate and at the same time, a telling example in this regard: a close analysis of the conceptual affinities between possible worlds and fiction reveals the attractive yet limited scope of usability of the philosophical concept for clarifying the literary object of research. Yet the full range of questions possible worlds legitimized, although not necessarily supplied the conceptual means for solving, can lead to a study of the structure of fictional worlds along the lines opened up by the possible worlds framework. Second, the aim of this study is to make a specific contribution to the ongoing theorizing about fiction. In this context the attempt is gradually to develop and formulate a set of conventions in terms of which the understander of fiction reconstructs a fictional world with its specific constitutive domains (of objects, characters, events, points of view and time). Since this study supports a pragmatic re-thinking on the notion of fictionality, the idea is to define this notion in terms of conventions that direct the reader in interpreting the global position of fiction vis-à-vis alternative world constructions. The second part of this book therefore "translates" the general model for fiction-understanding presented in the first half, into sub-models accounting for the way specific fictional domains are reconstructed.

By articulating these two aims I hope to clarify why this book seeks to present possible and fictional worlds in a way that should answer the concerns of philosophers and would satisfy the problems relevant to a literary enquiry. It is for this reason that the present study of possible worlds can not be an attempt to forge new tools borrowed from philosophy for literary critics. This latter worthy task has been executed already by literary critics and my purpose is to show what this forging led to on the conceptual level when guided solely by "literary" interests. In this respect the analysis of the concepts involved, as presented in this study, in a way "deconstructs" the theoretical presuppositions behind such interdisciplinary borrowings. My primary concern, in other words, is not "doing things with texts" but exposing inadequacies which emerge when interdisciplinary things are done with texts. In view of this concern, the "data" I use in this study cannot consist of literary texts. In order to reconstruct the interdisciplinary game at the first stage, and to formulate the conventions of fiction-understanding at the second stage, my data consisted of theoretical works produced by philosophers and literary theorists in relation to the problem of fiction. Theories of fiction are hence the elementary stuff from which a pragmatic theory of fiction can be deduced; even when the theories concerned do not in themselves forward one or another theory of fictionality, they reveal how the property of "being fictional" is interpreted by philosophers on the one hand, and by literary theorists on the other hand.

The point of view adopted for the present task is thus necessarily situated above, or better yet, outside the conceptual commitments of both philosophy and literary criticism. This somewhat unusual point of view might suggest one relevant domain where interdisciplinary theorizing and applications should be discussed. I believe such an interdisciplinary discussion should precede any actual borrowings across disciplines so that we can avoid producing what Jonathan Culler has described as "theory": studies which "exceed the disciplinary framework within which they would normally be evaluated" without mastering or enquiring after the traditions from which their tools were initially borrowed (1982: 7ff.).

Bibliography

Adams, Robert M. 1979. "Theories of Actuality," in: M. J. Loux (ed.), *The Possible and the Actual: Readings in the Metaphysics of Modality*. Ithaca & London: Cornell University Press, pp. 190–209.

Allen, Sture (ed.). 1989. *Possible Worlds in Humanities, Arts and Sciences: Proceedings of Nobel Symposium 65*. Berlin & New York: Walter de Gruyter.

Augustine, Saint. 1961 [397–8 A. D.]. *Confessions*, Book XI. Harmondsworth: Penguin Books, pp. 253–280.

Bal, Mieke. 1977. *Narratologie*. Paris: Editions Klinchsiedk.

1981. "The Laughing Mice." *Poetics Today* 2: 2, pp. 202–210.

Banfield, Ann. 1982. *Unspeakable Sentences: Narration and Representation in the Language of Fiction*. London: Routledge.

Barthes, Roland. 1966a. "Introduction a l'analyse structurale des récits." *Communications* 8, pp. 1–27.

1966b. *Critique et vérité*. Paris: Editions du Seuil.

Bell, J. S. 1989. "Six Possible Worlds of Quantum Mechanics," in: Allen (ed.), pp. 359–373.

Blocker, Gene. 1974. "The Truth about Fictional Entities." *Philosophical Quarterly* 24, pp. 27–36.

Bourneuf, Roland. 1970. "L'Organisation de l'espace dans le roman." *Etudes littéraires* 3: 1, pp. 77–94.

Bradley, Raymond and Swartz, Norman. 1979. *Possible Worlds: An Introduction to Logic and Its Philosophy*. Indianapolis, Indiana: Hackett Publishing Company.

Bremond, Claude. 1980. "The Logic of Narrative Possibilities." *New Literary History* 11, (Spring) Number 3, pp. 387–411.

Brinker, Menachem. 1987. "Realism, Pragmatism and Literary Theory." *Revue Internationale de Philosophie* 41, pp. 347–363.

1989. *Is Literary Theory Possible?* (in Hebrew). Tel Aviv: Sifriat Poalim.

Bronzwaer, W. 1981. "Mieke Bal's Concept of Focalization." *Poetics Today* 2: 2, pp. 193–201.

Brooks, Peter. 1984. *Reading for the Plot: Design and Intention in Narrative*. New York: Alfred A. Knopf.

Campbell, B. G. 1975. "Toward a Workable Taxonomy of Illocutionary

Bibliography

Forces, and its Implication to Works of Imaginative Literature."
Language and Style 8 (1), pp. 3–20.

Castañeda, Hector-Neri. 1979. "Fiction and Reality: Their Fundamental
Connections." *Poetics* 8, pp. 31–62.

Chateau, Dominique. 1976. "La semantique du récit." *Semiotica* 18: 3,
pp. 201–216.

Chatman, Seymour. 1986. "Characters and Narrators: Filter, Center, Slant,
and Indirect-Focus." *Poetics Today* 7: 2, pp. 189–204.

Chisholm, Roderick M. 1979. "Identity Through Possible Worlds: Some
Questions," in: M. J. Loux (ed.), pp. 80–87.

Cohn, Dorrit. 1990. "Signposts of Fictionality: A Narratological Perspective." *Poetics Today* 11: 4, pp. 775–803.

Cordesse, Gérard. 1988. "Narration et focalisation." *Poétique* 76, pp. 487–498.

Culler, Jonathan. 1975a. *Structuralist Poetics*. Ithaca, N.Y.: Cornell University
Press.

1975b. "Defining Narrative Units," in: R. Fowler (ed.), *Style and Structure
in Literature*. Oxford: Blackwell, pp. 123–142.

1980. "Fabula and Sjuzhet in the Analysis of Narrative." *Poetics Today* 1:
3, pp. 27–37.

1982. *On Deconstruction: Theory and Criticism after Structuralism*. Ithaca,
N.Y.: Cornell University Press.

Currie, Gregory. 1990. *The Nature of Fiction*. Cambridge & New York:
Cambridge University Press.

Davies, Paul. 1980. *Other Worlds: Space, Superspace and the Quantum Universe*.
New York: Simon & Schuster, Inc.

Doležel, Lubomir. 1976. "Narrative Semantics." *PTL* 1, pp. 129–151.

1977. "Semantics of Narrative Motifs." *Proceedings of the 12th International
Congress of Linguistics*, Vienna.

1979. "Extensional and Intensional Narrative Worlds." *Poetics* 8, pp.
193–211.

1980. "Truth and Authenticity in Narrative." *Poetics Today* 1: 3, pp. 7–25.

1985. "Pour une typologie des mondes fictionnels," in: Herman Parret,
Hans-Georg Ruprecht (eds.). *Exigences et perspectives de la semiotique.
Recueil d'hommage pour A. J. Greimas*. Amsterdam-Philadelphia:
Benjamins, pp. 7–23.

1988. "Mimesis and Possible Worlds." *Poetics Today* 9: 3, pp. 475–496.

1989. "Possible Worlds and Literary Fictions," in: S. Allen (ed.),
pp. 221–242.

Donnellan, Keith. 1966. "Reference and Definite Descriptions." *Philosophical
Review* 75, pp. 281–304.

1974. "Speaking of Nothing." *Philosophical Review* 83, pp. 3–32.

Dry, Helen. 1981. "Sentence Aspect and the Movement of Narrative Time."
Text 1: 3, pp. 233–240.

1983. "The Movement of Narrative Time." *Journal of Literary Semantics*
12: 2, pp. 19–53.

Bibliography

Eco, Umberto. 1979. "Lector in Fabula," in: *The Role of the Reader: Explorations in the Semiotics of Texts*. Bloomington: Indiana University Press, pp. 200–260.

1989. "Report on Session 3: Literature and Arts," in: S. Allen (ed.), pp. 343–355.

Edmiston, William F. 1989. "Focalization and the First-Person Narrator: A Revision of the Theory." *Poetics Today* 10: 4, pp. 729–744.

Felman, Shoshana. 1983. *The Literary Speech Act: Don Juan with Austin, or Seduction in Two Languages*. Trans. Catherine Porter. Ithaca: Cornell University Press.

Fine, Kit. 1982. "The Problem of Non-Existents." *Topoi* 1, pp. 97–140.

Forster, E. M. 1927. *Aspects of the Novel*. New York: Harcourt, Brace and Company.

Frank, Joseph E. 1945. "Spatial Form in Modern Literature." *The Sewanee Review*, pp. 221–240; 430–456; 643–653.

Genette, Gerard. 1972. *Figures III*. Paris: Seuil.

1982 [1964]. "Structuralism and Literary Criticism," in: A. Sheridan, trans. *Figures of Literary Discourse*. Oxford: Blackwell.

1983. *Nouveau discours du récit*. Paris: Editions du Seuil.

1988. *Narrative Discourse Revisited* (trans. Jane E. Lewin). Ithaca, New York: Cornell University Press.

1990. "Fictional Narrative, Factual Narrative." *Poetics Today* 11: 4, pp. 755–774.

Goffman, Erving. 1974. *Frame Analysis*. New York: Harper & Row.

Goodman, Nelson. 1978. *Ways of Worldmaking*. Indianapolis: Hackett.

1983. *Fact, Fiction, and Forecast*. Cambridge, Mass. & London, England: Harvard University Press. (fourth edition).

1984. *Of Mind and Other Matters*. Cambridge, Mass. and London, England: Harvard University Press.

Greimas, A. J. 1966. *Sémantique structurale*. Paris: Larousse.

1977. "Elements of a Narrative Grammar." *Diacritis* 7, pp. 23–40.

Hamburger, Kate. 1973. *The Logic Of Literature* (trans. Marilynn J. Rose). Bloomington and London: Indiana University Press.

Heintz, John. 1979. "Reference and Inference in Fiction." *Poetics* 8, pp. 85–99.

Hintikka, Jakko. 1967. "Individuals, Possible Worlds, and Epistemic Logic." *Nous* 1, pp. 33–62.

1979. "The Modes of Modality," in: M. J. Loux (ed.), pp. 65–79.

1989. "Exploring Possible Worlds," in: S. Allen (ed.), pp. 52–73.

Howell, Robert. 1979. "Fictional Objects: How They Are and How They Aren't." *Poetics* 8, pp. 129–178.

Hrushovski, Benjamin. 1979. "The Structure of Semiotic Objects: A Three-Dimensional Model." *Poetics Today* 1: 1–2, pp. 365–376.

1984. "Fictionality and Fields of Reference." *Poetics Today* 5: 2, pp. 227–251.

Hutcheon, Linda. 1988. "The Problem of Reference," in: *A Poetics of*

Postmodernism: History, Theory, Fiction. New York: Routledge, pp. 141–157.

Ihwe, Jens and H. Rieser. 1979. "Normative and Descriptive Theory of Fiction: Some Contemporary Issues." *Poetics* 8, pp. 63–84.

Ingarden, Roman. 1973. *The Literary Work of Art: An Investigation on the Borderlines of Ontology, Logic, and Theory of Literature.* Evanston: Northwestern University Press.

Inwagen, Peter van. 1977. "Creatures of Fiction." *American Philosophical Quarterly* 14, pp. 299–308.

Iser, Wolfgang. 1975. "The Reality of Fiction: A Functionalist Approach to Literature." *New Literary History* 7: 1, pp. 7–38.

Jakobson, Roman. 1976. "Closing Statement: Linguistics and Poetics," in: Thomas A. Sebeok (ed.), *Style in Language.* Cambridge: The MIT Press, pp. 350–377.

1978. "The Dominant," in: Ladislav Matejka and Krystyna Pomorska (eds.). *Readings in Russian Poetics: Formalist and Structuralist Views.* Ann Arbor, Michigan: Michigan Slavic Publications, pp. 82–87.

Jefferson, Ann. 1977. "Semiotics of a Literary Text." *PTL: A Journal for Descriptive Poetics and Theory of Literature* 3, pp. 579–588.

Kripke, Saul. 1963. "Semantical Considerations on Modal Logic." *Acta Philosophica Fennica* 16, pp. 83–94.

1972. *Naming and Necessity.* Cambridge: Harvard University Press.

Kuhn, Thomas S. 1989. "Possible Worlds in History of Science," in: S. Allen (ed.), pp. 9–32.

Labov, William. 1972. *Language in the Inner City.* Philadelphia: University of Pennsylvania Press.

Leech, Geoffrey N. & Short, Michael H. 1981. *Style in Fiction: A Linguistic Introduction to English Fictional Prose.* London & New York: Longman.

Lewis, David. 1973. *Counterfactuals.* Cambridge: Harvard University Press.

1978. "Truth in Fiction." *American Philosophical Quarterly* 15, pp. 37–46.

1983. "Counterpart Theory and Quantified Modal Logic," in: *Philosophical Papers,* vol. I, pp. 26–39.

1986. *On the Plurality of Worlds.* Oxford & New York: Basil Blackwell.

Linde, Ulf. 1989. "Image and Dimension," in: S. Allen (ed.), pp. 312–328.

Lotman, Jurij. 1977. *The Structure of the Artistic Text.* Michigan: University of Michigan Press.

Loux, Michael J. (ed.). 1979. *The Possible and the Actual: Readings in the Metaphysics of Modality.* Ithaca & London: Cornell University Press.

Lyons, John. 1977. *Semantics,* volume 2. London & New York: Cambridge University Press.

Mallory, William E. & Simpson-Housley, Paul (eds.). 1987. *Geography and Literature: A Meeting of the Disciplines.* Syracuse, New York: Syracuse University Press.

Malmgren, Carl D. 1988. "Worlds Apart: A Theory of Science Fiction," in: Arno Heller (ed.), *Utopian Thought in American Literature.* Tübingen: Gunter Narr, pp. 25–42.

Bibliography

Margolin, Uri. 1990. "Individuals in Narrative Worlds: An Ontological Perspective." *Poetics Today* 11: 4, pp. 843–871.

Margolis, Joseph. 1962. *Philosophy Looks at the Arts: Contemporary Readings in Aesthetics*. New York: Charles Scribner's Sons.

1977. "The Ontological Peculiarity of Works of Art." *Journal of Aesthetics and Art Criticism* 36, pp. 45–50.

Martinez-Bonati, Felix. 1981. *Fictive Discourse and the Structures of Literature*. Ithaca and London: Cornell University Press.

1983. "Towards a Formal Ontology of Fictional Worlds." *Philosophy and Literature*, 7, pp. 182–195.

McCawley, James D. 1978. "World-Creating Predicates." *Versus* 19–20, pp. 77–93.

1981. *Everything that Linguists have Always Wanted to Know about Logic, but were Ashamed to Ask*. Chicago: The University of Chicago Press.

McHale, Brian. 1978. "Free Indirect Discourse: A Survey of Recent Accounts." *PTL (A Journal for Descriptive Poetics and Theory of Literature)* 3, pp. 249–287.

1987. *Postmodernist Fiction*. New York & London: Methuen.

McNeil, Lynda D. 1980. "Toward a Rhetoric of Spatial Form: Some Implications of Frank's Theory." *Comparative Literature Studies* 17, pp. 355–367.

Mendilow, A. A. 1952. "The Position of the Present in Fiction," in: *Time and the Novel*. London.

Mitchell, W. J. T. 1980. "Spatial Form in Literature: Toward a General Theory." *Critical Inquiry* 6, pp. 539–567.

1986. "Space and Time: Lessing's *Laocoon* and the Politics of Genre," in: *Iconology: Image, Text, Ideology*. Chicago and London: The University of Chicago Press, pp. 95–115.

Nelles, William. 1990. "Getting Focalization into Focus." *Poetics Today* 11: 2, pp. 365–382.

O'Toole, Lawrence M. 1980. "Dimensions of Semiotic Space in Narrative." *Poetics Today* 1: 4, pp. 135–149.

Parsons, Terence. 1980. *Nonexistent Objects*. New Haven: Yale University Press.

Partee, Barbara H. 1989. "Possible Worlds in Model-Theoretic Semantics: A Linguistic Perspective," in: S. Allen (ed.). *Possible Worlds In Humanities, Arts and Sciences*. Proceedings of Nobel Symposium 65. Berlin & New York: Walter de Gruyter, pp. 93–123.

Paskins, Barrie. 1977. "On Being Moved by Anna Karenina and *Anna Karenina*." *Philosophy* 52, pp. 344–347.

Patrides, C. A. (ed.). 1976. *Aspects of Time*. Manchester: Manchester University Press.

Pavel, Thomas G. 1975. "Possible Worlds in Literary Semantics." *The Journal of Aesthetics and Art Criticism* 34: 2, pp. 165–176.

1980. "Narrative Domains," *Poetics Today* 1: 4, pp. 105–114.

1985. *The Poetics of Plot: The Case of English Renaissance Drama.*
Minneapolis: University of Minnesota Press.

1986. *Fictional Worlds.* Cambridge, Mass. & London, England: Harvard
University Press.

1988. "Formalism in Narrative Semiotics." *Poetics Today* 9: 3, pp. 593–606.

1989. "Fictional Worlds and the Economy of the Imaginary," in: Allen,
pp. 250–259.

Petrey, Sandy. 1990. *Speech Acts and LIterary Theory.* New York & London:
Routledge.

Pinto, Julio C. M. 1989. *The Reading of Time: A Semantic-Semiotic Approach.*
Berlin & New York: Mouton de Gruyter.

Plantinga, Alvin. 1974. *The Nature of Necessity.* Oxford: Clarendon Press.

1976. "Actualism and Possible Worlds." *Theoria* 42, pp. 139–160.

1979. "Transworld Identity or Worldbound Individuals." in: M. J. Loux
(ed.), *The Possible and the Actual: Readings in the Metaphysics of Modality.*
Ithaca & London: Cornell University Press, pp. 146–165.

Poetics 8: 1/2 (1979). "Formal Semantics and Literary Theory."

Popper, Karl R. 1982. *The Open Universe: An Argument for Indeterminism.*
London and Melbourne: Hutchinson.

Pratt, Mary-Louise. 1977. *Toward a Speech Act Theory of Literary Discourse.*
Bloomington: Indiana University Press.

Prince, Gerald. 1982. *Narratology: The Form and Functioning of Narrative.*
Berlin, New York and Amsterdam: Mouton Publishers.

1987. *A Dictionary of Narratology.* Lincoln and London: University of
Nebraska Press.

1988. "The Disnarrated." *Style* 22: 1, pp. 1–8.

Putnam, Hilary. 1983. *Realism and Reason: Philosophical Papers*, vol. 3.
Cambridge & London: Cambridge University Press.

1990. *Realism With a Human Face.* Cambridge, Mass. & London, England:
Harvard University Press.

Reinhart, Tanya. 1984. "Principles of Gestalt Perception in the Temporal
Organization of Narrative Texts." *Linguistics* 22, pp. 779–809.

Ricoeur, Paul. 1981. "Narrative Time," in: W. J. T. Mitchell, *On Narrative.*
Chicago and London: The University of Chicago Press, pp. 165–186.

1984. *Time and Narrative*, vol. 1 (trans. by Kathleen Mclaughlin and David
Pellauer). Chicago and London: The University of Chicago Press.

1985. *Time and Narrative*, vol. 2 (trans. by Kathleen Mclaughlin and David
Pellauer). Chicago and London: The University of Chicago Press.

Rigney, Ann. 1991. "Narrativity and Historical Representation." *Poetics
Today* 12: 3, pp. 591–605.

Rimmon, Shlomith. 1976. "Problems of Voice in Vladimir Nabokov's *The Real
Life of Sebastian Knight.*" *PTL* 1, pp. 489–512.

1983. *Narrative Fiction: Contemporary Poetics.* London and New York:
Methuen.

Ronen, Ruth. 1986a. "Poetical Coherence in Prose Fiction." *Style* 20: 1,
pp. 66–74.

1986b. "Space in Fiction." *Poetics Today* 7: 3, pp. 421–438.

Rorty, Richard. 1982. *Consequences of Pragmatism (Essays, 1972–1980)*. Minneapolis: University of Minnesota Press.

Rossum-Guyon, van Françoise. 1970. "Point de vue ou perspective narrative." *Poétique* 4, pp. 476–497.

Routley, Richard. 1979. "The Semantical Structures of Fictional Discourse." *Poetics* 8, pp. 3–30.

Ryan, Marie-Laure. 1980. "Fiction, Non-Factuals and the Principle of Minimal Departure." *Poetics* 8: 3/4, pp. 403–422.

1981. "The Pragmatics of Personal and Impersonal Fiction." *Poetics* 10, pp. 517–539.

1984. "Fictions as a Logical, Ontological, and Illocutionary Issue." *Style* 18, pp. 121–139.

1985. "The Modal Structure of Narrative Universes." *Poetics Today* 6: 4, pp. 717–755.

1991. "Possible Worlds and Accessibility Relations: A Semantic Typology of Fiction." *Poetics Today* 12: 3, pp. 553–576.

Sanford, David H. 1989. *If P, then Q: Conditionals and the Foundations of Reasoning*. London & New York: Routledge.

Schmidt, Siegfried. J. 1984. "The Fiction is that Reality Exists: A Constructivist Model of Reality, Fiction, and Literature." *Poetics Today* 5: 2, pp. 253–274.

Searle, John. 1969. *Speech Acts*. London: Cambridge University Press.

1975. "The Logical Status of Fictional Discourse." *New Literary History* 6, pp. 319–332.

Shen, Yeshayahu. 1985. "On Importance Hierarchy and Evaluation Devices in Narrative Texts." *Poetics Today* 6: 4, pp. 681–698.

1990. "Centrality and Causal Relations in Narrative Texts." *Journal of Literary Semantics* 19: 1, pp. 1–23.

Smith, Barbara Hernstein. 1980. "Narrative Versions, Narrative Theories." *Critical Inquiry* 7, pp. 213–236.

Smitten, Jeffrey R. 1978. "Approaches to the Spatiality of Narrative." *Papers on Language and Literature* 14, pp. 296–314.

Sparshott, F. E. 1967. "Truth in Fiction." *Journal of Aesthetics and Art Criticism* 26, pp. 3–7.

Stalnaker, Robert C. 1976. "Possible Worlds." *Nous* 10, pp. 65–75.

Stein, Gertrude. 1962 [1926]. "Composition as Explanation," in: *Selected Writings of Gertrude Stein*. New York: Vintage Books, pp. 511–539.

Sternberg, Meir. 1978. *Expositional Modes and Temporal Ordering in Fiction*. Baltimore and London: The Johns Hopkins University Press.

1981. "Ordering the Unordered: Time, Space and Descriptive Coherence." *Yale French Studies* 61, pp. 60–88.

Strawson, P. F. 1959. *Individuals: An Essay in Descriptive Metaphysics*. London: Methuen.

Todorov, Tzvetan. 1977. "The Grammar of Narrative," in: *The Poetics of Prose*. Ithaca, New York: Cornell University Press, pp. 108–119.

Bibliography

Tomashevsky, Boris. 1965. "Thematics," in: Lee T. Lemon and Marion J. Reis (eds.), *Russian Formalist Criticism: Four Essays*. Lincoln: University of Nebraska Press, pp. 61–95.

Toolan, Michael J. 1988. *Narrative: A Critical Linguistic Introduction*. London and New York: Routledge.

　1990. *The Stylistics of Fiction: A Literary-Linguistic Approach*. London & New York: Routledge.

Tynjanov, Jurij. 1978. "On Literary Evolution," in: Ladislav Matejka and Krystyna Pomorska (eds.), *Readings in Russian Poetics: Formalist and Structuralist Views*. Ann Arbor, Michigan: Michigan Slavic Publications, pp. 66–78.

Urmson, J. O. 1976. "Fiction." *American Philosophical Quarterly* 13: 2, pp. 153–157.

Uspensky, Boris. 1973. *The Poetics of Composition*. California: University of California Press.

Vaina, Lucia. 1977. "Les mondes possibles du texte." *Versus* 17, pp. 3–13.

van Dijk, Teun A. 1972. *Some Aspects of Text Grammars: A Study in Theoretical Linguistics and Poetics*. The Hague and Paris: Mouton.

Vilensky, Robert. 1982. "Points: A Theory of the Structure of Stories in Memory," in: Wendy G. Lehnert and Martin H. Ringle (eds.). *Strategies for Natural Language Processing*. Hillsdale, N. J. and London: Lawrence Erlbaum Associates Publishers, pp. 345–374.

Vitoux, Pierre. 1982. "Le jeu de la focalisation." *Poétique* 51, pp. 359–368.

Walton, Kendall. 1978. "How Remote are Fictional Worlds from the Real World?" *Journal of Aesthetics and Art Criticism* 37, pp. 11–23.

　1983. "Fiction, Fiction-Making and Styles of Fictionality." *Philosophy and Literature* 7, pp. 78–88.

　1990. *Mimesis as Make-Believe: On the Foundations of the Representational Arts*. Cambridge & London: Harvard University Press.

Wellek, Rene and Warren, Austin. 1973 [1949]. *The Theory of Literature*. England: Penguin University Books.

Wolterstorff, Nicholas. 1980. *Worlds and Works of Art*. Oxford: Clarendon Press.

Woods, John. 1974. *The Logic of Fiction: A Philosophical Sounding of Deviant Logic*. The Hague: Mouton.

　and Thomas, G. Pavel (eds.). 1979. "Formal Semantics and Literary Theory: Introduction," *Poetics* 8, 1/2.

Zemach, Eddy. Forthcoming. "Existence and Nonexistents."

Literary sources

Barnes, Julien. 1984. "Emma Bovary's Eyes," in: *Flaubert's Parrot*. London: Picador, Pan Books, pp. 74–81.

Flaubert, Gustave. 1969 [1870]. *Sentimental Education* (trans. Robert Baldick). Harmondsworth: Penguin Books.

Bibliography

James, Henry. 1986. "The Beast in the Jungle." in: Nina Baym et al. (eds.),
   The Norton Anthology of American Literature. New York: Norton,
   pp. 1457–1492.
   1963 [1881] *The Portrait of a Lady*. Harmondsworth: Penguin Books.
Nabokov, Vladimir. 1964 [1941]. *The Real Life of Sebastian Knight*.
   Harmondsworth: Penguin Books.
Robbe-Grillet, Alain. 1966 [1965]. *La Maison de rendez-vous*. New York:
   Grove Press.
Stendhal. 1953 [1830]. *Scarlet and Black* (trans. Margaret Shaw).
   Harmondsworth: Penguin Books.
Woolf, Virginia. 1977 [1927]. *To the Lighthouse*. London & Toronto: Granada
   Publishing.

Index

Index

Index

108–112, 114–122, 124, 126,
130–131, 136, 140–143, 202
Indeterminacy 65–66, 90, 93, 98–99,
101, 108, 115, 117, 119, 121–122,
141
Individuation 58, 115, 118, 131, 138
Inference
In modal systems 28–29
In fictional contexts 29, 33, 38–39,
63, 89–90, 169
Ingarden, Roman 97–104, 108, 112,
122, 203, 211, 221, 223–224
Integrationism (see Segregationism vs.
Integrationism)
Intensionality 28–29, 38, 98–99, 103
Interdisciplinary exchange of concepts
1–10, 14, 45–48, 71–72, 74–75,
229–230
Inwagen, Peter van 22, 119, 136–137
Iser, Wolfgang 81

Jakobson, Roman 2, 77, 80
James, Henry 224

Kinds (theory of) 117, 119
Kripke, Saul 4, 21–24, 34, 36, 39,
42–45, 51, 54, 58, 61–62, 97,
101–105, 133–135
Kuhn, Thomas 67–68

Leech, Geoffrey 81
Leibnitz 5, 30, 48, 56, 66, 102
Levi-Strauss, Claude 157, 165
Lewis, David 4, 22–24, 37–38,
49–50, 58, 63–64, 66, 70–71, 83,
200
Linde, Ulf 90
Literariness 80–82
Lotman, Jurij 97, 99–104
Loux, Michael 43, 49, 59, 62
Lyons, John 131, 145

Make-Believe (see Pretense)
Malmgren, Carl 154
Margolin, Uri 19, 111–113, 124
Margolis, Joseph 91
Martinez-Bonati, Felix 9, 19, 30, 176
Maximality (of Possible Worlds)
65–67, 90, 110, 116, 121
McCawley, James 67

McHale, Brian 9, 19, 53, 55, 77, 80,
141, 212
Mendilow, A. A. 211
Metaphorization of concepts 47,
72–75, 103, 215–216, 227
Mimeticism 52, 98–99, 106, 154–155,
217–219
Minimal departure (from the actual)
70–71
Minimal story 150–153
Modal logic
Modality 29, 38, 49–53, 58, 62,
88–89, 102–103, 105, 132, 210–212,
214, 219–220, 226–228
Operators 28–29, 38, 58, 89,
109
Quantifiers 22, 38, 62, 89–90
Motif 158, 177, 179

Nabokov, Vladimir 213, 226
Naming
Definite descriptions 42–45, 58,
131–134, 136–139
Identity problems 58–59, 132–133
Proper names 42–45, 58, 131–139
Rigid Designators 43–44, 53, 58,
60, 125, 133–137
Theories of 32, 43–44, 130–136
Naming (a narrative sequence) 156,
158
Narrative Domain 55, 57, 171
Narrative Focus 186
Narrative Grammar 148–150,
156–159, 161–163, 166–168
Narrative Logic 148, 152, 154, 160,
162, 164–167, 171–173
Narrative Present (also Fictive present)
204–214, 217–219, 222–228
Narrative Semantics 147–150, 158,
160, 164–169, 172–173
Narrative Unit 150, 156–159, 166,
177
Narrativity (fictional) 12–16,
144–147, 149–153, 156, 160, 162,
168–169, 171, 174, 180, 206–208,
210
Narrativity (historical) 147, 204
Narratology 13–14, 145–150,
152–153, 155, 159–162, 164,
166–167, 170, 173, 214

Index